True Confessions

True Confessions

Feminist Professors Tell Stories Out of School

Edited by Susan Gubar

W. W. Norton & Company *New York • London*

For information about permission to reproduce selections from this book,
write to Permissions, W. W. Norton & Company, Inc.,
500 Fifth Avenue, New York, NY 10110

For information about special discounts for bulk purchases, please contact
W. W. Norton Special Sales at specialsales@wwnorton.com or 800-233-4830

Manufacturing by RR Donnelley, Harrisonburg, VA
Book design by Brooke Koven
Production manager: Anna Oler

Library of Congress Cataloging-in-Publication Data

True confessions : feminist professors tell stories
out of school / edited by Susan Gubar. — 1st ed.
p. cm.
Includes bibliographical references.
ISBN 978-0-393-07643-1 (hardcover)
1. Feminism—United States—Anecdotes.
2. Feminists—United States—Anecdotes.
I. Gubar, Susan, 1944–
HQ1426.T786 2011
305.43'37812092273—dc22
                                      2011012327

W. W. Norton & Company, Inc.
500 Fifth Avenue, New York, N.Y. 10110
www.wwnorton.com

W. W. Norton & Company Ltd.
Castle House, 75/76 Wells Street, London W1T 3QT

1 2 3 4 5 6 7 8 9 0

In Memory of Carolyn Heilbrun

Contents

II
PROFESSIONAL VISTAS

Introduction

For the first time in history, women compose a sizeable percentage of the professoriate. Starting in the 1970s and 1980s, female scholars began to be represented not as tokens but as a considerable group among tenured professors and high-profile administrators in small as well as large institutions of higher education. At the same time, groundbreaking intellectuals, especially in the humanities, started offering new courses and generating new scholarship on women's issues and on the importance of gender as a conceptual tool in virtually all contexts. What private experiences prompted the professional activism of the women who transformed academia in the last decades of the twentieth century? Did the idiosyncratic roots of pioneering feminists shape their intellectual and institutional achievements? Which challenges most perplexed the foundational players in the first generation of women to revamp teaching and learning in America? By addressing their personal backgrounds or public careers, might these thinkers invigorate reflections on and within feminism?

With these questions in mind, I began emailing prominent and relatively senior women faculty across the country, limiting myself to those people whose publications in the past I had found original and riveting. High on my list were colleagues who had produced page-turners: books or articles I simply could not put down during the first reading or, then again, after it. Truth to tell, I had become a tad bored reading conventional feminist criticism and theory, but also alarmed that so many of the students, colleagues, and acquaintances whom I encountered in classrooms, at parties, or in supermarket lines assumed that "no one cares about feminism anymore" or "feminism is passé." Imagine my surprise at receiving an immediate outpouring of autobiographical essays, each more compelling than the next. Totally absorbing, they came in a flurry of electronic attachments.

As I scrolled down screen after screen, it became clear that a number of the essays being sent to me concentrated with a fairly narrow focus on one facet of family influence or a singular instance of intimate experience. How does it feel for a daughter to deal with her father's physical deterioration or to fear that a parent finds her body repellant? Why do a family's Christian or Islamic practices captivate or repel girls grappling with their relatives' faith? Others explored professional conflicts. What happens when a lesbian graduate student assumes she must be closeted, or when a female professor encounters hostility from other women on the faculty, or when a feminist professor is accused of sexually harassing her graduate students? Still others ranged more widely over an entire career to highlight conceptual breakthroughs that inaugurated not only academic changes but also profound shifts in our understanding of the nature of knowledge. Where, under what circumstances and by what sort of people, are breakthrough insights into sexual politics made in fields like African American or religious studies, music or art history?

Read together, the essays that I solicited tell us where pioneering academic feminists came from, what may have been some of the influences that grounded their activism within the academy as well as outside it, and how confounding were the perplexities they faced in the course of their training and their progress on the tenure track. A few of my correspondents sent me autobiographical sketches that had just been produced or that had been recently published, sometimes in hard-to-obtain newsletters or specialized journals. Still others decided to compose new essays for this book. Since the people I contacted have achieved international reputations as pioneers in their various fields, such introspections cannot but fascinate, for they illuminate the idiosyncratic personal origins or the equally eccentric professional quandaries faced by thinkers notable for grasping and illuminating the significance of gender in virtually all aspects of human interaction. Feminist thinkers extend themselves here, then, to elucidate some of the roots as well as some of the consequences of their commitment to feminism and of its institutionalization in higher education.

I therefore organized the table of contents of *True Confessions* around these two emphases—put simply, an accent on the personal as opposed to an accent on the professional. Yet all the essayists presented here engage the interface between the personal and the professional, and do so with exactly the quirky unpredictability and stylistic panache I miss in so much of the rigorous scholarship I dutifully peruse "to keep up in the field."

The emphasis my correspondents and soon-to-be contributors placed on the telling details of personal life or on the equally telling patterns of professional careers helped me free this book from an organization derived from the various fields represented by contributors. For the departmental addresses of the scholars in this volume vary widely: English, comparative literature, education, religious studies, fine arts, history, psychology, African American studies, philosophy, theater, anthropology, music, media studies, ethnic studies, and of course the interdisciplinary women's or gender studies programs many helped launch. Though they inhabit quite various institutional and disciplinary settings, for decades many of the contributors to this book have pondered and been influenced by or responsive to one another's words, as have innumerable readers in and out of college classrooms.

The authors included within *True Confessions* established their reputations by being "a first": one of the first women in a discipline dominated by male researchers generally insensitive to the absence of female colleagues in their schools or the absence of gender from serious consideration in their investigations. A number of the email correspondents who became contributors seem to have been animated by a sense of wonder at what has been achieved in their lifetimes, but also a poignant awareness that their work, at least their institutional work within academia, is coming to a close. Quite a few realize that a considerable proportion of their generation has retired or is now retiring and that others are struggling with disabling illnesses and limited energies, or they are dying or dead. Perhaps the electronic avalanche I received was prompted by a shared intimation of mortality, the need to catch the present moment before we and our cohort disappear.

But the profusion of responses to my queries may also have been impelled by insatiable curiosity and a fierce commitment to ongoing transformations, personal as well as professional. "I want my past to remain vital to me because I need to keep learning its lessons": this sentiment, so well expressed by Annette Kolodny, may have inspired the decision of other contributors to record lives that have made a significant difference to successive waves of undergraduate and graduate students. People who formulated new methodologies in the 1970s and 1980s could keep on learning from the sometimes approving, sometimes contentious commentaries and controversies their publications often sparked from the 1990s to the present moment. The passage of time has provided requisite distance, enabling some to discern the motives impelling investigations that have achieved canonical stature, stimulating others to perceive the sources of their commitment to feminist activism.

Besides registering intimations of mortality as well as insatiable curiosity and a fierce commitment to ongoing learning, the autobiographical reflections in *True Confessions* may also disclose rising levels of anxiety at the start of the twenty-first century. Surely the historic achievements of the contributors to this volume have made the academy more hospitable to women. But will successive generations of academic women be able to prosper in the future? What does it mean that the seismographic entrance of women into higher education coincided with the deteriorating material conditions many face within academe? The largest proportion of women entered humanities departments just at that point when the humanities began to be relegated to a third-class position with regard to the sciences and the social sciences, not to mention the professional schools. A feminized humanities, discussed by several authors in this volume, struggles with inadequate funding, hiring freezes, and budget crunches; the collapse of the PhD job market in many disciplines; inequitable teaching loads, advising responsibilities, and committee assignments—especially the exploitation of poorly paid junior faculty, adjuncts, and part-timers, often female; underfunding for so-called at-risk students as well as for at-risk doctoral students headed toward the miserably depressed job markets; and the proliferation of unemployed or underemployed ABDs and PhDs.

We live in a time in need of particularly nuanced and engaging voices that can deal with a barrage of forces deleterious to contemporary women's well-being. The thinkers presented in *True Confessions* provide an appreciation of the abiding relevance of a feminist perspective, on the one hand, and, on the other, of the need to make that relevant perspective persuasive inside and outside the academy. It may seem paradoxical to direct attention toward a group of elite American academics so as to revitalize prose for a general readership. But the contributors' combined answer to the question "What was one (or what were some) of the personal origins or repercussions of your professional work?" illuminates the diverse fears, desires, and hopes of feminists, as do their accounts of the learning they received and fostered. To those who directly address the threats posed by terrorism, poverty, warfare, environmental threats, and so forth, the writers in this book, contemplating their own circumstances, may seem relatively privileged. Quite a few of the contributors to *True Confessions* would admit that their personal trajectories gained them access to experiences in and out of schools that excluded many less fortunate.

Yet like the British feminist Mary Eagleton, I suspect that these essayists would "not want to circumvent the awkwardness and embarrassment of that situation," but instead "hold on to a sense of embarrassment and of ethics, not as a self-lacerating indulgence but as a necessary spur to political action" (19). In accord with Felicity Nussbaum's belief that feminism cannot be kept relevant through "a comprehensive view from nowhere" (85), the contributors to this volume adopt a specific view from somewhere in order to address psychological and ethical predicaments that spur activism. They do so in malleable forms of address and narrative accounts that might infuse feminist polemic with vibrancy, and in transnational as well as multiethnic contexts.

To a greater and lesser extent, a number of the contributors to *True Confessions* share an alienation from normative scholarly languages which have come to feel, as Leila Ahmed once put it, "almost like a prison." Varied in subject matter, many of the meditations in *True Confessions* spring from an urgent desire to find forms of writing less formulaic and tired than academic discourse as usual. Quite a few of the authors in this book attempt to transform critical prose in much the same manner as they earlier reinvented syllabi, courses, and degrees. A turn toward autobiographical perspectives allows contributors to attend to the specificity of their experiences. For, when embedded in anecdotal particularity, insights about gender and about race, ethnicity, class, age, sexuality, and nation seem to arise with more tonality and flexibility, a resonant timbre and honesty, with less reductive generalizing, than they do when cramped under the theoretical rubrics usually used to engage them.

Additionally, a host of different differences can surface in autobiographical reflections—differences not only of religious affiliation, for example, but within various historically inflected approaches to particular rituals or beliefs; differences not only in parenting, say, but also among parents with sundry temperaments, domestic practices, or health issues. Many contributors evoke the mysterious presence of the past: Gayatri Spivak connects her posture to the encouragement her father gave her to walk tall alongside the cows in Calcutta; Sandra Gilbert rejoices in the recipes brought from Liguria via Paris to her grandfather's kitchen in Queens and then through her husband and son into her own California kitchen; Hazel Carby weighs experiences of racism in Britain against her multiracial parents' faith in the virtues of a British education. Abstractions, transfigured into concrete instances and examples, bristle with evident vibrancy, as various dissimilarities surface and the borders demarcating the personal and the professional become malleable. The emotional complexities of private life as well as the pedagogic and collegial investments of feminists in academia, which have been severed from the scrutiny we generally accord the data of our disciplines, get stitched together again by the contributors to this volume.

In the sentence above I use the word "again" to stress the need to return—albeit by new routes—to earlier engagements with women's issues. From its inception, feminism attracted polemicists often outside (or on the fringes of) the academy who generally addressed a broad reading public. Indeed, until fairly recently, the vast majority of women only received what Virginia Woolf called "unpaid-for education," and therefore most of their reflections were composed at a far remove from the halls of academia. Such canonical texts as Alice Walker's "In Search of Our Mothers' Gardens" and Adrienne Rich's "When We Dead Awaken" provide models of criticism tapping the aesthetic pleasures that drew their authors toward literature in the first place. Feminist scholars have much to gain by exploring the techniques of the memoir and of other literary genres as well.

But why did I ask my email correspondents specifically for autobiographical reflections? Some time ago I was asked to respond to a day-long conference in honor of Carolyn Heilbrun, a year or so after her death. Because of teaching obligations, I could not travel to the CUNY Graduate Center, where a number of prominent women read portions of their completed or ongoing memoirs. From a distance, though, I shared the belief of participants that through her detective fiction as well as through her eminently readable critical prose, Carolyn Heilbrun epitomized what feminists gain from lucidity and integrity. What struck me after I received transcripts of these proceedings was how fascinating I found them, how quickly I raced through page after page of lyrical memoirs composed, in some cases, by people I did not know personally and suspected I never would meet. And yet I felt braced by their accounts of an intellectual journey quite distinct from my own, though somehow related, and in provocative ways.

Still, I did not ask email correspondents for excerpts from memoirs but instead for autobiographical essays, a fact that has quite a bit to do with the emergence of so-called personal criticism, a form pioneered by two writers included in *True Confessions*: Nancy K. Miller and Jane Tompkins. Each, in her own way, has melded personal retrospection with critical and theoretical speculations. A hybrid genre, not unrelated to Woolf's earlier achievement, personal criticism can veer toward pure autobiography or slip toward pure criticism—in precisely the manner many of the essays in this volume do. Personal criticism enables its authors to deploy autobiography in the service of critical or theoretical insights. The essayists in *True Confessions* explore their experiences as women who were part of a massive shift in colleges and universities. Their personal backgrounds fascinate in part because they function as idiosyncratic microcosms of the unprecedented entrance of women into higher education.

The opening essays of Part I hinge on the old slogan "the personal is political." Fathers, mothers, grandparents, aunts, great-aunts, siblings, husbands, children, and household intimates proliferate from every conceivable geographical locale to explain some aspect of the personal sources of the writer's engagement with feminist inquiry. *True Confessions* begins, then, by featuring literary scholars, whose preponderance reflects their investment in personal criticism. Since activism is now often staged inside classrooms, committee meetings, conference halls, and offices, the essays at the end of Part I and at the beginning of Part II explore how the personal translates into the politics of the professions, how the politics of the professions influences the personal. Contributors take up difficult questions pertaining to the depression and burnout of women in higher education; the friction between pursuing a career and feminine socialization, between academic success and marital as well as maternal obligations; careerism and competition affecting women inside the hierarchical world of the academy; the relationship between gender and mentoring; the vexed issue of sexual harassment; and the tensions between anti-racist and feminist activists inside institutions of higher education. The essays clustered toward the end of Part II explore the reasons why and the ways in which groundbreaking individuals transformed many different disciplines in the humanities.

Memory in *True Confessions* serves a host of approaches and enterprises: some psychoanalytic, others satiric; some sociological, others cautionary or self-cautionary. With remarkably different aims and tones, the essayists in both parts of the book return to formative earlier experiences. They therefore shed light on the gender dynamics especially prevalent from the 1950s to the 1970s. Perhaps because the contributions to this volume were composed at the present moment, when religious values play such a prominent role in the media and in politics, they also clarify a subject that has not yet received enough attention, the relationship between feminism and religion.

Any number of thinkers might have been included in the collective here, some of whom are just as important in the trajectory of feminist intellectual history as those represented. A few of the senior scholars whom I contacted were simply not ready or willing or able to participate in this project; many others could not be included because of space constraints. An entirely new book would be needed to represent feminists in the sciences. At the same time, one could easily imagine a succession of autobiographical collections from Africa, Europe, the Middle East, or South America since feminism has become a decidedly transnational endeavor, a fact registered by the international roots of many of the prominent people in this volume.

The personal nature of the material I received made *True Confessions* seem a fitting, if tongue-in-cheek title. Fitting because the popular magazine with that somewhat scandalous name—featuring articles about girls and family, romance and sex—targeted a female readership in the 1950s when many of the contributors were growing up, and fitting also because the confessional essays in this volume often flaunt the conventions of scholarly prose. Tongue-in-cheek because many of the contributors play with language to indicate that no confession can be truly true, mediated as it must be by the distance of retrospection and by the rhythmic, syntactic, imagistic nature of the prose in which it is transformed. My subtitle—*Feminist Professors Tell Stories Out of School*—draws attention to the academic networking, gossiping, and organizing that dismantled the old boy's club many feminists confronted in their graduate training, for quite a few of the contributors to this volume took classes only from male professors. Some of the stories told, therefore, mock the old-school practices this generation initially faced in a male-dominated academy. Others, though, tell stories that question the new-school practices established by feminists in the humanities and flourishing at the present time.

If, as some believe, feminism's prestige holds sway preeminently on college campuses today, it makes sense to examine the growth of political conscience in individual professors motivated by a passion for collective justice and equity extending to all women. In large measure, the credit for feminism's intellectual cachet goes to writers like the ones included in *True Confessions*. Readers who own and treasure the many essays and books produced by the contributors to this volume will gain from the following pages an intimate glimpse into the familial sources and professional conflicts through which feminists have managed to bring about one of the most momentous transformations in Western culture: the successful integration of women into higher education and therefore also into virtually all the professions.

WORKS CITED

Eagleton, Mary. "Who's Who and Where's Where: Constructing Feminist Literary Studies," *Feminist Review* 53 (Summer 1996): 1–23.

Nussbaum, Felicity. "Risky Business: Feminism Now and Then," *Tulsa Studies in Women's Literature* 26.1 (Spring 2007): 81–86.

PART ONE

Personal Views

My Father's Penis

Nancy K. Miller

WHEN I WAS GROWING UP, MY FATHER wore what we used to call string pajamas. Actually, I only remember the bottom part of the pajamas, which as their name might suggest, tied with a string at the waist. (On top he wore a ribbed sleeveless undershirt that tucked into the pajama bottoms.) The pajamas, made of a thin cotton fabric, usually a shade of washed-out blue but sometimes also striped, were a droopy affair; they tended to bag at the knees and shift position at the waist with every movement. The string, meant to hold the pajamas up, was also meant to keep the fly—just a slit opening in the front—closed. But the fly, we might say modernly, resisted closure and defined itself instead by the meaningful hint of a gap.

As my father wandered through the apartment in the early mornings, performing his domestic rituals (bringing my mother her coffee in bed, making my sister and me breakfast in the kitchen, shaving, watering the plants), this almost gap never failed to catch my eye. It seemed to me, as I watched him cheerfully rescue the burning toast and pass from room to room in a slow motion of characteristic aimlessness (memorialized in our family codes by the Yiddish trope of *draying*), that behind the flap lay something important: dark, maybe verging on purple, probably soft and floppy. I also suspected it was

3

hairy in there; I was pretty sure I had glimpsed hair (he had hair everywhere, on his back and shoulders, why not there?).

I don't think I wanted to see it—"it" had no name in my ruminations—but there was a peculiar way in which its mysterious daily existence behind the slit in the pajama bottoms loomed large in my prepubescent imaginary as somehow connected to the constant tension in our family, especially to my mother's bad moods. Growing up, I had only the vaguest notions of sex; I can still remember my utter astonishment when, sitting on the living room couch and feeling vastly sophisticated, I learned from my mother that a penis had to become "erect" to enter a vagina (I had never really thought about how the *man's* penis—in the redundant but always less than instructive language of hygiene classes—gets into the *woman's* vagina). Several years later, when in college I finally had a look at my first penis (this was no small surprise), I realized that I had never visualized the thing to myself at all.

Almost forty years after the scene of these memories, I find myself again, as a middle-aged, therapized intellectual, thinking about my father's penis. Now, living alone after my mother's death in the same apartment, my father, stricken with Parkinson's disease, shuffles through the room *draying*. Boxer shorts have replaced the string pajamas, but the gap remains the same, and it's still dark in there. But it's not the same: I have seen his penis. I have even touched it. One day when his fingers had grown so rigid he couldn't, as he puts it, "snare" his penis, he wanted to get up to go to the bathroom. It was late, and I wanted to go home, so looking and looking away, I fished his penis out from behind the fly of his shorts and stuck it in the portable urinal; it felt soft and a little clammy.

Shirley, the nurse's aide who takes care of my father, reported one day that when she arrived at the apartment in the morning, she had found my father in the kitchen "bare-bottomed" and cold. "His . . . was . . . blue," she said (the cadences of a slight Caribbean accent made the word hard to understand over the phone); "I rubbed it until it turned pink. Then he felt better." Rubbed his *penis*? But what else, in the vicinity of a bare bottom, of two syllables, could have gone from blue to pink? Did it respond to her rubbing? Become erect? The mystery returns. What do I know? Shirley and I talk about my father, his care. The apartment, despite her efforts, smells of urine. There's no missing this penis-effect. One day, in the middle of eating dinner, his back to me, he demands his urinal from Shirley. Shirley buys him new boxer shorts on 14th Street. Six dollars, she says. Apiece, I ask? No, three Fruit of the Loom in a package.

This is the condition of his remaining at home (he gives me a pained look at the mention of going to a "home" that silences me): to get out of bed and make it to the bathroom without falling, or to use the urinal that hangs like a limp penis from the walker he despises (he shows his superiority to his infirmity by carrying the walker in front of him instead of leaning on it). When these solutions fail, Ellen, the neighbor who brings him his daily *New York Times*, says "he peed himself" (my father always talks more elaborately about the "difficulty of urination," of responding in time to the "urgency of its call"). The newspapers now, like the *New Yorkers* to which he maintains his subscription and which remain unopened in their plastic wrappers, pile up unread in the living room; I throw them away in my weekly sweep through the apartment.

In "Phallus/Penis: Same Difference" (great title) Jane Gallop writes, "The debate over Lacan's and, beyond that, psychoanalysis's value for feminism itself centers on the phallus. Yet the *phallus* is a very complicated notion in Lacan, who distinguishes it from the *penis*. The distinction seems, however, to resist clarification" (125). For a while after touching my father's penis, I went around thinking smugly I would never again confuse penis and phallus, boasting that I had transcended the confusion. Phallus was the way my father could terrify me when I was growing up: throwing me across the room in a blind rage because I had been talking on the phone—endlessly, it's true—when the hospital called to say his mother was dying; knocking me down in the elevator for staying out late one night with my college boyfriend. Phallus was tearing pages out of the typewriter because I hadn't left wide enough margins on my term papers; making me break a date with the cab driver who had picked me up in London on my first visit there (but Daddy, he's *Jewish*, the son of a cantor!).

Penis was that dark-veined, heavy thing lying there against

strangely elongated, even darker balls; hanging between emaciated but still elegant thighs. It made problems for me, but they were finally prosaic, unmediated by concepts and the symbolic order. My father doesn't have the phallus; no one does, Lacan said. But, Gallop writes in *The Daughter's Seduction*, "the need, the desire, the wish for the Phallus is great. No matter how oppressive its reign, it is much more comforting than no one in command" (130–31). So now I decide, say no, and yell; I am responsible for the rest of his life ("It's for your health and welfare," he used to say as his cover for the exercise of an arbitrary authority); maybe I, failing the penis, have my chance at the phallus.

Months after writing this, I come into my father's room. I think I have put an end to all these speculations (penis, phallus, castration, etc.) but when I find him sleeping completely naked, stretched out like an aged Endymion across a hospital bed, I can't resist. His hand is resting in his lap, his penis tucked away out of sight, hidden between his thighs. I move closer.

"So what does it look like?" my sister asks. I don't answer, not only because I want to play big sister one last time, but because I'm not sure I can say what it is that I've seen.

When I wrote "My Father's Penis," I had been thinking more about penises than fathers (or so I thought at the time). Mira Schor, a painter and a critic, had done a slideshow lecture on representations of the penis in painting, and I conceived my piece originally as a kind of footnote to her panoply of members—the geriatric extension of her taxonomy. But I was also writing in the aftermath of an intensely charged academic performance in which the status of "experience" in feminist theory had been challenged with a certain phallic—what would a better word be?—insistence. When it then became a matter of publishing "the penis" (it seems impossible to invoke the title or its contents without getting caught in the spiral of catachresis) in *Refiguring the Father*, I felt that I had inadvertently found a destination for it: that the fragmentary essay, because of its mixed origins, born of the troubled intimacies of the autobiographical penis and the theoretical phallus, had unexpectedly come full circle back to feminist revision. But not perhaps back home.

Had my father still been able to read, I would never have written about "the penis." By going public with the details of domestic arrangements on Riverside Drive, I was flying in the face of the parental injunction not to "tell" that had haunted my adolescence and continued well into my adult years; the panic my parents felt that they would be exposed by us; the shame over family secrets. But he was down in his reading to the occasional newspaper headline and, I think, at his end, despite a finely honed personal vanity, beyond caring. He had become no longer himself, and I needed to mourn his disappearance.

My father died before this piece appeared in print. He died, I'm tempted to say, of the penis: at home, as he had wanted, after eating ice cream and watching public television, in the aftermath of a grueling seven-week stay in the hospital that followed a violent urinary tract infection. I dealt with—talked about, looked at, touched, raged at—his penis until the very end. And until the very end, the penis/phallus connection remained alive, impossible to sever. In the hospital, it was war between his penis and the doctors' discourse; or rather, my attempt to stand in as phallus for his penis—the rights of his body—against their authority to determine the course of his life; their wish for him to live, against his entire system's disarray (my wish for him?).

When I read one day on my father's chart in the intensive care unit "Responds only to pain," I found it hard to share the doctor's jubilation over the signs of life dotting the monitor above his respirator. "What do you want me to do," she hissed at me across the network of tubes mapping his body, "kill your father?"

WORKS CITED

Gallop, Jane. *The Daughter's Seduction*. Ithaca: Cornell University Press, 1982.

Gallop, Jane. "Phallus/Penis: Same Difference," *Thinking through the Body*. New York: Columbia University Press, 1988.

Yaeger, Patricia, and Beth Kowaleski-Wallace, eds. *Refiguring the Father: New Feminist Readings of Patriarchy*. Carbondale: Southern Illinois University Press, 1989.

A Reasonable Facsimile

Jane Marcus

MY FATHER HAD BEAUTIFUL FEET. The toes were long and well-shaped and the arch was high. He often went barefoot or wore sandals, showing off his lovely feet. He did this with a certain vanity that only enhanced his masculinity. It was his poor feet I thought of when I tried to imagine him dead. Would his feet, I wondered, in his Catholic way of thinking, be healed of the sores and scaly skin infections that plagued his last years before he met his maker? Keeping up appearances was a cardinal point in his lace-curtain Irish approach to the world. He truly worried, unlike anybody else I've ever known, about what other people would think. I'm imagining him embarrassed by his feet in heaven with a barefoot Jesus. They compare their wounds like two old war buddies. Do Catholics believe that the resurrected body returns to its former glories? Does it rise with or without its arthritis and psoriasis? I should know the answer to this question.

The Cathedral of Notre Dame in Paris is where I have come to have this talk with my dead father. We could actually talk about his feet. They were a safe topic and sure to produce a particular repertoire of stories. This was the only kind of conversation you could have with him, and I am doing this by instinct. Absurd details in Catholic ritual remained in his mind, and he could argue about angels gathered in

9

numbers on pinheads forever or explain why an act was a venial and not a cardinal sin. It was his Jesuit training that lasted when the rest of his brain was pickled in alcohol and people were just targets for the poison darts of his words.

I am embarrassed to be looking at the beautiful bleeding feet of Jesus on the cross. I try to feel what is happening here as a worshipper, not as the aloof tourist I have become—so carefully pretended to be—for many years in European Catholic churches. Lighting a candle gives no *frisson* of fervor. You must have to believe for those remembered physical thrills to work their magic—holy water, incense, bells. Probably it's not a good thing to think of my father's feet when I look at the wounded feet pierced by nails that churches offer to our eyes. On the other hand, it's perfectly logical in the culture that I grew up in to confuse God's feet with your father's.

My father was so taken with our Birkenstocks that he asked for a pair, a few years ago. He wanted desperately to be free of the socks and shoes he was made to wear, covering his wretched skin, causing his feet to fester, he felt. How triumphantly we produced the notorious hippie footwear. But he feared their foreignness, their apparent defiance of gravity. Why didn't they fall off? He was suspicious. Sports heroes don't wear Birkenstocks. Birkenstocks obviously meant queer feet. Queer feet were worse than losing his toes to gangrene. He wasn't allowed to wear them by his nurses, anyway. The naked feet of the old and ill are obscene to the young and healthy. Better to hide them.

The doctors had taken veins from his feet to use in a heart bypass operation. They left behind yards of plastic thread, like a fishing line, removed over a year later by another doctor after gangrene had set in and much pain had been endured. His caretakers tired of hearing that there was a wolf at the door or in his foot. A nurse had come to check his recovery a couple of times a week and never worried about the failure of his feet to heal. He told his doctors—always referred to as "my physicians"—but they probably resented being lectured on his previous dealings with other "physicians," the litany of their degrees and his knowledge of people in those august institutions: "He was on my board of directors"; "I knew him in Washington from HEW"; "We asked him to be on the board of trustees of Eckard College for

Retired Senior Professionals." His doctors in Florida were completely incompetent, whatever their credentials. Did he know? Was this word-crust that scabbed over his talk a substance exuded to heal himself? Was this recitation of the achievements of other people, strangers, his way of marshalling evidence before an imaginary family court that he expected to condemn him for fraud and malpractice as a father and a husband, as a man?

It was a charming vanity of his that fussed over his hands and feet. Their beautiful bones were evidence of his fairy-tale view of himself as the prince or as someone who had been accidentally assigned the wrong life, an actor given the wrong script and sent on stage in a play that meant nothing to him. We couldn't possibly be his real family. Like Cinderella's elegant foot, his elegantly boned appendages marked his difference from us ordinary peasants. How he mocked the ugly, the fat, the unfit, and his family's failures to be beautiful and aristocratic. What a serious concern for clothes and "looks," manners, "deportment" (as he called it; there was always a "D" in that box on my report card), and posture. (Slouching was a mortal sin. "Stand up straight!" an imperative that curdles the spine. Three slouching children complain that I lacked discipline as a mother, never taught them table manners. *Mea culpa.* Ah, what sadistic tortures can be practiced on one's self-esteem as "table manners." Better to gobble and grab when you're young.)

I know that he feels the ugliness of his feet more than the pain. As if his God might care more about how he cared for the body entrusted to him than the spirit. My sister Bonnie has his hands—long, beautifully shaped fingers skimming the raised dots in her braille books, completely at odds with the bloated, drugged, and sedated body of the suicidal, brain-damaged, blind person she has become. When we were young, our bodies clashed, making no claims to kinship. The ideal family body parts were distributed unequally. I was very tall and painfully skinny. Bonnie was blind but beautiful, and Kate, feminine and full-breasted as a girl, was trained young for professional tennis, and then, suddenly, just as she was getting good, was forced to give it up at fifteen. Her gaining weight and my losing it were part of the same game. The well-dressed anorexic teenager in the family pictures, myself when young, he called "Queenie," a grand, delusional name for collie dogs. They used to come running in airports when he called his pet daughter. He whistled, too, when he came home, and I came running, eager to walk to the bakery with him for his rye bread, to hear his stories.

But the name and my status as a royal pet disappeared when the flesh began to appear after menopause. How it disappointed him to have another fat female in the family. I lost my number one rating. I believe I was actually demoted to the rank of Sweetie Pie Number Three at Christmas at my sister's where he lived in rage and muttering. I went to say goodbye. He snapped his head away from a kiss. "When are you going to get thin again?" he demanded. "When are you going to stop beating your wife?" I retorted, answering back for the first time in my life. Fifty-eight, just, and now I finally fight back? Messing up the moment of the intended great emotional father–daughter reconciliation scene. Driving away, I told my children, in horror, of what I'd said. He would die, but would his mean mouth live on in me? God forbid. Serpent's tooth. In my own mouth.

He was so mean and hurtful that everyone tried not to respond to him. The doctors and nurses were only human, perhaps, and sensitive to insults. He practiced certain forms of discourse that assaulted the other person, and then kicked you when you were down. He made speeches and gave lectures—no interruptions tolerated, repeating word-for-word old stories, inflating his role in forgotten events. "How are *you*?" was not in his vocabulary.

Talking was a war, and he always had to win. Listening was for losers. Strangers who didn't know the Connor rules of conversation and tried to participate or offer an opinion were mown down summarily by a barrage of words. He didn't ask questions or listen to what people had to say. Overhearing conversations with other people, he learned a person's weak points the way a soldier learns the habits of his enemy, planning lethal surprise attacks for birthdays and weddings. Bombs and mortars full of words. For the granddaughter who has everything and is stunningly beautiful, he has a special present. He calls her ugly for a week until she begins to believe it. For the independent grandson in college, he has defined the rules of the visit: no driving. No car or bike. No escape. He must have worked for weeks polishing his weapons for Christmas and Thanksgiving.

Trying to imagine what it was like to be him, to live inside his skin, I am terrified by a wave of ice-cold loneliness, a chill in church that candles and holy water did not give. His mother was not very loving, I explain to myself; she was beautiful, vain, narcissistic, French. Accidentally run over by a train, his father was crippled in a wheelchair, solaced by whiskey. When I was a child I went after school to read chapters of Balzac to him. My father had two brothers, one ten years older, the other ten years younger—as children in a small town, we were not allowed to speak to our cousins because of his feud with one of them. His own family was anything but a haven in a heartless world. It was the heartless place from which one fled to the warmth of the world. And that was the kind of family he made for us—to flee was your only hope of survival.

It is Ascension Thursday, coinciding with the French national holiday celebrating the end of World War II, the morning after I hear the news of my father's death. It seems somehow appropriate to go to Notre Dame to try to make peace with his spirit. But I keep thinking about his body, his Christ-like bruised feet, somehow preserved unmarked by the mean-spirited scornful tone with which he addressed the world and his family alike, though he was known to have been charming to total strangers on occasion. His high-arched feet dance in my imagination marked, scarred, wounded, and unmarked, the crucified feet of a bland Jesus figure. A marked man. An unmarked body. How will it rise? Will his feet disappear above me in a cloud over Paris? Should I try to negotiate a peace with the marked man before his feet disappear?

As a high school teacher with children, my father was exempt from fighting in the war, one of the few men left at home. He practiced the tactics of war in family life. All was fair in that war. Rare forms of subtle torture and treachery were rehearsed. On the playing field where he coached the football and basketball teams, he preached fair play. As the high school coach he drew the respect of all the young men in town. Once I was walking with him in the evening, and he silently knocked a cigarette out of the mouth of a boy who was dropped without another chance from the team. On the kitchen table, he wrenched dislocated shoulders back into their sockets, his one year of medical school cited as authority. He was a handsome man, in a black Irish way, like the film star Tyrone Power, and he still looks handsome in the last photograph I took of him at Christmas with my son, his grandson, who has inherited some of his grandfather's good looks. His eyes are empty, though, at eighty-three. When were they full of life, unclouded by drink and spitefulness?

In the cathedral in Paris, my Jewish husband and son comfort me with their presence. Michael weeps tears of forgiveness for the sins of an unloving father-in-law and urges me to forgive him too, to begin to mourn my loss. But I cannot cry, or even do more than bring myself back to the scene of his culture out of a willed respect. He never went to church, but he was saturated in Catholic culture; its curses were his curses; its enemies were his enemies; its language was his language. Irish Catholicism is a crude and vulgar structure of feeling, but it's tenacious, and I find I have not wholly forgotten it or rooted its fatalistic glooms out of my life.

Paul's letter to the Ephesians is the text. Live up to your calling. Be humble always and gentle, forbearing with one another and charitable. It is about community, and even Mark's more threatening version of the Ascension is about the gift of tongues to the apostles; we are instructed to understand one another across the boundaries of language. These values were the opposite of the ones my father lived by. He isolated himself and his family from communities that claimed allegiance. Never trust anyone. We were individuals, solitary sinners sinking or swimming on our own. When he was drunk he talked about survival of the fittest, and whether the blind and crippled should be allowed to live. Ties of blood or nation did not move him. Kinship was an alien concept. You knew as a child that he would live up to his words and disown you on a moment's notice if you disobeyed or embarrassed him in public. His refusal to speak to his own brother was a lesson to us all. Master of abandonment. Even when he actually hadn't abandoned you, you felt he would.

Relatives belonging to my mother, to whom she tenaciously held on despite his contempt for them, were figures of ridicule and jokes. His way of keeping her in line was to insult her mother and her sisters and their husbands and their way of life. Paul wrote to the Ephesians from prison, assuring them of one Lord, one faith uniting them. My father's faith was the Roman rule of "divide and conquer." He set us against one another, sisters and mother, mocking any signs of affection among us lest they turn into signs of rebellion. He wheedled confessions of discontent out of you on private walks, when you were supposed to be learning the names of trees and plants, and then he told your secrets and broadcast your complaints.

He was a colossal troublemaker. An expert at sowing dissension. He taught us how to hate, using the language of humiliation against the harmless. He could bring a blush of shame to anyone's cheek, reduce all cousins and unsuspecting friends and visitors to wounded animals with his magic mirror for looking into your soul and ferreting out vanities and pretensions, harmless prides and self-delusions. Deadly accurate strikes shut mouths, dissolved family occasions and porch conversations with the neighbors. At our last Christmas together, he responded to "Isn't Bridget a lovely girl?" with "Little bitch."

My mother's eldest sister had married a Northern Irishman and, like some of my mother's family themselves, his family had come to the United States through Canada. My father's worst term of abuse, the ultimate swear word in the family language, was "dirty Nova Scotian." Just writing it brings a blush to my face. He insulted Uncle Fred with this phrase to his face and behind his back, while boasting about his Jewish and black friends. He could then use the term "Nova Scotian" in a conversation with others, signaling to us who the enemy was. Words could be filled with private meanings and deployed as weapons. Like Wagner's leitmotivs, certain notes were sounded throughout our childhood to announce his opinion of characters arriving on the family scene. The sound of a toilet flushing indicated my mother's other sister, her modesty a source of laughter, as she flushed to hide the sound of peeing. How mean he was.

My sisters and I developed our own language for dealing with life in the family. Part pig-Latin and part words with our own ascribed meanings, it protected us for a while. Some words were completely made up. We would say them and burst into laughter. Bonnie still remembers the whole vocabulary. She can still, in fact, speak it. But

Kate and I have lost it, our child's tongue for making a place safe from our elders.

The crossed feet of Christ, the priest tells us, having risen from the dead and walked the earth with his apostles, will soon be lifted from the ground as his body ascends into heaven. These words—ascend and descend—were mysterious holy words in my childhood and I was always surprised to meet them in a secular context; used about elevators, for example, they seemed sacrilegious. It was Jesus who ascended and descended; people and elevators went up and down. Is Jesus being lifted into heaven because his feet are still hurting from the nails?

I see a cobblestoned street. My dad is walking with Jesus. He is leaning on his elegant cane, the other beautiful hand gesticulating, talking nonstop. The guy in the gown, the interlocutor, has his hands in his pockets, his head bent to listen, totally taken in by the old man. My instinct is to warn him. Oh, boy, I think (my father always said "ohboyohboyohboy"), is he going to get you. Long hair, sweet face, dress; good Christ, you'll be cremated.

Actually, it is my father's body that's going to be cremated. He used that word, cremated, that word now nailed to the history of the Holocaust as Christ's feet were nailed to the cross, and the word "murdered," too, in ordinary conversation, Irish exaggeration producing goose bumps of fear. Christ ascended out of it, though, whether his feet were intact or still bloody from the nails, I don't really know. My father asked to be cremated, and I am forced to think about this while searching for a "notaire" in the twentieth arrondissement in Paris to witness my agreement to his wishes. He gave us cremation as a text to interpret; my sister, the ex-nun, would object to the burning of the body on religious grounds. Certainly, my younger sister, a born-again Christian, believes in the resurrection of the body, head to feet. She'll be shocked at his disrespect. Kate said that as she dialed our blind sister Bonnie on the phone, she half expected the news of our father's death would produce a miracle, that it would cure her of her blindness and her craziness. She imagined for a minute that Bonnie would magically turn into the real person who had been imprisoned in a blind and alienated body by the wicked king. And now the king was dead.

I wonder why it never occurred to me to disobey his wishes?

These things are taken very seriously in France, and lawyers charge real money for their services. The notary's office is near Père Lachaise cemetery, the place where we walk to grieve, my family. It is raining, of course, and we stand under the chestnut trees, grandly blooming pink and white. Paris in May. Academics like us are also in leaf, on leave, in cafés under the trees, their work blossoming in the Paris air. The streets, one always forgets, are paved with dog shit. A pigeon's droppings dribble down my shoulder. Oscar Wilde's tomb, carved by Jacob Epstein, is a horizontal naked angel, penis broken off by vandals, weighed down by heavy stone wings done in modernist primitive imitation Aztec. This falling angel would make a perfect tomb for D. H. Lawrence, perhaps. But Oscar Wilde was a man of style. What a witty deconstruction he would have done of this mistaken monument to someone else's blood-consciousness. He would certainly have insisted on being dressed for the occasion, in velvet jacket and suede gloves at least. And this grim avenging angel should be replaced by an amusing version of Walter Benjamin's angel of history wearing a hat and gloves, a bunch of lilies in his arms.

You could call Epstein's figure "Aborted Ascension." My father, too. Wasn't his life an earthly aborted ascension? That's too simple for the ups and downs of class and race in his family history, I suppose. Being Irish in Boston then was to be a race apart, the object of cartoons about monkeys, marked in puritan New England for always being late, dirty, lazy, and boisterously drunk and violent—stupid animals. A refrain from the speech we were given about studying hard was the threat of the "No Irish Need Apply" notice appearing again to single us out for God's punishment, lifted whole out of his childhood into our own, though it was no longer relevant. No wonder he taught the repression of the body and its pleasures, the stress on books and the contradictory ethics of self-sacrifice and willpower warring in the soul. He taught. Yes, he was a teacher. How many young people besides ourselves were shaped by his rod? Cremation recalls the Inquisition, the auto-da-fé, Joan of Arc, GBC the martyr. He did a good martyr act about being the one man in a house full of women, never able to get into the bathroom, our presence felt as emasculating.

Cremation. Into the oven. Saints and martyrs. Your own private, painless holocaust. The funeral home has sent a pamphlet, "Crema-tion Facts." My father was meticulous about grammar. It seemed a harmless fetish, correction being a habit in certain types of teachers. He would have written a letter to correct their bad grammar, when he was in good form, or had a day's talk about instructing them on their mistakes, pointing out the double-noun construction, the horror to "all civilized persons," he would have said, of using cremation as an adjective.

"Inurnment," defined as "placing the cremated remains in an urn or other container in preparation for final disposition," was surely invented by a man after his own heart, playing on "internment"'s suggestion of forced captivity in wartime and the idea of burial buried in "interment." But there is so little verbal motion in the word "inurn-ment" that it makes me think of my father's body imprisoned against his will in a giant flowerpot, inurned. "Technically, these fragments are not ashes," the pamphlet intones. They are bones. These are bones and splinters of bones that were my father's frame. Sir Thomas Browne (but I don't have *Hydriotaphia* on hand to check) would ask, "But who were the proprietaries of these bones?" ever skeptical about ascension himself. The flesh evaporates, though "occasionally, excess body fluids escape from the cremation chamber during processing." The "human remains," not "ashes," weigh between four and eight pounds. Is this fact supposed to be a comfort? Could one claim "My father's bones were heavier than your father's bones," as he always competitively announced the weight of the Thanksgiving turkey?

Families who have "chosen cremation" are warned about scattering the ashes (I mean bones) in the sea or in a "scattering garden": "The decision to scatter should be made carefully in that it is irreversible." The decision to scatter. To scatter or not to scatter; that is the ques-tion. Whether 'tis nobler in the eyes of men to bury, to scatter, or to inurn. Those are pearls that were his eyes, pulverized bones that were his feet. If burnt bones aren't ashes, what are they? "The Big Fellah," over six feet tall, strong and terrifying to children, captain of his Bos-ton College football team, card-carrying member of the hod-carriers' union, unloading ships at night during the war, is now pulverized to powder, weighing in at, say, the seven and a quarter pounds he was when his mother gave birth to him, her middle child, at home in her bed in Cambridge, Massachusetts, on September 29, 1914. She named him Gordon for George Gordon, Lord Byron, my grandfather's favorite poet—Gordon Benjamin Connor, GBC: he always had his initials stamped on his luggage and his briefcase, on his stationery, and inside his clothes. Kilroy was here.

(Is there another chance for those sinners who had themselves cremated to be reconstituted for the Last Judgment? Just add water. Or, like the decision to scatter, is it irreversible?)

His mother's name was Florence Touchet. Her father owned a livery stable in Cambridge. When I first read Henry James, I used to think of her as cousin to Ralph Touchett. Her sisters were called Beatrice and Lily, and my father made fun of their ladylike ways, their teacups and flower gardens. Florence, my Grandmama, pronounced with a French accent on the last syllable, was tall and elegant and smelled of face powder and rouge. She carried a scented handkerchief and wore silk stockings and high heels, glamorous fur coats, breathtaking hats with veils, and had a gorgeous handbag full of treasures that snapped shut with a loud and definite click when she had finished flinging out divine presents for you—used kid gloves, satin shoes and earrings, old lipsticks for dressing up. The clothes came from her patients. She worked as a nurse until she was very old and broke her hip in the subway after they took away her driver's license. She was full of energy and laughter and always threw up her skirts on entering the house; her greeting and opening line to "get my mother's goat" was, "Look at my legs. Aren't they something!" And indeed they were. And indeed my mother was scandalized, and pursed her mouth and turned her head. "Are my seams straight?" she'd ask with a wink as she was leaving in a cloud of perfume, as we rushed to help straighten the seams, touching the magic silken legs. She gave us French china dolls—too nice to play with, said my mother.

Grandmama had run away from home (always described as a place where she drove a pony cart and, in winter, a sleigh) to become a professional ice skater. Like going on the stage, this was a wicked thing to do and led, eventually, to her marrying an Irishman, Benjamin Franklin Connor, a pharmacist from western Massachusetts, where his father,

Black Mike, had settled to work on the railroad after emigrating from Ireland during the Potato Famine. Connor's Drugstore was still there in Hadley when I was a child, but my grandfather then worked in a drugstore in Swampscott, across from the beach. We walked on the boardwalk while my father visited his father, sometimes dressed in our Sunday best, eating a roll of pastel candies called Necco wafers one by one, saving the licorice ones for last.

He worked so many shifts, going to classes in between, that we scarcely saw him. But one Saturday, he took us on a real train from North Station, in Boston, to Lynn. We met the engineer, my sister Kate and I, in our matching homemade camel-hair leggings and coats with leather buttons, and boasted about our excursion for weeks. He signed us up for monthly visits to the Natural History Museum for a series of children's plays, sponsored by society women, I suppose for the "underprivileged." How we feared and loved these outings with my father, these terrifying lessons in "being on your own," where we were tested for endurance like soldiers in the field and failed utterly. Live theater was magical, and it was worth anything to go, to be transported in the dark on a velvet seat to other worlds, to live other lives that we dreamed about for weeks and acted out ourselves.

Dressed in the matching leggings and coats, my mother showing society that we were poor but respectable, we took the bus and the train into the city. My father dropped us at the door and went off "to see a man about a dog." He was drunk when he came back and always late. Once it got very late. Everyone had left, and the museum doors were locked. It was snowing very hard, and we both had to urinate desperately. Miserably cold and wet in wet pants and leggings, we didn't know what to do. I had finally gotten up the courage to ask a policeman for "car fare" when he showed up asking us to promise not to tell that he'd been late, bribing and wheedling. We agreed, but then we told him that it was no use trying to fool my mother since she'd have to clean and dry our fancy outfits; the tale would be told by the wet camel-hair leggings scratching and irritating our legs all the way home. For the rest of our lives, he told a funny story about how he, the blundering father of girls, took his daughters to the children's theater in Boston. He made people laugh by saying, "Of course, whenever you take them out they have to pee. What's a poor father to do?" And he recited his adventures accosting nice women at the doors of ladies' rooms, to help unzip and zip up those impossible leggings, to take us to the toilet. Everyone laughed as he acted the helpless male stuck in a public place with daughters whose braids came down, whose noses ran, while we were thinking, "whose fingers and toes froze, whose hearts beat so wildly, waiting for him to come (or not to come)?"

My father was totally unreliable. We children tried to cover up for him, being more upset about his untrustworthiness than about waiting hours for him. Fathers were supposed to be dependable. What had we done?

We wanted bicycles as presents for a certain Christmas. For months, we were given hints and led to believe that miracles on wheels would soon be ours. Instead, a long gleaming red metal cart with four wheels close to the ground, a seat barely above ground level, and pedals, was unwrapped with great fanfare and taken out to ride. We were the laughingstock of the neighborhood. The thing was called an Irish Mail. My father had seen one and ordered it instead of a bicycle because it would be different, he said. It was very showy and un-American, we thought, as we swallowed our lumps of disappointment. Like the camel-hair coats and leggings, it made us stand out as snobs. The Irish Mail was a great letdown, especially when we recalled how he had built up our expectations for weeks and was enjoying our discomfort and inability to handle an unwelcome gift. Where were our bikes? He really had them out in the back somewhere, didn't he? We weren't getting bikes at all. The Irish Mail was "a reasonable facsimile" of a bike, he said. It was an approximate copy. No matter that we were humiliated and embarrassed by it. For the rest of our lives, he told the story about himself, as a great joke and lesson to us children. "A reasonable facsimile" came to mean wishing for what you cannot have, "getting too big for your britches." We were to learn to be satisfied with the substitute thing, the reasonable facsimile, to control our craving. It was like the lesson of "The Fisherman and his Wife," a moral utterly beyond us. "I am in charge," said the father bear. "You will want what I want you to want."

Somehow, there was another level to it all, and that was how vulgar it was to want what everyone else had. Your reasonable facsimile of the required school gym sneakers or notebook was never really a reasonable facsimile. Its difference made you stand out. This is the way to train consumers of the real thing, loyal customers who will never be satisfied with anything but the object with the mark or label that says it's not a copy, though it is one of millions with the same mark. I need the Chanel label, even at a discount. The Irish Mail was replaced by a scooter. It had two wheels, but it didn't count as a reasonable facsimile. Maybe the whole thing was about keeping your feet or your seat on the ground?

The trouble with GBC was that he wasn't even a reasonable facsimile of a father. Oh Dad, Poor Dad, Mama's Hung You in the Closet, and I'm Feeling So Sad.

I'm a literary critic. How is having an unreliable father in your life like an unreliable narrator in a story? That narrator makes the reader work to figure out what's going on. Suspicious of motives, I mistrust authority. I need community. There is no such thing as a reasonable facsimile. All facsimiles are unreasonable. Let's face it: a facsimile is just a fake. But not all fathers are unreliable. This story would be better with an unreliable narrator, some playful backtalk, or sidestream action. When are you going to stop beating your wife? What would be a reasonable facsimile of cremation? All fathers are definitely fakes. Ashes, ashes, we all fall down.

The process is irreversible, but I keep imagining a great kitchen in limbo for unurning the inurned remains of all Catholics or all fathers or all reasonable facsimiles of fathers. If you pour water on dem bones, dem dry bones, that white powder, bone dust—not, remember, to be mistaken for ashes—reconstitutes itself in two easy steps. First a skeleton appears. Then it puts on flesh. But—and this is a point of dogma about which there has been serious ecumenical debate—it is not your real father who is reconstituted, but a reasonable facsimile. All the faux-fathers (faux-papas) have long elegant hands and feet, developed in an evolutionary process that takes place during inurnment and fits them for the task of riding the red Irish Mails to deliver facsimiles from earth to limbo and back again. They are always on time. Through sleet and snow. Old Reliable and Young Reliable. Good names for whiskey labels. One last message, Dad.

Feet, don't fail me now.

Coming home at night on the Watertown streetcar as an adolescent, I used to change at the switchyard for a short trip through Newton to the edge of Brighton, where we lived. Every night, a pervert followed me and exposed himself and harassed me. The streetcar drivers could do nothing. One night, I called you from a phone booth with his face leering in the window, begging you to get in the car and pick me up, for I was frightened out of my wits. "No," you said. "You're a big girl now. You have to learn to take care of yourself." The man was drunk and dirty and abusive. He enjoyed my fear, and he teased and tormented me until the streetcar came and I jumped on board, out of breath from running, crying hysterically. I smell it now, the tar from the old railroad ties next to the trolley line. Walking up the hill, wiping my tears, I tried to breathe regularly, regaining my composure for the scene you would make and the laughs to be had at my expense. "Who would go after a skinny scarecrow like you?" or he would sing a chorus of "Charley on the M.T.A." That man wasn't you. Just a reasonable facsimile of you. An unreliable father.

Whose feet are we talking about here?

What have I done? ("What hath God wrought?" he used to ask when you wore a new outfit.) I've made a portrait of my own private fascist father, daddy the dictator, the wicked king. It does no good, sticking pins in his effigy. Worse evils happen every minute, to children in Palestine, to whole countries and ethnic groups in Africa, Kurds in Turkey, ordinary people in Iraq, child prostitutes in Thailand. Power is abused. The powerless lick their wounds.

The worst thing is that I loved him. I really loved him. We always love them, don't we? You can rely on that.

Answering for the Consequences

Tania Modleski

I HAVE READ MEMOIRS OF WOMEN WHO have unusually coherent dreams in which they are fighting off monsters and saving the world. When they tell the dream to their wise old grandmothers, the response is something like the following: "Someday you will be a warrior. There are many battles and many kinds of warriors. You shall be a great one, fighting for a great cause."

The only dream I can remember from early childhood when I was, say, three or four is a recurring one in which my life-size little-girl doll Susie would come to life and go off somewhere on her own without telling me; when she came home I would beat the crap out of her. I experienced the most intense erotic sensations as I whaled into her. Every night I hoped to have that dream again, craving the perfect blend of Walt Disneyish childhood innocence (toys coming to life) and Sadean revelry.

My grandmother may not have been prepared to interpret this dream, but she would have known in her bones what it meant, for abusiveness was part of the legacy she would pass on to her progeny. The words spoken to me by my grandmother that I recall most vividly had nothing to do with prophecies of my future greatness. What I remember was the time—I was around ten years old—she called me a "goddamned little cheat" when we were playing Crazy Eights. This from a woman whose daughter swears her mother cheated at bingo.

Instead of feeling bitter about this traumatic incident (and exasperated when every time I tell the story people ask, "Well, were you cheating?"), I shall choose to see these words as in fact foretelling my fate: I was to become a legendary outlaw cursed by many, a maverick gambler who understood that you had a right to hold back any eights that came your way when the cards were stacked against you.

So, let's begin by paying "homage" to our ancestral mothers, who one way or another, by example, counterexample, or some jumbled mixture, propelled us into a movement which changed or tried to change the rules of the game.

Ellen Hughes

My mother's mother, who was called Ella, was a loud, big-boned, jowly woman who had a propensity for falling out with people, including her own children, whom she was capable of cutting out of her life for years on end. She quarreled with the priest when my mother was a girl and vowed never to set foot in church again. She kept that vow, although she went to the church bingo games and sent her children to Mass regularly. Other than going out to play bingo, she ruled from her rocking chair, while her youngest daughter, Bobbie, anxiously ran around doing her bidding. My grandmother's speech, delivered in sharp, strident tones, would bear down on you with tremendous force and speed like the trains that clattered by just a few yards behind her house. These trains were about the only thing that made her stop talking, and she waited impatiently for them to pass. When, to be conversational and also to prove how closely I was listening to her, I would try to interject a comment as she spoke, she would holler "Hark!" and glare. She sat in her rocking chair and rocked with increasing velocity as she got wound up, railing against the neighbors or cursing her children, interrupting herself now and then to bark "Quit slacking that gum!" at me. As the tempo and volume of her monologues intensified, the parakeet in the cage behind her would become increasingly agitated and chirp louder and louder until my grandmother, maddened by the competition, would command, "Bobbie, shut that bird up," and Aunt Bobbie would leap up to cover the cage.

I would sit happily for hours listening to my grandmother talk, though mostly she gossiped about people I didn't know, filling in as she went along with details of their family tree ("Joyce Hunt had a baby last week, a little boy—she used to be Joyce Johnson, doncha know, her mother was a Van Alstyne, that's the Van Alstynes who lived on Old Mill Road; Doris Van Alstyne—she married, let's see, who *did* she marry, Bobbie?—had a daughter who ran off with a married man: them Van Alstynes never amounted to anything, doncha know. Once Doris called to tell me my son Mart was picking on her son at school, and I told her, 'You've got some nerve to call me about that; everybody knows your son is no good, always getting in trouble with the police.' Her daughter was nothing but a goddamn tramp.")

When her children were young, if a teacher did something she didn't approve of (she believed it was her own job to slap her kids around), Ella would get them ready and walk them down Main Street for a face-off with the teachers at Chatham High.

To me she was a brave, brave woman, not afraid to speak her mind in the coarsest language possible to anyone—priest, school principal, whomever. I wished I could cut loose and say things like she said, that I could speak that way to my parents, my teachers, Joe Curcio the school bully, and even at times to my friends Geraldine and Janet—goddamn lying tramps. And indeed in my efforts to avoid becoming my mother the doormat, I have to think there are ways I've imbibed Grandma's spirit—for example, attacking so many people in print I don't have enough friends in high places to ask for a letter of recommendation. There'll be no Guggenheim for this project.

Little Lulu

I loved visiting Grandma's house, a house that always smelled of mothballs, a place where you were criticized constantly—for chewing gum, having hair in your eyes, turning over in bed (I slept with Aunt Bobbie). I loved being talked at for hours at a time, loved shuffling around in Grandma's huge sheepskin slippers when I got cold (what big feet you have!). It was with great excitement each time I would pack my bag and go off to spend the weekend with my Aunt Bobbie and Grandma. My aunt took me down each visit to Main Street for ice cream sodas and gave me a dollar to buy ten comic books. I'd buy all *Little Lulus*. With her perennial attempts to integrate the tree house, on which Tubby and the other boys posted "No girls allowed" signs, and the babysitting stories she would make up for Alvin about Witch Hazel and her niece Little Itch, Little Lulu was a great role model. She and the witches of her imagination seemed an integral part of the matriarchal world of my grandmother. Once, my brother packed his bag, anticipating that if he asked to spend the night he would certainly be allowed to do so. "Another time," Grandma said with a cold smile. No boys allowed.

Barbara Hughes

Unfortunately, Aunt Bobbie, whom Grandma kept at home to take care of her needs, didn't live up to her literary avatar Witch Hazel, being malignant only in small ways. Over the years I watched her go from being an attractive, cheerful, and hopeful young woman, who in my memory is always singing, "Every time it rains it rains / pennies from heaven," to a spinster in the most stereotypical sense. She worked for forty years as a clerk wrapping meat and vegetables in the local grocery store, never learned to drive, and never developed any interests outside of gossiping—not even watching television. When Grandma died, Bobbie left the house, as unmarried women will do, and in a small town where there were almost no apartments, rented a huge, dark, stuffy railroad apartment over a soda fountain. It faced an alley on one side and a long, dimly lit hallway on the other. She filled it with dark furniture of green, yellow, and blue plaids and kept the shades pulled low on the windows overlooking the alley so the light, dim as it was, wouldn't fade the fabrics. She kept a sharp lookout for any trash you might have created, like an empty soda can, and ran it out into the big bins so as not to dirty her pristine garbage cans. She had fussy knickknacks everywhere: Hummel figurines, dishes and ornaments with rooster motifs, and magnets that covered every inch of her refrigerator—magnets that she said were her "pride and joy."

Now that Grandma was dead, it was Aunt Bobbie's turn to hold forth with visitors, but while her speech was carping and critical like Grandma's, it somehow lacked the potency. It was more like a constant whine than rage. When you went to see her, it didn't matter how long you stayed; she was always upset that you were "in a hurry" to leave. Her desperation only increased your desire to get out of there, and as you walked down the dark corridor, practically feeling your way out, you felt you were abandoning her to the void and had narrowly escaped it yourself. Indeed, Aunt Bobbie fully rose to the pathos of her solitary condition, even holding herself up to me as a bogey figure, asking me through the passing years when I was going to get married, wrinkling her nose and warning, "You don't want to be an old maid like your Aunt Bobbie."

Well, that was for sure. Nobody would want to be an old maid like Aunt Bobbie. And let's face it, just about nobody wants to be an old maid. Women who came of age with the feminist movement, women who gleefully and relentlessly attacked the family as institution, still seem to be as anxious to escape that fate as women of former times. And how could you not, when the world outside of your various small communities views you with pity and contempt? "So, you never did marry," said a man from my youth, sorrowfully, seeing me (then in my thirties) at a wake. As if it might just as well be me in the coffin. The Ella in me might have responded, "So, you never did write a book, you goddamn pathetic loser." But even now, though some may not believe it, I have to struggle to keep Ella's spirit on call and to keep Aunt Bobbie's at bay.

Little women, romance heroines, and Deborah Kerr

In my preteen years, Little Lulu receded into the background, and romance heroines emerged front and center. From desiring to batter down the doors to the boy's club in the tree house, I shifted to fantasies of men battering down my barriers and conquering me by sexual force. The most thrilling line from my first romance, Emily Loring's *Stars in Your Eyes*, was uttered by the hero to the heroine, "If you keep looking at me that way, I won't be answerable for the consequences." Actually, I still think that line is pretty sexy.

After I discovered Emily Loring and then Harlequin Romances, I took to spinning my own romantic tales in my head at night before I went to sleep and at all hours of the day—in class, on the school bus or in the car, doing household chores, etc., and I continued telling them to myself for many years. The narratives were full of male bronco busters with names like Todd Fallon or Boyd Ballinger (taken from Harlequins) and pert, saucy young women. In a typical episode, the tempestuous heroine, riding bareback on an untamed stallion, would gallop away from the hero, furious because he had been laughing at her lack of common sense (this last bit was taken from my father). He would catch up with her, though, since his stallion was a little bit faster and his horsemanship just a little more skilled than hers. Driven crazy by the prospect of the harm that might have befallen her as a result of her reckless riding, he would yank her unceremoniously off her horse and crush her to him with a punishing kiss that left both of them panting. My stories would last for weeks and even months, and I would take my lovers through the early years of their marriage, the birth of their first-born son and other children as well—perhaps a little girl whom her father would worship because she was as adorable as her mother—but perhaps five or six sons and no daughters. Inevitably, however, the challenge of sustaining the eroticism through marriage proved too much for me, and I would reluctantly abandon the happy couple and begin a new story.

Meanwhile, Jo March became less important to me than Meg March and the latter's "progeny" in women's magazines, which, like Marmee in *Little Women*, instructed women in how to be selfless wives and mothers (while still taking ten minutes or so a day to pamper themselves, a pampering that in the end was sure to benefit the rest of the family, so no need to feel guilty).

One of the most potent images in my fantasy life was of me standing with the front door open greeting my husband with a smile as he returned from work (busting broncos or doing whatever it was he did for a living). I looked something like Deborah Kerr, whose picture I had seen on the cover of the Sunday magazine section; my raven-colored hair was coiffed and shining, my dress crisp. I scorned those slatterns whose husbands would come home after a hard day's work to find their wives in housecoat and hair curlers.

My husband would lift me in his arms, sit down on the sofa, and cradle me in his lap. He would kiss me passionately, murmuring erotic things in my ear in ersatz nineteenth-century English. For a man, he was surprisingly loquacious.

If dinner was a little late on such nights, the boys didn't mind.

Clare Hughes Modleski

In marrying my mother, my father, whose first marriage was to a woman twice his age, was canny enough in his widowerhood to choose a docile woman, softened up by years of enslavement to her mother, a woman much younger than he. My brother, my mother, and I were all in a sense my father's children. "Is he still mad? Did he start speaking to you yet?" my mom would whisper, trembling. Whenever he left the house angry, if she hadn't been around to see him go she would run to look in his closets, fearful that he had packed up everything and left her.

The way my mother figured it, men weren't for the most part "answerable for the consequences" of even the most extremely brutal behavior. A case in point: years before I was born, my father's brother Anthony, a policeman in Brooklyn, shot his wife and children and then killed himself. Of course, this horrifying skeleton was kept tightly locked up in the family closet (I'm surprised I was ever told about it at all). Once I asked my mother if anyone had an inkling of what drove Uncle Tony to commit this atrocity, and she said she didn't know, "but they do say his mother-in-law was a terrible woman."

If Uncle Tony wasn't answerable for the consequences of his actions, it's hardly surprising that my father was not considered responsible for his. Not that his was the worst behavior imaginable. I'm sorry to disappoint any experienced reader of memoirs who may be expecting a revelation of incest (as if men had to commit the most heinous acts imaginable before we hold them accountable for behaving badly: they get that much of a walk).

When my father mysteriously lapsed into one of his moody silences punctuated by sudden outbursts against us that seemed to come out of nowhere, my mother, ceasing to be my "sister," would order me to go to him and apologize.

"But Maaaa," I would bleat, "I didn't *do* anything."

"I know, but would it kill you to try to make a little peace? You know how moody your father is; that's just his way."

"But Maaaa, it's *my* way not to apologize when I didn't do anything wrong. What about *my* way?"

"Can't you just forgive? Why do you always have to be so stubborn?" Then the ultimate insult: "You're just like him."

When she would point out that no matter who the source of his anger was, she was sure to come in for some of the blame (which was true), what could I do but try to propitiate him, just as she did? So I found myself playing all the roles in the drama: the one who apologizes and the one who forgives, while my father admitted to nothing, forgave nothing.

For a few blissful years starting when I was about ten years old, my father got a job which required him to live away from home during the week, so we saw him only on the weekends. Then we had great times. When my father was home, he would often curtly order us to turn off the TV so he could go to bed early or listen to a game on the radio, usually maddeningly full of static. But on nights he was gone, we would get into our nightgowns and pajamas early, make fudge and well-buttered popcorn, and stay up late watching shows like *The Fugitive*, the story of accused wife-slayer Dr. Richard Kimball relentlessly hounded by authorities to atone for a crime he didn't commit.

Dennis Brorup's Penis

Given this family background the anecdote I am about to relate is at least understandable, if improbable.

Around the time I reached puberty I became convinced that I had committed the "sin against the Holy Spirit that cannot be forgiven."

I came across the enigmatic reference to this sin in the Bible, which I had taken to reading at night. My mother said that Catholics do not read the Bible on their own but rather look to priests to interpret it for them. So I had to sneak it into my room when my parents were asleep, just as young boys sneak the much less pornographic *Playboy** into their beds.

My intense relation with Catholicism was largely self-imposed. We were not sent to Catholic schools; we attended Mass no more than was required, never discussed religion, and went to confession only once or twice a year. Yet I pored over religious documents, fantasized about becoming a nun (when I wasn't fantasizing about being the Happy Housewife), and, relying on missals that were fast becoming out of date, learned all the laws pertaining to sin and damnation. The older teachings of the Church held that there were three places (putting limbo aside) to which one could go when one died: heaven, hell, or purgatory. The chances of one's winding up in purgatory for a short time were very great, since it was the place where souls would be purified of the venial sins that in all likelihood were still attached to them at death. Of course, when I say "a short time," I mean short by the standard of eternity. A soul could be in purgatory for several billion years, suffering even worse torment (on the grounds that the pains were ultimately destined to end) than the torment of the damned. And I learned that it was in the power of the living to procure time off for the inhabitants of purgatory through our good offices: each rosary we said would subtract a few years from the sentence being served by the object of our prayers.

Now, I figured that my little Polish grandmother (my other grandmother) might possibly be in purgatory (hell was out of the question). And of all human beings, I was most attached in my childhood to this woman, my father's mother, who lived with us for the first two years of my life and died the day after my third birthday. So one of my many fantasies of rescuing maternal beings from paternal ones centered on my attempts to extricate my grandmother from the clutches

---

*After all, Hugh Hefner never suggested daughters should be offered up by their fathers to be raped by other men.

of an angry God. Taking the Church's teaching to its logical conclusion, I indeed judged it to be a horrifying sin not to be saying *constant* prayers for a sweet little old lady whose excruciating sufferings it was in my power to cut short. Therefore, I prayed every time I had a few moments, and I have a vivid recollection of saying rosaries on the bus to an out-of-town basketball game.

My mother, who couldn't drive, wished that my father would take her to confession more often than he did, and I heartily concurred, though unquestionably for different reasons. The infrequency of our visits, rather than making me see confession as relatively unimportant, actually made it much more of an ordeal. So, for example, our missals instructed us to specify the number of occasions on which we had committed a given sin since our previous confession. It was hard enough to remember and have to admit to the number of times over a six-month period that I fought with my brother and "entertained unkind thoughts" about him; but how did I overcome my shame to confess to what seemed innumerable "impure thoughts and acts"? In reflecting on her impure acts, how was a young girl supposed to calculate acts of masturbation (the only "impure acts" I as an eleven-year-old had engaged in—not counting practicing movie-star kissing with my friend Geraldine Kubeck, which, come to think of it, didn't strike me as sinful at all)? Was it one sin per individual orgasm or per session? Here I was, a budding young feminist already grappling with the problem of reckoning multi-climactic female sexuality in terms of what we feminists once called patriarchal law (one God, one erogenous zone, one climax). I decided to take no chances and to count each orgasm separately, as one mortal sin. But what to do about the fact that you couldn't possibly remember what the total was over a half-year period? My theory was that, however mortifying, it was not wrong to overstate the extent of your wrongdoing (whereas if you guessed low on the numbers you received communion in a state of sin that meant you were actually cannibalizing the body of Christ). Therefore I always inflated the figures. "Bless me Father, for I have sinned; it has been six months since my last confession. I committed impure acts with myself 2,479 times." (As when estimating your income tax deductions, it seemed important not to give round numbers, not to say, for example, I committed impure acts with myself 2,500 times.)

One day, as I have said, I thought I had stumbled upon the sin against the Holy Spirit that can never be forgiven. In Matthew, Jesus is quoted as saying, "He who blasphemes against the Holy Spirit never has forgiveness, but is subject to eternal condemnation." I became convinced that this sin consisted of seeing in one's mind a picture of God's naked body. Once I became convinced that this thought damned you to hell for all eternity, it naturally flickered before my mind incessantly: God the Flasher. (For some reason, I tried to banish this unforgivable image by substituting a lesser impure thought—picturing Dennis Brorup's penis. Dennis was the boy next door and was not anyone to whom I was especially attracted. The unfortunate result was that I developed a kind of tic, and to this day pictures of Dennis Brorup's penis will from time to time appear unbidden to my mind's eye.)

When I tell people this story, they always want to know what God looked like naked. Of course, I believe His phallus was huge, but the crux of the issue is that I can't be sure, because focusing on the picture was forbidden. Impure thoughts, my missal instructed me, came in three categories. First, there were the kind that you rejected immediately when they occurred to you and hence were not sins at all. These were simply thought morsels Satan dangled in front of you, and if you could banish them on the spot, you were fine. Then there were those which you allowed into your mind but did not dwell on: these were venial sins. And finally there were the ones you "entertained": they were the mortal sins. I figured that the act of picturing God naked damned you to hell only if you held the thought in your mind, rather than dismissing it immediately. But what minuscule fraction of a second constituted immediacy? And did the distinction between venial and mortal sins even obtain in the case of seeing God naked? And if so, how could you ascertain the level of sin you had committed without reviewing in your mind the very thought you were not supposed to contemplate? And how could you confess to the priest something you couldn't even think about, much less say out loud? So you referred to it indirectly: instead of saying, I keep seeing God's member, I said, "Bless me Father, for I have sinned. I had impure thoughts about God

7,778 times" (adding the review sessions to the total count, of course). And when the priest said, "Say three Our Fathers and one Hail Mary," I thought, he just doesn't understand.

I was caught up in the toils of these paradoxes for about a year, certain of my own damnation. I couldn't talk to my mother because she was frightened of my fanaticism and, I think, terrified that I might be a little demented.

Since then some people have told me with enviable certainty that the sin against the Holy Spirit that cannot be forgiven is despair. But it turns out other people besides me have been unsure about the nature of this sin. In *A Portrait of the Artist as a Young Man*, James Joyce's hero Stephen is tempted to go into the priesthood just to find out what the unpardonable sin is. Coming across that passage in college gave me a kind of retroactive comfort, as did the discovery in the seventies of the comic book *Binky Brown Meets the Holy Virgin Mary*, in which Binky thinks that every time he passes a statue of the Virgin Mary, rays from his hands shoot out to touch her breasts. I doubt, however, that touching the breasts of a woman, even Mary herself, would have incurred the penalty of eternal damnation.

I don't care what people say; I know I was right. I had hit upon and been in danger of violating the cardinal law of patriarchy famously articulated by the French psychoanalyst Jacques Lacan: "The Phallus must remain veiled."

The Historian, Her Mother, and Her Dead Women: Past, Present, and Places In Between

Dyan Elliott

A T SOME UNSPECIFIED DATE TOWARD the end of the fourteenth century, the English matron, Margery Kempe, awoke to the sound of celestial music. She jumped out of bed and announced to no one in particular, "It is full merry in heaven"—the implication being that there was little fun to be had in her husband's bed. And in fact, much of Margery's subsequent spiritual odyssey was devoted to getting out of her husband's bed and staying out. After fourteen children, she finally succeeded in talking him into a vow of chastity.

Some six centuries later, the Canadian matron, Helga Elliott, experienced something similar at the christologically portentous age of thirty-three. Lying in bed beside my father, she received a vision of such clarity and power that it altered the entire course of her life. Nor does it seem incidental that while my mother was experiencing this infusion of grace, my father, asleep beside her, was beset by a horrendous nightmare—almost as if he knew what was in store for the rest of us.

When my mother found God, all hell broke loose.

My mother told her conversion experience to whomever would listen, as well as to those who wouldn't.

My mother continued to see things (my favorite was the angel dressed like a policeman).

My mother attended divinity school, which eventually broke her heart.

My mother would study until she dropped, rarely making the trip upstairs to her husband's bed.

My mother stopped cooking and cleaning.

My mother was never home.

My mother would grin puckishly when her children complained, reminding us that Helga meant *heilige* (holy) and that she had her priorities.

My mother made it a priority to chase us around the house every night in order to read from a dreaded book called *Our Response to God*.

My mother rewarded our begrudging attention to this book with a tautological dose of C. S. Lewis's *Chronicles of Narnia*.

My mother would drag her four children, still drugged with sleep, to the convent for Mass several times a week.

My mother filled the house with leering unbeneficed clerics and smug bewhiskered nuns.

My mother ensured that there was at least one nun at every family function (including birthdays) who would demand the tribute of a kiss on each of her hoary cheeks.

My mother was told by one of her nuns that the TV show *Bewitched* made light of the devil's work and advised that all my teenage books on the occult be burned. (Years later my niece refused to kiss this nun, claiming she was a witch, which served her right.)

My mother somehow requisitioned my body as a temple for the Holy Spirit, who was seemingly afflicted by an aversion to Tampax, shaving above the knees, fishnet stockings, and dating.

My mother gave much more to the church than she ever received
back.

My mother attempted to give me to the church.

My mother tried to stimulate my piety by threatening that the Hound
of Heaven would eventually get me.

My mother predicted I would become a nun.

My mother's bizarre tutelage convinced me that God was a thug, the
Holy Spirit his spook, and Christ's church the font of all misogyny.
I had to do what I could to share the news with other women!

Perhaps my mother's predictions generated a certain amount of appre-
hension about the future. This could explain my inclination to go
back in time. I scrambled backward as quickly as I could until I came
to a thud in the Middle Ages. I have been here ever since.

If my purpose was to get away from my mother, God, and his
misogyny once and for all, I seemed to have come to the wrong place.
Every medieval endeavor seemed to begin and end with an invoca-
tion of God, who created woman as an afterthought, and made the
entire human race live to regret it. Female intellectuals were few on
the ground. And the occasional woman who did become visible within
the historical record was often afflicted with the same mystical mal-
aise as my mother. But I must have realized, at least unconsciously,
that I had reached a place where my liabilities at last could become
strengths. My mother's vocation had ensured that I lived a life where
the familiar had always seemed a little strange; at last I had discovered
a place where the strange was familiar.

So I did what any writer would do—I wrote what I knew. My doctoral dissertation was on spiritual marriage: instances in which a married couple either agrees to abstain from sex on their wedding night
or in which one party convinces the other to take a vow of chastity
for purposes of piety. (As suggested in the above instance of Margery
Kempe, this was almost invariably the wife.) Even the lofty rhetoric
of hagiography couldn't disguise the unattractive subtext to many of
these tales: a family's dysfunctionality in the wake of the wife finding
God. My next book, written at a time when my mother was strug-

gling for ordination in the Anglican church (she was made a deacon but never a priest), focused on clerical efforts to create a female-free zone—whether in their own psyches or in sacred space. And the next examined how female mystics were used to promote the church's theological agenda, only to be discarded and even persecuted once this objective was met.

My research trajectory might suggest that I had gone to the past explicitly to relive the trauma of my mother's religiosity—accepting the grim comfort that Freud assures us comes with hysterical repetition. Who can say? It is only retrospectively that I have become aware of parallels between my work and my mother's restive spiritual quest. My professed reason for burrowing into the past was the desire for information: I had to find out more about the church to understand its macabre hold on women, to expose it to the world, and, although it was a little late to pry my mother free, at least I could have the satisfaction of taunting her for being so gullible (read "selfish") in the first place. My life story had equipped me with a strange kind of historical empathy that, I believe, simultaneously made me both sensitive to, and profoundly suspicious of, women's religious experiences. So occasionally I found myself wondering: suppose I did find the women I was looking for? Would they talk to me?

As it turns out, I was an expected guest, patiently awaited by my dear dead women (which was how I eventually came to think of them). The terrain which they inhabited was a familiar alterity: an anomaly captured by the mystic Marguerite Porete who characterized her spiritual destination as the kingdom of *Nearfar*. *I had gone back into the past for an exorcism, only to come away newly possessed.* But our communication was never exactly relaxed. There were always strict guidelines that had to be observed.

My dear dead women didn't write; didn't know the Latin in which their words were preserved; and it was too late for them to learn. So I learned.

My dear dead women revealed themselves slowly (my Latin is proportionately slow).

My dear dead women were patient with me, and I am learning to become patient too.

My dear dead women had time to kill; I spent longer cultivating our relationship than I did any other.

My dear dead women gradually moved closer to me than all others.

My dear dead women were subdued by my empathy, which was a key to their past.

My dear dead women cautioned that historical empathy could also distort the past, and warned me to beware.

My dear dead women taught me that the dead deserved the same respect due to the living.

My dear dead women insisted that the past shouldn't be used as my personal laboratory, therapy, self-medication, padded cell, or ammunition.

My dear dead women have no historical agenda, and they make me leave mine at the door whenever I wish to speak with them.

My dear dead women acknowledge that, from where I stand in the present, I can see things about their relationship with the church that they cannot see.

My dear dead women insist that I be very careful when I stand in the present and write about things in the past that they cannot see.

My dear dead women have never told me about the joys of the spiritual life, but I have never asked them.

My dear dead women agree that there are others who do a much better job writing about the joys of the spiritual life than could I.

My dear dead women are *gradually* teaching me not to use my mother's religiosity as a punching bag.

My dear dead women can't resist the occasional visit to the present to take a playful punch at me on behalf of my mother.

And here is their latest punch. My mother was, and continues to be, a woman of charisma and charm. But I always considered her more successful as a disciple of devotional disarray than as pious prophetess. If the Hound of Heaven did come a-calling, I was apparently not at home. My projected vocation as a nun also seemingly came to naught.

But my dear dead women choose to think otherwise. They remind me of the time when I was interviewed for a job at a celebrated, but very nasty, divinity school and asked the (illegal) question whether or not I believed in God. My answer was "No. But I literally think about God all the time." My dear dead women think this indicates that God may have plans for me yet. (I hope they are wrong.)

Fleeing and Pioneering Women: Matrophobia and My (Asian American) Feminist Praxis

Shirley Geok-lin Lim

ANY FEMINISTS HAVE NOTED WRYLY or mournfully that women who have visibly achieved some new notable pathway often exhibit close attachments to supportive fathers and critical rejection of mothers whose lives and actions had set up obstacles for their daughters as the young women attempted to break away from established gender roles and social constraints. I take up the challenge of writing as a mongrel academic-creative writer, between and in between the two institutionally-differentiated identities of scholar and poet, to talk about the psycho-sociological dynamics that arguably link these two acts, between fleeing the mother and breaking gender molds/roles, the former being wholly even if cruelly inevitable for many women in order to achieve the status, no matter how little conscious, of social pioneer.

The subject of matrophobia as the nodule for a notion of feminism is not original; Adrienne Rich dealt with this subject in her book *Of Woman Born: Motherhood as Experience and Institution* (1978). While matrophobia is usually defined as the fear of becoming one's mother, I understand that fear differently and therefore reject Rich's concluding formulation that only by embracing the mother does the daughter learn to love her body and other women. I define mother-fear as the antipathy to the actual figure of the historical mother, whose social weakness, whether exhibited as cowardice or cruelty, has had actual harmful repercussions on the children encircled inside her domestic domain. To embrace this mother, Rich suggests, is to understand, forgive, and, to my mind, reproduce her actions. Naomi Wolf, speaking as a third-wave feminist and with a sharper, less sentimental voice on fraught mother-daughter relations, notes, "No matter how wise a mother's advice is, we listen to our peers" (281). In a similar fashion, I see mother-fear as powering the young woman's restlessness for other forms of community—sometimes a quest with deleterious consequences, sometimes leading to a search for peers, even if in the form of older women, who offer an alternative and new form of gynolove (a woman-based, woman-centric homosociability separate from lesbian love).

The fear of mothers and the rejection of older feminist generations by younger women have not been examined of late (despite the rejection of Hillary Clinton by many women under thirty in the recent primary campaign for Democratic Party presidential candidate, and despite the decades-long ongoing complaints by second-wave US feminists and academics on being disrespected by their "daughterly" generation). Rich's critique of a hapless mother whose model sets up her daughter for unhappy compulsory heterosexuality is seldom referenced today. After all, contemporary women are hardly restricted to their mothers for gender models, but via the technologies of popular, mass, and instant culture receive overt and subliminal messages on their bodies, sexuality, talents, self-esteem, etc., from women as diverse as Oprah Winfrey, Madonna, Britney Spears, and Paris Hilton. A central issue, if not problem, facing any would-be pioneer or mold-breaking woman is the ancient problem that continues to befuddle women: the age factor. Except in exceptional societies more mythified than anthropologically recorded, old women are commonly viewed, even among themselves, as being over the hill. No longer capable of attracting heroes into their beds, birthing prized offspring, intimidating sons- and daughters-in-law, bearing sole witness to significant history, instantiating wisdom of the ages, or possessing healing herbs and cures, old women, particularly in the US, retreat to senior-citizen communities and, somehow, in flocks of thousands and more, survive publicly invisible and silent. And, even as I myself am looking down this darkened well of oblivion, there is a part of me that does not only not contest this ending but rejoices in it. Remembering the decision that Carolyn Heilbrun made in 2003, to set her own deadline for leaving the world, I understand and empathize with her choice, although I am uncertain that when I enter the stage of social decline I shall be as heroic and steadfast.

My seemingly irrational complacency at the inevitable giving way to the young has everything to do with my early separation, emotionally and physically, from my mother and the mothers before her. Indeed, of my father's second mother, the only grandmother I was acquainted with, this is how her image has imprinted itself on my moral sensibility, as drawn in the only poem I've written on her:

AH MAH

Grandmother was smaller
than me at eight. Had she
been child forever?

Helpless, hopeless, chin sharp
as a knuckle, fan face
hardly half-opened, not a scrap

of fat anywhere: she tottered
in black silk, leaning on
handmaids, on two tortured

fins. At sixty, sons all
married, grandfather bought her,
Soochow flower song girl.

Every bone in her feet
had been broken, bound tighter
than any neighbor's sweet

daughter's. Ten toes and instep
Curled inwards, yellow petals
of chrysanthemum, wrapped

in gold cloth. He bought the young
face, small knobby breasts
he swore he'd not dress with sarong

of maternity. Each night
he held her feet in his palms,
like lotus on the tight

hollows of celestial lakes.
In his calloused flesh her
weightless soles, cool and slack,
clenched by his stranger's fever.
(What the Fortune Teller Didn't Say, 13)

Does the poem contain fictional elements? Yes, for how can I know the relationship between a grandfather, dead by the time I was four or five, and this girl-child he brought into his household, who was still a physical although aged figure when I was ten and eleven? How can I even now intimate the sexual exchange between the two? Could I instead in the poem have imagined his tenderness toward her, her mixed feelings as a childless concubine, her complicated status in the household where the six sons borne by his first wife must have paid her the customary respect as their father's "second wife" while treating her with the male rudeness that was legendary in our small town concerning my grandfather's gang of boys?

The poem does not talk about Ah Mah's (the Hokkien term for "grandmother") well-known addiction to opium, which made her much more a figure of pathos; my memories of her occasional visits to our impoverished, unkempt household to beg for money; the way she took off her tiny embroidered cloth shoes, sighing at the relief of being seated, and the pungent salted-fish odor that came out of her wizened, deformed, three-inch feet. She was "my" grandmother only in filial association, and emotionally, wholly in dis-identification. My memories of such Chinese-based matriarchal figures can only be written as apophasis: these women's lives as they interacted with mine can only be deemed actively absent, and, like begging ghosts, shunned. Even now, berthed in a more secure contemporary American middle class, I fiercely deny any relationship to this grandmother, so Chinese in recollection, so much a victim, such an irreducible figure of social despair, of a cultural past which is claimed, if and when, only in a deep psychic revulsion, to reject. To the Western feminist who urges that we may yet recuperate some female heroic in this grandmother, I say, give me a break! Keep your orientalizing romanticizations to yourself. This rejection of the grandmother of sexual bondage, bound feet, opium addiction, and beggary forms a major wheel in the engine of my ambitions. To attempt to change such primal fear to admiration, albeit intellectualized, is ill-conceived, for the effort may well muck up the dynamics of (counter-) self-actualization.

As for my birth mother, of whom I have written many poems, imagined many versions, and discussed at some length in my memoir, *Among the White Moon Faces*, the ambivalence often expressed is chiefly intellectually constructed, while the emotional charge is, I argue and feel in my bones, totalizing. There was, before she left one day forever, another mother in my story. This mother was present and presence. She was the hand who combed and braided, so that once she was gone, I never did learn to comb or braid my hair, not really, not so that the unruly curls, split ends, and breakaway strands even today will stay neatly tucked. She was the mother who ensured we ate, no matter how mingily, so that even when I went to sleep hungry, there was a faint promise of something to be had tomorrow. I see this woman, with her mixed smile, half of hope and half of skeptical social knowledge, who must have been a loving figure. I use "must," knowing that I cannot in fact imagine this figure. She's been gone so long—mother of childhood, a type of woman many of us conjure in the very word itself, reified in Western mythology as Demeter, who faced death to recover her daughter, and as Mary, faithful, mournful, redeeming— that the memory of this mother's love, faded, cannot be trusted.

Does this deadweight of estrangement make me a bad daughter? Yes, of course. A bad daughter to a bad mother, and there's no prettifying the verdict. I am now older than my mother was when she died, so forgiveness is not a concept that needs to be batted about here. She will not benefit from it, and as an intellectual woman committed to integrity of mind and emotion, I prefer not to confuse desirable conditions and goals with actual facts on the ground. Would I prefer to be a more forgiving daughter? Of course. Someone said to me once, and I then thought he was acute in his perception, "You will never be happy until you have forgiven your mother." I think now that his statement was both presumptuous and fashionable psychobabble. Even as I do not in fact recall my mother as a loving figure, so the meaningfulness of her story—as a mother who abandoned six children, the youngest barely five, leaving them permanently to an unemployed husband, a man prone to violence who'd recently lost the family home and, destitute, was forced to live with his always hungry children in temporary shelter, such a woman, who went far away—lies beyond my ken. Her weakness may be understandable, but because my brothers and I suffered from her weakness, I am often tormented by the question, should the child forgive the tormentor? The yet vivid, rankling memory of this mother drives the engine of my fervor for social justice, the heat of my anger against cruelty, my knee-jerk responses to issues of human rights for all: the right to food, shelter, protection against evil, economic justice.

With these foremothers, for the abandoned, solitary girl-child to survive was already fiercely to enter pioneerhood, breaking decisively away from the female domestic history of victimhood and victimization. I dislike stories of victimhood, and I am uncomfortable with

narratives of reconciliation. With what, I ask, are we reconciling ourselves? So matrophobia drives me away and forward. One might para-
phrase T. S. Eliot's question in "Gerontion" to ask, after such mothers,
what forgiveness?

It does not surprise me, therefore, when young women laugh
at, disdain, and openly disrespect an older generation of feminists.
The sisterhood of the pantsuits? Playing the gender card? Not again!
Watching the ways in which public discourse over Hillary Clinton's
campaign for the Democratic ticket ran, the patent falsehood over the
18 million cracks in the glass ceiling, and Geraldine Ferraro's take that
sexism is worse than racism in the US, I know we deserve the threat of
Sarah Palin as the first US woman president. Women owe no stronger
loyalty to women on account of their common gender, at least not
more than we owe loyalty to every human on account of our common humanity. Yes, I am a feminist, but I am a humanist first.

In this way also, I do not set myself up as a pioneer Asian American
feminist. Every immigrant woman crossing the border into the terrifying paradise legally constituted as the United States of America
is a pioneer. The nation's history is a catacomb of pioneering bones.
Legend has it that the earliest Chinese in the US, generally male, were
tasked with the solemn duty to dig up the bones of Chinese dead to be
returned for proper burial in their South China native villages. Some
historical records bear testimony to this practice, but it has been over
a century now since such reburial was common. That is, even many
bones buried outside of the United States belong to American pioneers. American pioneers are everywhere and everyone.

When I am attributed pioneering status as one of the first Asian
American women to write on Asian American women's representations, to edit Asian American women's literary works, and to participate in academic conversations concerning Asian American women's
cultural issues, I think back, not only on the matrophobia that has
driven me toward the new world, a new social order, a new body of
writing, a new canon, a new image of the United States as a non-
white-supremacist nation, but also to the many US women who made
a professional woman like me—contentious, argumentative, restless,
contrary, questing, not always nice, not always right, and, yes, not

white—possible in the United States. Although they may not wish to have me claim their influence on me, I count Nancy Miller, Florence Howe, Claire Moses, Susan Lanser, Rachel Blau DuPlessis, and many other second- and third-wave feminists as pioneers who went on to mentor sister-outsiders. Many Asian American and other ethnic women writers have modeled the way forward: to name a few out of a telephone-directory-large generous community, Amy Ling, Elaine Kim, Maxine Hong Kingston, Mitsuye Yamada, Meena Alexander, and those whose words rang the bell of instruction loudly, writers such as Toni Morrison, Sandra Cisneros, bell hooks, Gloria Anzaldúa, Louise Erdrich, and many, many more.

While I reject my natal (grand)mothers, I admire and love many women. The one does not contradict the other. Nor do I disrespect the hard work involved in mothering, which stands alone and above all other human acts of generational care. It is, after all, the only family-relational word in the English language that possesses a full spectrum of grammatical usage. "Mother" and "father" function as both nouns and active verbs, but the gerund "fathering" does not function in English in the way "mothering" encompasses a panoply of verbal and adjectival significance and associations. (It is interesting that "parenting"—a gender-neutral gerund—takes the place of "fathering" in English usage.) I know many good mothers and have felt an occasional pang at observing the enormous social capital such mothers endow on their children. But in my feminist praxis I hold on to the constructed (not naturalized) claims and institutions of sisterhood. If we are of mothers born, we are also, more and more, of sisters formed. Sisterless, nonetheless, it has been sisters and sistering that have shaped me in the new world. Sistering is all about reciprocity, equity, equality in our storytelling status, loving each other through the years of famine and plenty.

There is a value to valorizing certain female cultural figures in the world of representation, figures such as my own beloved Jane Austen, for me the first among sisters, Virginia Woolf, Maxine Hong Kingston, Susan B. Anthony, and Susan Gubar. But, at the same time, I do not accept these historical women as inhabiting a hall marked "Pioneers." Reading their texts and about their lives, I imagine them working through bouts of doubt, beaten by fatigue, days expended on netting sentence after sentence together, unraveling and unstitching to follow those partial glimpses of thought and to tie down those feelings that were never intended for speech. Some of us are brave, but many more of us are tired, and sisters understand this existentialist condition literally. If scientists stand on the shoulders of giants, as Isaac Newton famously claimed, then pioneering feminists stand in the birthing room with a grand gynology branching every which way. I imagine this complex intellectual topography, a map of the universe of US feminist discourse, in which the Milky Way of women's lives as narrated shines with seemingly infinite points of light. If I am an Asian American feminist pioneer, it is as only one infinitesimal point among the starry hosts by which the dark night that is the condition of our existence is lit.

WORKS CITED

Lim, Shirley Geok-lin. *What the Fortune Teller Didn't Say*. Albuquerque: West End Press, 1998.

Wolf, Naomi. *The Beauty Myth: How Images of Beauty Are Used Against Women*. New York: Morrow, 1991.

Labial Politics

Patricia Yaeger

To start at the beginning means unearthing a deep-seated embarrassment. I feel uneasy about the sources of my feminism because they belong to subterranean fissures I've disavowed. From sixteen until the age of twenty-three I was what experts now call bulimic. I hate this word with its quick consonants and slimy vowels, but I hated even more the state it describes, so much so that I have not claimed this history. As a closeted ex-bulimic I refuse to talk about my hyper-agitated bodily despair with anyone—not my colleagues, not my students or children. My closest friends know, but in a minor, incidental way. It's just something (just my being) that happened a long time ago. And I respect this abstracted desire for silence. Writing this I'm abhorring each word and force-feeding this paragraph—but coughing it up nonetheless because I'm trying to tell this quick truth: bulimia was my path to feminism.

Amidst the buzz about Sandra Gilbert and Susan Gubar's *The Madwoman in the Attic*, I picked up their heavy book and found in the first chapter a description of female maladies. These syndromes were, they said, social in origin. Depression, hysteria, the vapors—any symptom that made women leave husbands or children and live in bedrooms, sanitariums, or faraway spas: these were nineteenth- and early-twentieth-century exits for angry women who refused their anger but also refused to commit suicide or live with *petit mal* normalcy. What? These maladies were not the product of individual bodies or weird psychic residues? Who knew? And then Gilbert and Gubar listed eating disorders among the socially induced maladies of the twentieth century, and I stopped reading, opened a small door in myself, and joined the sisterhood.

Okay, so I'm writing now, and I love the image of that little door, but this exercise also feels "hateful"—a word my mom used to describe all her children; and tears come, unsummoned. Eating salt, blinking back, I can't abide this old epiphany; it seems painfully obvious. Everyone else must have known. Not about my hungry secret but the world's secret: that this self-directed malady is social in origin, that we dress ourselves, helplessly, in the stigma of the social. And now the old obsession with reordering my body has become an intellectual as well as a somatic embarrassment. When I was a young woman, I couldn't bear the thought of not controlling my body. And now that I'm older, I can't bear the thought of not controlling my mind. I feel humiliated by not having known that my hell was social and shared.

Although my feminism began in extremis, it has continued in happier forms. I remain interested in the bodily asymptotes that obsessed me during late adolescence: gigantism, fragility, the pleasure of making a mess. But instead of focusing on these private cacophonies, my recent work follows the trajectories of unruly women who trash infrastructures, who leave patriarchy's armor in shreds: from Thelma and Louise when they blow up an oil truck in the southwestern desert, to Sigourney Weaver as a shoot-'em-up space girl in *Alien*, to the Ethiopian American artist Julie Mehretu, whose canvases—massive, intersecting blocks of architecturally drawn buildings disintegrating into flows of people or surging with advertising logos or national signage—show a world subject to erasure. I'm fascinated with Yin Xiuzhen's sculptures that take Shanghai or New York cityscapes and make them disposable: crafted out of thrown-away old clothes so that myriad buildings can fold into a single suitcase.

Pushed into a corner, I admit that my mother is also in this work. One year as an early adolescent I refused to clean up my closet, and she refused to buy me clothes. I went to school in the hand-me-downs of my cousin Mary Llew—dresses too long and a decade out-of-date, clothes that drooped on my droopy frame. We have always been twins. When Mary Llew and I were younger, our mothers entered us in the Little Miss Daytona Beach pageant in Florida. Neither of us won a thing, and afterward my mom kept harping, "Patsy, you were the cutest, but you were just too tall." I have never shaken off this feeling of taking up excess space, and I'm fascinated by mess-making women because they take up space and remain powerful, even when their closets aren't clean.

Size matters. But instead of writing about sublime mess-makers or my feelings about being too fat or too thin, I want to write about the spatial indelicacy of skin, about what folds, and folds into me. This essay will not be dedicated to being a tall girl, or to a ghostly bulimia, or even to my father's inability to throw anything out, but to a set of sibilant l and b membranes: to my labia.

On the day my mother taught me to use tampons, she looked at my genitals and gasped. "Oh, they're so big, so . . . you'll have no trouble having babies." She stared. What was the matter? Was I malformed? Eight years later, it was Little Miss Daytona Beach all over again. Could this be a compliment? I didn't think so, but wasn't she saying I was perfectly designed for rapturous reproduction? What was it about my labia that guaranteed easily emerging babies? These questions must have hung in my hair and curled my ears, but they floated out of sight until one day I started writing and dreaming about a compensatory animalia in the most unlikely creatures, sea slugs. Not those phallic-shaped, mile-long, all-over slimy creatures, the land slugs—like nothing so much as slow-crawling penises—but diaphanous, floaty, multicolored, always-undulating sea slugs. Sea slugs are also known as Nudibranchia, a taxonomic clade of "soft-bodied, shell-less marine opisthobranch gastropod mollusks which are noted for their extraordinary colors and striking forms." On TV's *National Geographic* I watched them dominate the screen, far superior to the seahorse, the manta ray, the blowfish, the dolphin. No creature was so beautiful or so much like me. I kissed the waters they swam in and imagined their constant adventures, in which nothing happened, really; they just swam and swam and then undulated like liquid crinolines—rippling and crinkly and always moving.

The mind is also an undulating thing. It compensates for old hurts with fantasias, and the very fact that a name as ugly as "sea slug" could seem so glamorous (no, not even "glamorous," not even "alluring," words connoting other people's desire, but self-ruffling, serene)—the serenity of this creature as it furled through the sea was consoling—and only now does it occur to me that these creatures don't live in the water unimpeded. They are, after all, food for fish.

Any number of feminist artists have addressed the aesthetics of the vulva; I don't claim originality for retinting my own labia as aqueous ruffles. What I do claim is that my labia have their own autobiography, their own life in my mind, and that this is important to me, just as other women's labia are important to them. Sex comes into this story, and also masturbation, but to write about these particular acts seems too generic. I want to be more personal.

Many years ago, when my daughter Victoria was one, she watched me in the bath, my pubic hair floating above the water like a bush baby taking a drink, and she waved at this floating fur as if it was a small animal. I laughed at our shared fantasies of the lower body's zoology. This was not the world I had shared with my mother, but a realm where genitals might be metamorphic. In fact, since I hadn't given birth to, but adopted my daughter, I never thought of my labia as her passageway or embroidered crown. Instead of opening for progeny, my labia stayed child-free.

A year or two later when my daughter saw a naked man (or a picture of a naked man, I'm not sure which), she asked, "Why does he have that frog on him?" I smiled and said that this frog was attached to the body and called a penis—although her vocabulary seemed more apt than my own. No Freudian fantasies for this little girl. Men were like women, except for their anomalous animality: the addition of a hanging amphibian. I explained that boys' sex organs were quite visible, while girls also had beautiful genitals that were secret or hidden and asked if she wanted a closer look at her own. When she nodded emphatically, I got out a mirror and held it in front of her stretched-out legs. And then every six months or so she would ask again to see herself in the mirror, until one day she asked to see, but told me to turn away—and I waved goodbye as she swam into her own private aquarium. While we, as women, share a labial intricacy, each of us may be bordered by different species of nudibranch.

In talking poetically and factually about labia, my language leans on French feminists who invented a labial language in the 1970s and 1980s that I found thrilling and useful. Luce Irigaray's "When Our Two Lips Speak Together" reimagines women with two mouths, each of them eloquent. Monique Wittig imagines the labia as simply one body part in a cast of thousands. These stories created new ways of thinking and feeling about our bodies for legions of feminists. Still, for me, there was that nagging voice, the worry that something was wrong— that instead of looking like a billowing nudibranchia, I resembled another kind of sea slug: the *Aplysiomorpha* or sea hares, "rather large, bulky creatures," including the largest of the gastropod species.

Not that I thought about this all the time. My labia floated up and floated down—sometimes coming to consciousness and sometimes not. And I could and did talk about women's right to experience their full sexuality (whatever that means) frequently, and with gusto. When my daughter was in junior high school, a boy and a girl were expelled because the girl sucked the boy's cock in an obscure corner of the playground—oblivious to a grown-up walking by. Talking this event over with my daughter, I decided not to protest these kids' sexuality, but to protest their inequality. It's not right, I said, that when young people hook up the way those students did, the boy's penis gets all the attention, and the girl's pleasure, her nudibranch, stays out of the picture. "Mom!" my daughter protested, and the subject was closed forever, but not before I struck a blow for clitoral sisterhood.

Each of these interactions involved a kind of labial pedagogy—but I still hadn't addressed the problem of my difference. What clade or suborder or species was I? And then one clear autumn night, a friend and I were waiting on the roof of a tall Ann Arbor building for a lunar eclipse, and we started murmuring about the size of our genitals and the uneasy feeling that they might be too large, or embarrassing, or lack the requisite ruffles or gills. We'd both enjoyed wielding a feminist speculum to discover the glistening orderliness of the cervix (it was surprisingly tidy and round), but we'd never figured out what to think about the outer walls of our genitals. Instead of undressing on the spot to compare size and color, we began by intellectualizing the problem: is there greater variety in men's or in women's genitals? And then we were joined by the feminist anthropologist Gayle Rubin, and as we watched the sun take bites of the moon, I asked Gayle whether men's or women's sexual bits were more divergent. In her line of research with gay men, Gayle said, she had probably seen more male than female genitalia, but she speculated that there was more variety among women and cited an exhibit of labial paintings by the feminist artist Tee Corinne. Four days later, what arrived in my mailbox? Tee Corinne's *Cunt Coloring Book*.

I ran around my department showing everyone willing to stop in the hall, until a graduate student almost fainted and I dived for cover. *The Cunt Coloring Book* was filled with page after page of clitoral, labial, urethral, and vaginal variety in pen and ink drawings that looked like—ah, were these new species of nudibranch? You name a shape, and it was there.

As the Wikipedia site on sea slugs explains, the orders of sea slugs go far beyond Nudibranchia:

> Cephalaspidea sea slugs include the colorful Aglajidae, and other heterobranchs such as the Sacoglossa, the sea butterflies, the sea angels, and the often rather large sea hares. The term sea slug is also sometimes loosely applied to the only very distantly related, pelagic, caenogastropods within the superfamily Carinarioidea, and may also be casually used for the even more distantly related pulmonate sea slugs, the Onchidiidae.

Shape after shape, name after name. Even among the nudibranchia there is not a wide enough terminology. Whenever we see Spanish Dancer, False Pyjama Sea Slug, or Three Striped Phyllidia, "these common names cause problems. Nobody can be sure, which animal you are really talking about. . . . But what is more important: more than

95 percent of the sea slugs don't have 'common' names. The authors [of guidebooks] are forced to create them."*

I, too, would like to create names and new pleasures for a multiplicity of labia, as I attempt to approximate the feral differences among families of outer lips (*grande lèvre, labio externo, grosse Schamlippe*) and inner lips (*petite lèvre, labio interior, kleine Schamlippe*), not to mention clitoral hoods (*prépuce clitoridien, tapa del clitoris, Vorhaut des Kitzlers*) and perineums (*perinée, perineo, Damm*). Each of us swims in this water, folding or unfolding in an extravagance of super-pelagic tissue. To celebrate, I need a tub of crayons and open seas.

*http://www.philippine-sea-slugs.com/general.htm.

The Piano Lesson

Jane Tompkins

THE WAY IT BEGAN WAS, WE WERE IN Woodstock for the summer: 1945, long before rock music made Woodstock famous. My parents had rented a cabin on a dirt lane next to Tannery Creek, which runs through the center of town. The cabin had two tiny bedrooms, a bath, a kitchen with an icebox cooled by an actual block of ice and, in a corner of the living room, an old upright piano. Nearer the creek lived the Magafan sisters, artists who wore their dark auburn hair in bangs cut straight across the forehead. They went to Mexico in the winter, and on the driver's door of their wooden station wagon they had painted the words *No tengo rancho* (I have no ranch): that was when poor artists could still afford to live in Woodstock. My mother was fond of saying the town was so bohemian you could walk down the street wearing nothing but a diaper and no one would notice.

She likes to remember how much it rained that summer. "It rained for nine days straight," she says. "You can imagine how damp it was." My father only came up on weekends, so, cooped up in that cabin and desperate to find something for me to do, my mother looked for a piano teacher. She'd thought of having me take art classes offered by friends who lived on the lane, but that didn't work out. I always felt my life would have been easier if it had. Drawing and painting seemed so much less fraught than piano-playing. For one thing, there would have been no recitals, and you couldn't make a mistake—at least not in the same way.

The teacher my mother found was Clara Chichester, who lived on the Glasco Turnpike with her ancient father and an English setter. Over the phone Mrs. Chichester had said she didn't take children as young as five, but when my mother explained that I could already play a song, she agreed to an audition.

On the appointed day we made our way up some stone steps and into a charming cottage where I was introduced to Mrs. Chichester's father, who sat with a white face and a bit of whiter hair, knees covered by a gray plaid shawl. Mrs. Chi referred to him, improbably, as "Dad." I promptly sat down and played and sang the tune my Aunt Margaret had taught me: "Do you remember the place where we met, long, long ago, long, long ago? Something and something I'll never forget, long, long ago, long ago." Mrs. Chi thought well enough of my playing that she took me. She would come to our cabin at such and such a time each week, and I, as it turned out, would "practice" in between times, learning the pieces and exercises I had been assigned. There seemed no harm involved. I didn't mind picking out the notes—it was rather like solving a puzzle—and people were impressed by it. Besides, my mother wanted me to. What harm could there be?

I learned to read music and to play pieces from a book called *Teaching Little Fingers How to Play*. "Off I go to music land, training ear and eye and hand." "Here we go, up a row, to a birthday party." "Dolly dear. Sandman's near, you will soon be sleeping." Even at five, the words seemed babyish, but I can recite them all. The old upright piano in its corner of the living room became my space, and I received attention because of what I was doing there—though what I did had no particular meaning for me beyond the occasional appeal of the sounds and the satisfaction of figuring out how to make them. It was a job, and at first, I progressed quickly from one task to the next.

At what point fear entered, and in its train a long coil of painful experience, I'm not sure. At some point, I must have grasped the idea of the mistake, by which I don't mean the ability to recognize a wrong note, which anybody could do, but rather the damage to one's self-image inflicted by the public commission of an error: I mean the mistake as producer of shame. At any rate, by the time I played in a recital at the end of that first summer, I knew what a mistake was, and the fear of failure in public performance was already set.

Before the recital, I had an attack of diarrhea. Mortified, and fearful of being late, I waited for the toilet along with another pupil of Mrs. Chi's, Jane Nehr, a fat girl, older than me, who boomed out, "If ya gotta go, ya gotta go." I didn't know exactly what that meant. I didn't know exactly what a recital was, either. The grand piano loomed on the stage of the Woodstock Town Hall. You were supposed to walk across the stage, sit down on the strange bench, and play your piece from memory on the huge instrument. The spaces on the stage were cavernous, brown and black; in the direction of the audience, I couldn't see a thing. But somehow, I walked out there and got it over with, another job of work, though why it should have to take place in a darkened hall in front of a lot of strangers I had no idea. I did what I was told.

From then on, fear is entwined with all my memories of the piano, for gradually, from being a mildly enjoyable activity, piano-playing became a problem and a burden, and I, from being a promising student, became a person perpetually guilty as charged—one who had not practiced enough, could not keep the tempo, could not play without stumbling and missing notes, and who didn't (though I only realized this later) display a proper feeling for the music. I knew Mrs. Chi meant well, I knew that in some way she even liked me, but the thought of her brings a sensation of imminent disaster. With her dyed blond hair coiled on top of her head, her small, piggish blue eyes and tweezed eyebrows, her large pores and gravelly voice, her black knit dresses—very smart, according to my mother—she would fish her eyeglasses out of their case, put them on and lean over to mark my music with her little red pencil; as she bent close I could smell her perfume. Years later, whenever I caught a whiff of it at the theater or in an elevator, I got a bad feeling in my stomach.

Though in school I was a star student who never disappointed, at home, on Tuesday afternoons when school let out, I was dead meat (for of course the lessons continued into the winter, since Mrs. Chi lived in the city then, as we did). The perfect scores I was able to maintain on my tests in math and spelling, the correct answers I could always give to the teachers' questions, the model deportment for which they regularly commended me—I behaved towards my teachers as if they were angry gods—caused me to believe that in life a spotless record was both mandatory and achievable. But on Tuesday afternoons, that expectation was crushed, and my ego along with it.

When I got home they would be having tea in the living room, my mother and Mrs. Chi. They were in cahoots. With their cigarettes and their superior taste—they drank lapsang souchong—they had discussed my case (I assumed) quite thoroughly and knew all that there was to know. I would cross the living room, sit in the yellow chair, and wait, stomach churning, until it was time for the lesson to begin.

The feelings of doom and shame, the struggle to play correctly, a frustrated Mrs. Chi beating the time on my shoulder, the embarrassment at my mistakes, the awful ticking of the metronome (I detested the metronome—my mother had bought a fancy one with a silver inlay that she had made into a lamp), the red markings on my music were repeated, week in week out, fall, winter, and spring, with just enough passable lessons to keep me from revolting and Mrs. Chi from dismissing me—though it's possible she needed the money and kept me on because of that. The myth was, and would continue to be, that I had "talent," though where it lay or in what it consisted I had no idea. At any rate, come May, there was the recital at the Park Avenue apartment of some rich student, and in summer, lessons in Woodstock. I hated it all.

Then, why did you do it? Why didn't you tell your mother you didn't want to take piano lessons any more? Were you so beaten down that you didn't have a voice of your own? Surely if your mother had known how you felt she wouldn't have made you continue.

I'm not sure, really. I've no idea what my mother's investment in the piano lessons was. For myself, I clung to the idea that I was "talented" and liked the attention I received—none of my friends or relatives played the piano—and of course, I didn't want to disappoint my mother and Mrs. Chi. I felt that not to continue would be letting them down, a betrayal. And after a while there were pieces I liked to play—a Clementi sonatina here, a Mozart minuet there—and later something called "The Dream of Olwen" that I loved, as it was romantic and not too hard. When we left the city and moved to the Jersey suburbs, I continued taking lessons because it seemed part of my identity; when everything else was changing, the piano provided continuity, even if it was painful.

I sometimes think there is a fatality in children's lives that is nobody's fault and that no one can stop. We blame parents or teachers or other responsible parties for damage done, when really it was just a combination of circumstance that caused the harm. I think of my sister-in-law, Rita, who told me when I asked how she'd felt about school, about a teacher who had announced to the class at the start of a question period that people shouldn't repeat one another's questions. Rita, a shy soul but very bright, listened for a while and finally got the courage to raise her hand. When she was called on, the teacher thought her question resembled one that had already been asked and reprimanded her sharply. She never raised her hand in school again. Some things acquire a momentum that can't be stopped.

And so when we moved to New Jersey, I found myself in the living room of Manfred d'Elia, a once handsome fellow who, I suspect, was disappointed to be giving lessons to ten-year-olds instead of appearing at Carnegie Hall. He had an imposing profile and an imposing grand piano, though the students played on a spinet in a den on a side of the house that had a separate entrance. Mr. d'Elia was rougher around the edges than Mrs. Chi, paid no court to my mother, and certainly paid less attention to me, which was refreshing. But he was no more satisfied with my playing than she had been, and lessons soon turned into the same round of anguished anticipation, tortured execution, and, when they were over, blessed relief.

Sometimes Mr. d'Elia would impatiently push me aside and sit down at the piano to show me how my piece ought to sound. He'd stumble over the notes at first, blowing air through his nose as if he had something stuck in it, but once he got going there was so much energy coming through his hands onto the keyboard, a power that forced the notes to fall into place and the composition to sound fresh and bracing, that I could feel it in my own body as I stood there listening. It was as if I had never struck a note in my life, so great was the difference between his playing and mine.

That power was the thing that was missing when I played the piano, a live connection, physical and spiritual, between my body, my spirit, and the keys, something electric that ran from the center of my being into the notes and flowered in music—that strange mystical blossom that hid itself from me. Every now and then I sensed its fragrance in a passage I played, and at long intervals I felt myself caught in the arc of an impulse that carried me through an entire piece—music, divine and unrepeatable. It could be present in a single chord or series of chords, it might linger in a haunting succession of notes, or sound in the harmony of a certain interval, say the F sharp major thirds in a Schumann Romance. But it kept itself scarce. Like a wood nymph or a satyr, it never showed itself except under certain extraordinary conditions, evoked by magic, disappearing without a trace.

One day while Mr. d'Elia was showing me how something ought to be played, I had to go to the bathroom. I stood there in agony as he played on and on, afraid to interrupt the maestro as he demonstrated for my benefit. Finally, I just let go. When he saw what had happened, he was disgusted, but set about matter-of-factly mopping up the rug with an old cloth and sent me off to the bathroom to make what improvements I could. He was decent about it. Looking back, I wonder what fear made me stand there mute, what inability to be for myself. Whatever it was, something had so sapped my courage at the piano lesson that I couldn't ask permission to meet my bodily needs, not even in order to avoid humiliation.

The more I think about it, the more it seems that playing the piano was all about the body and one's relation to it, by which I don't mean the tedious instructions on how to hold one's wrists, fingers, elbows, and so on—every teacher had his or her own formula, guaranteed to produce results, and if you didn't adhere to it, you were damned. No, it was the body electric that was needed at the piano, the body of instinct and desire, whose energy was connected to the atoms and the constellations. It was related to sex, that body, ironically and unfairly: the thing that was forbidden was exactly the thing that you needed to have.

Around this time I discovered a paperback novel lying around the house called *Woman of Rome* by Alberto Moravia, and started reading it. This book gave me feelings I felt I shouldn't be having, obscure, pleasurable feelings that were somehow not right. The story was about a prostitute who falls in love with a man who doesn't love her and, toward the end, is raped by a murderer. It was full of sex, which I didn't understand, and full of humiliation for the female protagonist. She ends in degradation and hopelessness, a fate which, as far as I could tell, she'd done nothing to deserve, and for which she received little or no sympathy from the author. It was a bad introduction to sex and not a good recipe for a young girl who already had problems with self-esteem.

Mr. d'Elia fell asleep one Saturday morning while I was playing Mozart, something I suspect had occurred more than once, only this time there was no getting around it; the snores were loud and clear. When I told my mother, she terminated the lessons at the end of the school year and found another teacher for the fall.

By this time the piano had gotten a grip on my psychic life and entwined itself with a general feeling of entrapment and a caving in to authority. In tenth-grade English class I wrote a short story about a young man whose gift for the piano has been discovered early and is sent by his parents to the best teachers. When the story opens, he's sitting in the green room of a theater where he is about to give a concert, thinking about his life. Governed entirely by the need to practice and perform, it appears to him in the guise of a long corridor down which he must walk, looking neither left nor right. Doors line the corridor on either side, some closed, some ajar, beckoning; none of them is he allowed to enter. It's a hot summer day, and on the counter stands an electric fan, its face turning back and forth. The young pianist hates performing and fears it but sees no alternative. As he sits there watching the fan, it occurs to him that by sticking his hand inside the grille that guards the whirring blades, into the soft fog that could shred his fingers in an instant, he could end his misery. But there's a knock on the door, it's time to go. He gets up in defeat, walks onto the stage and there, on the shining black concert grand, right on the piano itself, its face turning back and forth, is an electric fan . . .

You'd think that having written a story like this and having escaped Mr. d'Elia's lukewarm grasp, I would have managed to get out of taking any more piano lessons, but no. I was caught up in my mother's idea that I deserved a better teacher. And there was one.

Doris Frerichs lived on Mountain Avenue—Ridgewood, New Jersey's premier address. Her pale, wide-set green eyes pierced you from under a broad brow, and her big mouth full of teeth smiled with a combination of aggression and glee. Me she hypnotized, and as for my mother, who knew a good teacher when she saw one, there were enough airs and graces, classic furnishings, and high culture references knowingly dropped to satisfy her. A whole new world was opening up; from now on my talent would receive the cultivation it had long deserved, and I would ascend to a pianistic empyrean there to realize the essence of music.

Of course, there was the Method to be mastered—fingers just so, wrists, arms, et cetera—but always there wafted in front of me the angel wing of Miss Frerichs's rhetoric on which I was shortly to ascend. This was serious, the stakes unimaginably high. To fail, inconceivable for souls as rare and illuminated as ours. I was cast in the role of disciple and felt specially chosen. As long as Miss Frerichs talked, eyes gleaming, hands gesturing grandly, and I listened, borne aloft by her conviction and enthusiasm, all was well.

Well, it *was* better. Miss Frerichs talked to me as one adult to another, albeit adults of different stations in life. Though many times I fell short of expectation and my playing limped along with neither fire nor conviction, she could always galvanize me again. I came to enjoy the lessons that consisted entirely of her inspired preaching, even though they were occasioned by failure on my part; it relieved me of the burden of performance and the risk of falling short yet again, and I felt flattered to be the recipient of so much intense concentration. At these times I believe Miss Frerichs saw herself as my ally, bucking me up and giving me courage, and even, perhaps, underneath it all, trying to free me from my mother's domination. But she could never succeed. For in my universe, Miss Frerichs was an extension of my mother, another instantiation of adult authority, and therefore could never really be on my side. Still, I felt flattered by her attention, flattered, exalted, and unworthy.

For I knew, mere ninth- or tenth-grader that I was, that I was not the material Miss Frerichs deserved or was looking for. She spent hours preparing me and her other pupils for auditions, presumably the first step on a ladder that led to glory, held in small practice rooms at the back of Carnegie Hall, auditions in which (I don't know how the others did) I played poorly. It was too bad. I wanted to fulfill her dreams, to rise on wings of song and be consumed by the flames of musical passion. But that was it, you see. Whatever passion I had was artificially induced by *her* passion, which would suffice for the two of us for only so long. It wasn't that I didn't like music in general or the piano in particular; it was that I didn't love it. There was an exercise I was supposed to do in rising thirds, CEDFEG, DFEGFA, to which she urged me to sing "I will *love* my music, I will *love* my music." But though I practiced the exercise, I never sang the words. I didn't love the music in the way she meant and didn't want to be forced to—couldn't be, in fact, it wasn't possible. I simply felt deficient and slogged on.

Miss Frerichs was a great teacher, in that she saw the potential in me and tried with everything she had at her disposal to elicit it. She was passionate, committed, willing to take risks in the service of her students, but time and chance were against her. Just before my senior year of high school, we moved to Pennsylvania. The next year I went away to college and stopped playing altogether, sensing that attending Bryn Mawr was enough of an accomplishment and that I no longer needed the piano to make me special. But one day years later, I was shopping for shoes in Manhattan on Christmas vacation and looked up from my seat in a Fifth Avenue store to see none other than Doris Frerichs by my side. I was shocked to see her, and a dart of fear went down my spine. I told her about my life—husband, PhD—feeling guilty that the piano figured nowhere in my account and sorry that she, a spinster, had poured her life into pupils like me who didn't bring much return on her investment. She maintained her pride, boasting somewhat reproachfully of a former student who had written a dissertation on "The Marriage of Music and Poetry in Renaissance Something-or-Other," the implication being that *he* (or she) had carried the torch successfully into later life. Well. We said our good-byes, she rose, reached the door, and just before exiting, turned and let fly with: "I guess your mother won't have *you* to ride herd on any more." The parting shot zinged across the room and into my heart, a direct hit.

As for the piano, excellent a teacher as Miss Frerichs was, it turned out that what I needed was something quite different. The summer after graduating from high school, I got a job in a music camp in the Adirondacks where one of the perks was free piano lessons, so I took. The teacher, a Hungarian named Joseph Wittman, didn't care if I played well or not. His indifference was balm to my soul. He just smoked cigarettes, looking preoccupied and darkly interesting. After listening to me play, he gave me practical tips on how to improve my technique—what a relief!—and critiqued my interpretation of the first movement of a Beethoven sonata I'd been working on. Though my vanity was piqued, it didn't hurt much because I understood that what he said wasn't about me, it was about the music. For eight weeks I related to the piano in a workmanlike way: no tears, no self-flagellation. I even had an inkling of what it might be like to play, as it were, in another key, one in which I would become an extension of the music, body and soul so bent to its requirements that the piece would simply play itself through me. I envisioned this possibility, even if I didn't quite realize it, and the recognition set me free. I felt I need not struggle with this angel any more. I went to college, bought a cheap guitar, and taught myself to play. It was the era of the Kingston trio and Joan Baez and I loved sitting around the dormitory with my friends, singing and accompanying myself in a rudimentary way ("She was a lass from the low countree . . . "). I was playing only for myself. I swore I would never take a guitar lesson in my life.

———

Years pass. If this were a movie it would show me, in short order, going to college then graduate school, teaching, getting married—once, twice, three times—and ending up in a house in North Carolina in my mid-forties, superintending the moving of my parents' piano (an old parlor grand) into my living room. My parents had moved out of their home of many years and into a retirement community. Though I no longer played, who knew? Maybe some day I'd learn to sight-read—from time to time I'd had visions of myself playing Christmas carols with people standing around singing their hearts out, like characters in a scene from *It's a Wonderful Life*.

This never happened. But not long after, a houseguest who stayed for seven weeks wandered into the living room one day and started playing. It sounded wonderful, and he seemed to derive so much joy from it that for a moment the dream of entering the realm of successful performance opened before me again. Martin showed me his teacher's method, a sensuous stroking of the key in slow motion that allowed each tone to reverberate, so you could feel the sound travel up your arm as well as hear it. You played a scale that way with one hand, slowly, then with the other hand, then with both hands, a sonorous, meditative involvement with vibration and touch that absorbed the attention completely. I sensed the wisdom of this technique, but it was a wisdom I couldn't appropriate because the problems it touched—lodged in my body, my hands, my arms, my back, a muscular memory of fear and failure—felt too old and painful to address.

But not long after, when a friend at the university decided to take up the piano for the first time, I saw what it was like to play without a history. Barbara was fiercely intellectual, competitive and combative—I loved to hear her argue a point. She was in her late fifties or early sixties and had never played the piano before. She bought a Steinway baby grand, found a teacher, and never looked back. Immediately she learned to sight-read, bought CDs of piano performances, sent away for music, and soon was making her way through the literature of the piano, relishing every note.

Now and then, she would invite me over for tea. She lived in a sturdy, many-windowed house in the forest, full of earth tones and shining wood surfaces. Sometimes we'd walk in the woods first along the banks of the New Hope Creek. After tea, which always featured some delicious sweet, I would end up lying on her sofa listening to her play the piece she was working on at the moment. I loved hearing her play.

Barbara moved steadily through her piece, playing with gentleness and persistence, sometimes feeling for a note, sometimes having to start over; there were "mistakes." None of that mattered. Her love came through, and the effect on me was magical. Her playing had an innocence and purity about it. She wasn't anxious, and she wasn't afraid; as far as I could tell, she had no hang-ups at all. At whatever level of competence she was able to play it, she appreciated the music thoroughly. "Play some more," I'd say, and I'd hear again the true, clean sounds of the Steinway. There was something poignant about her playing that moved me and gave me exquisite pleasure. I've often thought that the times I spent lying in her shadowy living room hearing the pure notes were my finest moments in relation to the piano.

One night my husband and I attended a concert on campus given by a visiting pianist. In the intermission we ran into Barbara. We greeted each other effusively but never got around to discussing the performance, though just before it was time to go back in, Barbara indicated that she had decided opinions about the concert. I've since wondered what she was going to say. The performer's technique was beyond brilliant; he turned the piano into some other instrument, almost, with gossamer webs of sound, impossibly delicate glissandos, contrasted with furious percussion and the precision of a stiletto. His virtuosity made me gasp, but soon, it left me cold. It was all pyrotechnics without a spark of soul. Music, I'd begun to learn, in part from listening to Barbara, was not just in the notes.

Some time shortly before leaving North Carolina, where I'd lived for almost fourteen years, I took it into my head to take a piano lesson. It turned out that I already knew someone in the music department at the university who taught piano. A mutual friend told me that she was a wonderful teacher. Her name was Jane.

Jane's personality was soft and light, and I was immediately comfortable in her office, a large, pleasant room in the music building. She was full of humor and seemed to take everything lightly, which is to say, gaily, without drama—her teaching hadn't the faintest trace of self-importance or high seriousness. Mostly we laughed. And what we laughed about was the insanity of my education in the piano which, no matter what my teachers may have said, had always emphasized the avoidance of mistakes. From the age of five to the age of seventeen, I'd been terrified of making a mistake and as a result was never able to open up to the instrument. Short-circuited by fear, that current of energy, the energy of creativity and desire I'd seen coursing through Mr. d'Elia's fingers, seldom had a chance to flow through mine.

And this energy, I discovered at the lesson with Jane, didn't have to be heavy or intense; there could be whimsy involved, even nonsense. For her, playing the piano was fun! I sat on the piano bench dazed with disbelief. It couldn't be. You mean . . . after all these years . . . I didn't have to do it perfectly? I could *not care* if I played a wrong note? And not only that, it was okay to make *lots* of mistakes? We were giddy, I was dizzy, unable to get my bearings. It was too good to be true. My whole experience denied it. How could it be true? But it was. We practically danced around the office with elation.

This happened some time in November. In December, we moved to Chicago, I fell ill, and my plans to take lessons never materialized. But one day, after seeing the movie *Shine*, about a concert pianist from Australia who overcomes family obstacles to become great, I went home, sat down at the piano, which I hadn't touched seriously in years, and played for two hours without stopping, enjoying every minute. Something got into me, some fearlessness, some devil-may-care that propelled me through every piece I knew and some I didn't.

Last spring, after moving to Florida, I started playing again. I had breakfast with a friend of a friend who taught piano and who knew just what to prescribe for a traumatized one-time, would-be piano player. Try sight-reading really easy things for about ten minutes, she advised, to build your confidence, then switch to scales and exercises for as long as it's interesting, then work on a piece you'd really like to play. The sight-reading built my confidence; the scales and exercises made my hands feel good. And every time, the piece I chose to work on was one of the *Eighteen Short Pieces* by Johann Sebastian Bach I happened to have on hand. I made no progress. The Bach pieces never got any better than when I started and so I gave up trying to play them the way I thought they ought to sound; I just practiced, slowly, first one hand, then the other, then both hands, and the beauty of the individual notes as they floated up into the air and out the windows of the house and into the neighborhood was a delight. No one complimented me on my playing. No one objected. I just played for the sake of doing it, for the beauty of the notes as they wafted through the air, and for the feeling of doing something purposeful with my hands. Now and then I get discouraged because there is no "point"—so conditioned are we to self-improvement, so enslaved to accomplishment—but when I miss a week or two, I notice the difference and start playing again. The sounds are satisfying, no matter how simple, and my fingers feel better than when I'm not playing at all.

So what is the lesson, Jane? What did the piano teach you? Can't you give us a nugget to carry away?

When I think about the piano now, I see it less as a musical instrument that I'm supposed to know how to play and more as a mysterious object set down in the middle of my life, tantalizing, inviting inspection, and at the same time warning me away. I think of pianos I have known. The piano in the perfume ad from *The New Yorker* of my childhood, in which a handsome violinist passionately embraces the lovely young accompanist half risen from the bench, shoulders bare, gown flowing gracefully behind her, hand still resting on the keys. Ah! That is not my piano. Nor is it the piano of my Christmas carol fantasy, the bourgeois piano of fellowship and good cheer. It's not the concert grand of the doomed young soloist in my story, nor the spinet at which the heroine accompanies herself in a British novel of the eighteenth or nineteenth century, charming her suitors while she sings in a clear soprano. None of these.

And it's not the piano in the movie of the same name, played by

Holly Hunter on the New Zealand shore, pouring forth an iridescent skein of sound that tumbles over the beach and into blue air, and plays again in Harvey Keitel's bungalow while he stalks around the room naked, the piano beneath which they later fall to make love. These pianos, full of romance, entangled in desire, despite their imaginary status are more solid than mine. Woven of circumstance and accident, my piano waits to ambush me in various guises. Less of an object than a psychic space, because it was not my natural instrument and didn't come easily to me as so many other things did, the piano became my ally in the way that hardship can sometimes do, making me see myself from an angle that few other experiences had. It was and is a kind of a proving ground, a place where things turn up in my life, a locus of pain and frustration, opportunity and promise, calling forth curiosity, obedience, striving, wonder, the urge to please, vanity, diligence, and sometimes, when it incarnates as music's emissary, fulfilling the desire for connection to a higher realm, becoming the source of a few pure notes that cleave the air and vanish into it, dissolved in the flux of time.

The summer I was at the music camp in the Adirondacks, the senior counselor in my cabin had two records I'd never heard that she played over and over. One was the Four Freshmen singing songs like "Street of Dreams" and "Mood Indigo"; the other was Glenn Gould's first recording of the *Goldberg Variations*. Over the eight and a half weeks of camp, it worked its way into my mind, becoming and remaining my favorite piece of music. Beginning with a statement of the theme, simple, pure, untroubled, given to Bach by his patron, it runs the gamut of mortal possibilities—frenzied, peaceful, bumptious, playful, witty, pedantic, sonorous, trilling, Gould throwing himself into each one with total abandon—and finally comes to rest in the theme's restatement, all the pieces of the puzzle falling into place, conflicts resolved, turbulence soothed, worries relieved, reminding us that all is order and beauty, as the poet said, and that our souls can be at rest.

In My Family,
We Spoke in Tongues

Rayna Rapp

Father, the gods endow men with good sense,—
Highest of all things that we possess

—HAIMON in *Antigone*, L.737

IN MY FAMILY, WE SPOKE IN TONGUES. "Progressive," we said, and "People with good values." Like the Yiddish to which they turned when they wanted to keep secrets, my parents surely used this language not only as an intimate code for themselves, but also to protect me: they had vivid memories of children interrogated by demon FBI agents who forced them into betrayal; they never wanted me, small fry in the rank and file, to know too much. Whatever one knew might be inadvertently dangerous: affectionate family parables taught me to watch my words and my back. On a trip from our then-suburban home to the city, I was always reminded, for example, about how I piped up in my shrill ten-year old voice while standing on the rail platform among scores of presumably conservative commuters to query, "Daddy, did you remember to bring your Communist ticket?" And heartfelt kindred humor included the story of a young cousin who asked his mother for a definition of "aristocrat." After providing a didactic explanation that began with the French Estates and moved toward Thorstein Veblen at a rapid but very detailed clip, Judy finally paused to take a deep breath and remembered to ask her son where he had learned the word. "I read it on the back of the toilet bowl," he replied.

It was only on a family vacation to Quebec, across an international border, that we overtly used the C-word. I was halfway through high school by then, impersonating a cheerleader in the hope of passing. The following year, I got sent to the principal's office when I refused to duck and cover in the bowels of the school's air-raid shelter during the Cuban Missile Crisis. Children of friends who were then old enough to be in college found scores of their opposite numbers on the trains they all silently boarded into the city from SUNY–Stony Brook at the same time: wordlessly, they all had assumed that their parents were about to be rounded up and interred, and they were going home. Cautious activism wrapped in reflexive paranoia had by then been bred in the bone.

Being a red diaper baby was not without wit and empathy: it's an endlessly told story of worldview vertigo in which no one ever felt the need to say "God bless America," although we thought of ourselves as the greatest of patriots. More than the unsuspecting masses, duped into opiate stupor, we intended to patiently preach the rational interests of the working class until they finally coincided with common sense. Then, as my first ex-mother-in-law so cheerfully put it, "we'll make a picnic on the White House lawn. Only please don't tell anyone just yet. If you do, they'll come to arrest us." As many have noted, we believed our cause just because it spoke to the real heroes of American society, those who produced its abundance but failed to benefit from its profits. Our values made good sense. Only they didn't quite correspond to reality: as the South Asian dad in My Beautiful Laundrette would later proclaim, "The working class has been such a disappointment to me." Its own myriad rationalities were beyond our ken. Among ourselves, we "just" neglected to think through the menacing irrationality and murderous brutality of the Stalinist terror, although we read Victor Serge with avidity. When I, a confused visitor to American culture, finally waltzed off to college, anthropology was a natural major. There, I might meet other Martians and learn the local language.

Family values also inclined us red diaper babies to rationalize hard work and to work harder still whenever we discovered an error in our ways. Long before Maoist tendencies brought the Trojan Horse of criticism/self-criticism to our beleaguered movement, we Commie kids knew that you had to learn from your mistakes and soldier on. At early women's movement meetings, I was affectionately known as a Stalino-feminist, committed to keeping democratic order and making sure our work got done, despite the passionate and personal meltdowns often caused by the intensity of our politics; Stakhanovite might have been a better term for my commitment to hard labor and self-effacing leadership. While my parents and I had our hard times over the Weather period in SDS, I felt endlessly supported for my civil rights, anti-war, and early women's movement activities. Unlike almost everyone else's family, mine backed me to the hilt. We might engage in bitter disputes over strategy and tactics, but my family certainly understood the need for immediate social change. Often, we'd make a rendezvous in New York or Washington DC when I bussed in for anti-war marches and rallies; they were as likely to be there as anyone else I loved. So it made perfect sense that these values of hard work, rationality, and confidence in the importance of making history with and for righteous others would be carried directly into my early feminism. So far, so good.

It is hard now to convey the headiness of early women's movement utopianism: we truly believed that if we worked hard enough, the world would immediately transform under our direction. Health activism was my passion, reproductive freedom my cause; it was all of one piece, as we broke into the statehouse to hex the Michigan legislature as WITCHes (Women's International Terrorists Conspirators from Hell) and provided abortion counseling that moved women from the Midwest to New York clinics in the year between local legalization and the bittersweet federal victory of *Roe v. Wade*. In an early 1970s' photo, I stand, long-haired and sandaled, holding a huge sign that reads "free legal abortion on demand" on one side and "end sterilization abuse now" on the other. But my work life would eventually be tied to practices I then considered as immediate as the air that I breathed. We founded women's studies because it was urgently imperative—as the poet Audre Lorde would later elegantly describe it—that we revise all masculinist systems of knowledge beginning with anatomy and ending with zoology. Anthropology was near the top of the list.

We had our work cut out for us as we invented feminist methodologies for the science of man. Some of us feminized the classic charts of kinship; others set off to reinvent the ethnographic corpus. Collectively, we interrogated work, nationalism, development, violence, expressive culture, and a vast array of other topics as if women mattered. Increasingly, they did. We thought long and hard about our achievements, and our failures, as well. It is one of the big success stories of our interdisciplinary assault on the ivory towers that anthropology proved a more-or-less early and willing ally as we redrew its boundaries and transformed its content. We faced our share of ordinary contempt and resistance, but the field as a whole was remarkably open to our demands. I remember shaking in my shoes as I strode up to a formal professional meeting attended by thousands in the grand ballroom of a Hyatt or Hilton, intent on presenting a resolution against the sexist hiring practices of a bunch of universities including Harvard, only to have several male old-timers provide a crash course in Robert's rules of order, so that our voices could not be silenced on the grounds of a rational technicality. We won, to considerable cheering from the floor, having learned to separate our allies from our enemies. This was another form of good sense. And we carried the theory/practice couplet into our intellectual work.

In my part of the forest, an early focus on bodies as they were culturally assigned to nature led quickly to an examination of authoritative medicine and science as "man-made" fields. Collectively, we dragged the antinomies of nature/culture, reproduction/production, irrational/rational, female/male under the microscope of critical thinking and quickly pronounced these pathological. It did not take long for us to realize we were mucking about with the moorings of Cartesianism, intent on parsing the great Greeks, taking aim full-tilt at the basis of scientific thought. We knew, too, that we could ill afford to throw various babies out with their bathwater: responsible in the way of all mothers of invention for rethinking our origin tales and substituting a better story, we were committed to making critical spaces in the house that Franz Boas built without demolishing the edifice of rationality on which our foundational worldview had been erected. But partial deconstruction proved to be a tricky matter.

My own contribution to this collective reworking of anthropological practice entailed a close look at the social impact of what were then dubbed the new reproductive technologies. Taking the perspective of pregnant women and mothers drawn from diverse racial-ethnic, class, religious, and national backgrounds, I tried to document the multiple forms of thought and decision-making with which women faced a new scientific technology that turned them into "moral pioneers" as they debated the consequences of using amniocentesis, assessing fetal and child disability, and choosing or rejecting abortion on the basis of biomedical diagnosis. Science may consider chromosomes and genes to be pre-cultural, but when viewed through the eyes and expanding bellies of pregnant women, these carriers of heredity also bear the marks of diverse social histories and cultural resources. Women have no choice but to make a choice; in the process, their constrained agency reproduces scientific rationality in potent and vulnerable contexts.

Trained to think of anthropology *as* science, many researchers moved toward an anthropology *of* science. In that prepositional substitution, an interrogation of the biases inherent in scientific rationality quickly came under scrutiny. Without rehearsing the evolution of debates in science and technology studies (STS), this relatively new (or at least renovated) field witnessed its venerable background in the history and philosophy of science incorporate the infusion of social science and, specifically, interdisciplinary feminist influences that interrogated its position, practices, and politics. Whether indexing glass ceilings in Japanese physics, the murderous limits of "harm reduction" programs in HIV/AIDS policy when applied to "maternal vessels," or military "missile envy" (in Carol Cohn's felicitous phrase), a congeries of researchers took the passions of Women's Studies to the heart of science itself. There, we discovered what had conveniently been left unspoken: the reflection of scientific rationality entailed more than a ripple in the pool of powerful narcissism, as the limits of its traditions and practices were explored.

Close to home, feminists in medical anthropology, postcolonial studies, and STS often found themselves researching in laboratories and clinics, negotiating the politics of insurance, inclusion, and exclusion, the political economy of globalizing drug markets, and coming to grips with what was so antiseptically entitled "health disparities" by our government's funding agencies. We discovered colonial medicine abroad and *Medical Apartheid* (Harriet Washington's apt title) at home, in conversation with many others. Gendered medicine constitutes a vast terrain of heterogeneous practices, as some struggle to attain the benefits of pharmaceuticals while others move to lessen their own medicalization.

These differences manifest class, race, and national privilege/disprivilege; the prejudices of ablism and normative heterosexism; comfort with biomedical etiquette; religious conviction; and a host of other ordinary forms of social support and discrimination. When viewed as a whole, they index the vast social Darwinism at the heart of scientific, biomedical thinking. Although Western biomedicine has developed powerful theories and practices to treat all bodies in universal, pre-cultural terms, our work continually pointed to the differences in how bodies count: who thrives, who falls ill and from what causes, and who has or lacks access to relevant expert healing resources are matters not only of biological vulnerability, but of culture and power. In the intersection where health, culture, and political-economic power meet, feminist researchers, teachers, and activists had to consider not only intellectually challenging materials on health and disease cross-culturally, but also our own personal and social beliefs about bodies and the causes and responses to their vulnerabilities, as well.

It was at this intersection that the problem of rationality reared its ugly head. Although respectful of Lorde's injunction that we could not use the master's tools to dismantle the master's house, we nonetheless had to build our own home on the rock of coalition with many others: were there tools that hadn't already been imprinted on our diverse and various masters? "They" may hold the statistical keys to meta-analysis and lab-based studies of epigenetics; we've got accounts painstakingly collected outside the clinic that bring the limits of clinical understanding into focus. Laboratory rationality in a petri dish is not necessarily rationality in what we so fondly used to call the real world: bodies that are "treatment naïve" (read: poor and desperately unable to access medical care) may not respond to pharmaceutical or other technological interventions precisely as do those that are well-fed (indeed, increasingly overfed on empty calories, but that's another, if related, story) and hyper-medicalized, too. Are we being irrational when we say, "Some people tell us their bodies are different from ours. Let's pursue their claims"? Or might we just be enlarging the sphere of democratic action by following the leads thrown to us by women and their supporters who require another kind of (pick one): fertility control and infertility aid; HIV/AIDS protection or diabetes prevention; emergency hydration for their dying infants or food for their starving children. The political economy of greed is an old story continually resuscitated by globalization; might a parsing of hegemonic scientific rationality be a newer story owed in large measure to feminism and its heterogeneous alliances?

Feminists have lost a lot of sleep on this one. But one possible strategy entails getting inside the lab to watch scientists at work, systematically parsing their rationality as only one among many. It is only when we watch them—women scientists as well as men, increasingly those drawn from international and multiethnic backgrounds (hey! biomedicine is no longer white man's medicine in any clear-cut fashion)—that their ellipses can be dissected. In my own work, I've become comfortable in cytogenetics laboratories, tracking DNA searches for small genetic changes that lead to large disease consequences, and watching scientists run scans of children's brains in search of cognitive difference. In each case, I've had to suspend my disbelief in order truly to shadow scientists at work, querying their thinking and practice. And in every instance, I've been privileged to develop working friendships with key scientists, immeasurably complicating any too-simple notion of "critique." Their passions, commitments, and findings are no less engaged than my own.

Yet even as I've investigated new scientific knowledge production, I have never been far from the real-world testimony of those far less likely to be the beneficiaries of scientific/biomedical progress than we researchers are. And I've also experienced many unanticipated adventures on the Möbius strip: we anthropologists come in search of interviews, but activist/policy/project innovators spot our arrival a mile down the pike. From their perspective, we represent other possibilities, and they are quite skilled at putting us to work. This heady mix of learning our way through powerful scientific theory and empirics without losing our own sense of praxis is far from a guarantee of success. Sometimes we fall on our faces. At other times, we use our resources to help enable something new to emerge. Practice makes perfect? Hardly, but at least practice makes practice.

Antigone's claim is always with us: we cannot know when we're just looping through the dominant assumptions of science, constructed on conventional (dare I say it?) patriarchal grounds, sustaining them through our very resistance, and in the process, making the case for conventional rationality stronger. Indeed, is it even possible to discover another kinder, gentler rationality outside their own? Is there an outside, and how/might we discover a pathway toward it? Recognizing the philosophical naïveté to which our re/searches place us "at risk," we've become knowing in the art of staying discomfited. We acknowledge the potential irrationality of insisting on the historic horizon on which certain powerful forms of rationality are placed. We learn the science and become its acolytes, even as we seek to shake its foundations. This is messy business, at best. But—with gratitude to feminism—at least now I no longer have to speak in tongues.

Confessions of a Culinary Transvestite

Sandra M. Gilbert

For the late Bob Griffin, who made shepherd's pie while I sat at the computer.

In the overwhelming majority of societies cooking is the woman's work. No doubt this stems from practical considerations—since the woman has to stay home with the baby, it is convenient for her to perform the chores centered in the home. But if it is true, as Lévi-Strauss has argued, that transforming the raw into the cooked may represent, in many systems of thought, the transition from nature to culture, then here we have woman aligned with this important culturalizing process, which could easily place her in the category of culture, triumphing over nature. Yet it is also interesting to note that when a culture (e.g. France or China) develops a tradition of *haute cuisine*—"real" cooking, as opposed to trivial domestic cooking—the high chefs are almost always men. Thus the pattern replicates that in the area of socialization—women perform lower-level conversions from nature to culture, but when the culture distinguishes a higher level of the same functions, the higher level is restricted to men.

—SHERRY ORTNER (81)

The good woman nurtures men; the bad woman feeds off them.
——JANE GALLOP (230)

STRANGE ARE THE WAYS OF FEEDING
and eating in this brave new world
of sex war, sex change, and gender-bending. My son, for instance, does
almost all the cooking for his family; he even makes school lunches
for his son. Yet why should I be surprised at that, since my husband did
most of the cooking for our family, including the preparation of school
lunches for our children? Nor did that seem odd to me, because when
I was growing up, my father did much of the cooking for me and my
mother, and in fact he made my school lunches. This did not appear
peculiar to either of my parents, since my father's father had also regularly cooked for my grandmother, my father, and my aunt when
they were kids and still routinely produced many a holiday feast for us
as well as many a daily supper for his household. And I guess this long
and nourishing patrilineage has made it, from my point of view, perfectly natural that since my husband's death, the one person who has
most persistently broiled and baked, braised and simmered for me has
been my old friend Bob, himself an expert cook of long standing,
though the heir to a very different culinary genealogy.

Even if my personal gastronomical history is aberrant—and I suspect it may not be utterly eccentric—it would seem to put in question a number of standard assumptions about the engendering of life
and, for that matter, love in the kitchen. Like most feminists of my
generation—those of us who started our work in the early 1970s—I
was first aided in my theorizing about the history of sexuality by two
especially seminal (or shall I say ovular?) essays that were collected in
Woman, Culture, and Society, the wonderful anthology edited by Michelle
Rosaldo and Louise Lamphere in 1974: Nancy Chodorow's "Family
Structure and Feminine Personality," a precursor to her now classic
The Reproduction of Mothering, and Sherry Ortner's still classic, if somewhat
controversial, "Is Female to Male as Nature Is to Culture?" Both pieces
are elegantly argued and in many ways meticulously documented, so
much so that when I first read them I wholeheartedly assumed their

validity, indeed their absolute truth, without particularly bothering to refer them to my own experience.

That women were, as Ortner asserts, the primary nurturers of almost all families everywhere, the principal converters of raw to cooked, seemed obvious to me, and it seemed equally obvious that this was at least in part so because of the ways in which, as Ortner also notes, quoting Chodorow, "the structural situation of child rearing, reinforced by female and male role training, produces . . . differences, which are replicated and reproduced in the sexual sociology of adult life" (80). Yet as one minute of introspection would have demonstrated, Ortner's general claim had comparatively little relevance to my own life, especially to a number (though not all) of my childhood memories—those recollections of early pleasures or pains of the table that novelists and memoirists from Marcel Proust to M. F. K. Fisher have long understood to be powerful constituents of identity.

My grandfather's kitchen in Kew Gardens, for example, is probably the first kitchen I remember with any clarity as a place of magical culinary transformations. Redolent of garlic and cigars—for Grandpa chewed incessantly on large, quite good Cuban cigars as he cooked—it was considerably larger than the narrow little alcove, barely the size of a walk-in closet, that graced my parents' Jackson Heights apartment. Grandpa's kitchen was white and square, lined with cabinets that held all kinds of mysterious instruments: a polished wooden potato masher, an elegantly carved chocolate beater, countless wooden spoons, mortars and pestles of various materials, terrifyingly sharp chef's knives, glittering colanders, porcelain canisters, strainers in many sizes, wire whisks in abundance, two or three egg-beaters, several meat grinders, chopping blocks, pastry boards, and even an enigmatically beautiful wood and metal rod and bowl thing (I don't know how else to describe it) that hangs on my kitchen wall today and which my friend Bob just now speculated might possibly be some kind of a fruit pitter, though I guessed it may have had something to do with wine-making.

And Grandpa's kitchen had not one narrow window, as our apartment kitchen did, but two tall windows looking out on a rather scruffy Queens courtyard—since his was also an apartment kitchen—both of which windows, fortunately, could be flung wide on the rare occasions when the aroma of garlic and cigars, or the blissful odors of sau-téing onions and mushrooms, peppers and eggplant, got too strong. (They hardly ever did.) And in the center of Grandpa's kitchen was the relatively small white metal worktable where he performed his culinary legerdemain in honor of such ceremonial events as Thanks-giving, Christmas, New Year's Day, Easter, and oddly enough (if I remember correctly) the Fourth of July.

To be fair, Grandpa's kitchen was also Grandma's kitchen. She too was mistress of the porcelain canisters; she too wielded a mean whisk, twirled a canny chocolate beater, and reduced an innocent onion to a hundred glistening particles faster than an eight-year-old's protest-ing tears could form. Here, as I sat at the white metal table, she made me scrambled eggs for breakfast when I was lucky enough to stay over (she did them the French way, in the top of a double boiler, or in a heavy cast iron ramekin); here she rolled out homemade noodles on the floured marble pastry board; here, on the day after Easter, she produced her shepherd's pie, with its artful rim of mashed potatoes, and on the day after Christmas, ravioli from the same delicate pastry dough out of which the noodles were cut for her chicken soup; here she strained chicken soup through cheesecloth to purify it of fat for me, and here, speaking still of chicken soup, she unfurled Grandpa's big black umbrella and braved a scalding rain of broth that seethed from the ceiling the infamous afternoon when the pressure cooker exploded. And here, too, she produced—though usually in collabora-tion with Grandpa—the fabled eggplant caviar that she had learned from her Russian childhood but which her husband's family had modified, in Nice, into a savory Provençal concoction.

For—and perhaps this is crucial to my meditation here—both Grandma and Grandpa were immigrants, they were really very for-eign, they were emphatically Not American (which is no doubt at least one reason why our ritual celebrations of the Fourth of July bemuse me). Can it have been this cultural difference that shaped our culi-nary family's culinary difference? Grandma was a White Russian, who journeyed at the age of twelve to Paris, where she lived not far from the Parc Monceau with her émigré mother and the Russian priest for whom her mother kept house, and where she eventually met my grandfather, a nineteen-year-old aspiring art student from Nice. They came to this country, so far as I can tell, because Grandpa finally resolved to study art here (in 1908 or so) rather than in Paris—a decision not unlike Rick's explanation in *Casablanca* that he went there to "take the waters" because he "was misinformed." In the event, when they got here, Grandpa worked in, and eventually owned, a restaurant in the New York City market district (on the Lower West Side) where he was lovingly called "Frenchy" by waiters and truck drivers, produce vendors and union organizers.

But it was not, in my opinion, because he was a restaurateur that Grandpa was a cook, and really (despite Grandma's skills) the primary cook in his household. He didn't, after all, do the cooking in the Franklin Street Restaurant, with its bentwood chairs and sawdust floors, and he wasn't in the least like the classic French chef who spends his days toiling amid saucepans full of hollandaise, bordelaise, and béchamel, only to return home, thankfully, to a platter of boiled beef prepared by his good and conscientious wife. *Au contraire*, so far as I can tell it was because he was neither a hierarchically "professional" French chef nor a "regular" American he-man that Grandpa was able to regard cookery as a normal mode of masculine expertise so that he was quite often the chef at home, with Grandma at best the sous-chef. His revisionary version of eggplant caviar was the one the two of them dictated to me and my husband when we got out our graduate student notebooks and asked for recipes; he was the one who roasted the lamb out of which the shepherd's pie evolved (and, no doubt, he was the one who devised the recipe for the brilliant mashed potatoes that surrounded the pie); he was the one who knew, beyond question or controversy, how to make the custard that appeared, variously, in little cups at the supper table for me, especially if I had a cold or the flu, and in an exquisitely fluted tube pan as the world's greatest crème caramel on special occasions (a crème caramel against which my family and I have always measured all others, even in Paris); and he was the one, he was most certainly the Elect One, who made what has come to be called, even by those who are not his grandchildren, "Grandpa's stuffing."

For feast days, Grandpa would produce many things: *hors d'oeuvres variées* of lobster salad, stuffed mushrooms, marinated artichokes, "alligator pear" (a.k.a. avocado) salad, marinated mushrooms, roasted red peppers, eggplant caviar (with Grandma's help), and so on; roast lamb, beef, or turkey, depending on the occasion; asparagus and strawberry shortcake (in the spring); marrons glacés or Mont Blanc (chestnut purée and whipped cream, in the winter). And sometimes there were minor solecisms. He devoutly and wrongheadedly believed, for instance, that his *boeuf bourguignonne* would be better if he made it with an excellent cut of steak—even a filet—in honor of his little granddaughter. According to my husband, moreover, he consistently overcooked the turkey, and there were, to put it mildly, many debates between them on that subject, debates which usually issued in my husband's arriving early at any turkey feast—Thanksgiving and Christmas, as a rule—in order to invade the kitchen and forcibly turn off the oven, despite Grandpa's protests. But Grandpa's stuffing was without question beyond compare, as all who have ever tasted it would probably agree.

Grandpa's stuffing was and still is a comparatively simple Genovese filling, no doubt transported to Nice several centuries ago by his Ligurian forebears. Bread (or was it bread crumbs?), sausages, mushrooms, onions, garlic, parmesan cheese, and spinach. Enough spinach so the stuffing turns green. Enough sausage so it doesn't taste bready. Enough cheese, garlic, mushrooms, and onions so that it has some other lovely resonance one can't quite place. Every turkey, always, was stuffed with it, and every turkey in my family—indeed in a very extended family—still is. And if there's some left over, as Grandpa always ensured there would be, and as any provident cook would certainly agree there ought to be, it can be eaten cold (with leftover turkey and homemade mayonnaise), or made central in the creation of those ravioli whose suave envelopes Grandma would pinch together every December 26.

Because Grandpa—small, bald, with a dragging foot and (eventually) a bankrupt restaurant—was throughout his long life the culinary master of all he surveyed at home, my father didn't dare to compete with him in the realm of, say, stuffing, or, for that matter, crème caramel, Mont Blanc, marrons glacés, etc. At the same time, from *his* father my dad clearly learned not only that it's okay for a man to cook but, more to the point, it's incumbent on a man to cook. Even while he must have suffered from a kind of gastronomic anxiety of influence, therefore, Daddy nurtured me and my mother. In fact, except in unusual instances, he was the one who produced our daily fare while I was growing up.

Perhaps because the Depression had at various points put my father temporarily out of work and forced my mother to pursue an ambivalent career as an elementary school teacher (I say "ambivalent" because on the one hand she claimed to want to stay home and "bake cookies"—a process of which she knew nothing—and on the other hand, she declared that she wished she could have gotten a PhD and become a clinical psychologist), my mom was for a while our family's principal breadwinner. Can that be why my father cooked so routinely and so well? I don't think so, really. Recent sociological observations in both eastern Europe and contemporary America would suggest the opposite: that no matter how many professional burdens women have to bear they still tend to do most household chores, including of course the preparation of food. Thus, my father cooked because his father cooked, because, in short, there was a culinary patrilineage to be maintained.

What my father cooked, however, was emphatically normal and modest fare: pot roasts, stews, Sunday joints or chickens, steaks, lyonnaise potatoes. Then, sometimes, things like chocolate pudding or—alas—Jell-O. And though he didn't much care for vegetables (he was a red-blooded American man who had been an undergraduate at Cornell!), he responded with exuberance to my childish passion for mashed potatoes by becoming an expert at such modern taste treats as Potato Buds and other instants. When frozen foods appeared on the market, moreover, he—an engineer, after all, a prototype of Technological Man—was the first to celebrate the joys of Swanson's petite peas, cut green beans, broccoli spears, and chopped spinach.

School lunches: my father made these for me with the same matter-of-fact acquiescence to his culinary destiny that marked his Saturday afternoon labors over pot roast or lyonnaise potatoes. The breakfasts he offered often featured, from my point of view, solecisms as grave as my Grandpa's *boeuf bourguignonne*: lumpy oatmeal, scrambled eggs hastily tossed in a pan with what I plaintively called "the tails" still in them. (Unlike my grandmother's eggs, they were cooked too fast and not properly mixed, so that the whites asserted themselves in alarming ways.) And the school lunches, too, were often problematic, especially after a fancy allergist in Brooklyn decided that I should only eat bread that had been toasted. Consider, after all, the horrors of ham sandwiches on cold toast! The very concept, many years later, sends a shiver down my spine. Yet my father, nonetheless, was capable of extraordinary inventions for my fifth- or sixth- or seventh-grade lunch box: my favorites included cold roast lamb with mayonnaise and various other condiments (yes, unfortunately, on toast); Grandpa's turkey and stuffing, left over from some holiday or other (ditto on toast); and—most curious of all—a remarkable sandwich of lettuce, nothing but pure lettuce (and iceberg at that), mounded high with lots of good mayonnaise and accompanied by an apple and maybe a piece of cheese.

Like my grandmother, my mother also tried to cook, but at best she became a kind of sous-chef, prepper of vegetables, and bottle-washer. Indeed, like my grandmother, she became in the ordinary course of things the one who cooked when the Man was Out. For example, when my father went to meetings of the Queensborough Civil Engineering Society (of which he was long president) or of the local Democratic Committee (on which he served for many years), my mother and I would furtively eat the foods he detested: liver, fish, kidneys, and various Sicilian treats she hazily remembered from her childhood—*escalore in brodo* (with lots of garlic), garlicky stewed tripe (it made me sick), and endless spaghetti marinara (into whose sauce my mom would put an entire head of garlic). On these occasions, though, I think we must have had the abandoned, even depraved feelings that American men are said to have when their wives are away from home and they get to drink too much bourbon, concoct strange hashes, and eat lots of unlikely sundaes. Certainly, as soon as Daddy was back, we resumed our normal regimen: pot roast, mashed potatoes, lettuce sandwiches.

In the meantime, of course, I was as deeply embedded in American culture as anybody else. Or perhaps more so. My parents were inveterate readers of the *Nation*, the *New Republic*, *The New Yorker*. When I attained the ripe old age of thirteen and my father thought I might possibly turn into a real poet and intellectual, he immediately got me a subscription to the *Partisan Review*, in the interest, I dare say, of fostering my transcendent rather than immanent impulses. In reaction against such perverse (or so it seemed to me) nurturing, I started secretly buying supermarket magazines along with copies of the *Ladies' Home Journal* and *Good Housekeeping*, which I'd hide in the capacious pockets of my winter coats when I brought them home. Both my parents shuddered at the thought of such screeds. Even though we did celebrate the Fourth of July and imagine ourselves as a family with a Cornell lineage (that was where I eventually went to college), we really weren't Americans, and all those odd recipes for yams with marshmallows or tuna casserole with crushed potato chips on the top were so utterly alien that my parents were deeply unnerved by my fondness for them.

But fondness it was: I knew I was supposed by both the *Ladies' Home Journal* and Marynia Farnham (anti-feminist author of *Modern Woman: The Lost Sex*) to learn how to cook, but I also knew that there was probably some strange genetic glitch in my family that made men into cooks and women into consumers. Thus, when I finally did go away to college, I resolved to change, to be modern, to be womanly and American. At the dinner table in my dorm, I heard one girl talk about the extraordinarily interesting-sounding dishes she claimed her mother produced with, of all things, Campbell soups. You could put Campbell's tomato soup on pot roast, she said, and Campbell's cream of mushroom soup on chicken, and Campbell's cream of celery soup on your tuna casserole (to which the crushed potato chips would later be added). I wanted to learn all this; I wanted to try it out.

With my first serious college boyfriend, I did: all the changes that could be rung on canned goods were rung by me, in his little dank Ithaca basement apartment, and tried out not just on him but on his two vaguely sullen and jealous roommates, each of whom seemed to hold cryptic things against me—though all those things might well have added up to my willful fondness for sauces derived from Campbell's cream of mushroom soup. Even then, though, our most serious meals were made by my boyfriend, Ralph, whose parents would now and then send him brown paper parcels of kosher salami and matzohs, the ingredients, he declared, for a classic *matzoh brei*: all he needed to do was add eggs, fry, stir, and it was perfect. After hours in organic chem. labs, too, he'd stroll down College Avenue to his part-time job at Ithaca's only Jewish deli—Zim Zim's—where, with HCL-soaked hands, he'd expertly mix up a huge batch of coleslaw, vinegary, oleaginous, and utterly delicious, HCL and all.

In the inexorable course of events, such batches of coleslaw were eaten by my husband-to-be, then a graduate student in English at Cornell, who was at that time, for his part, subsisting in an Ithaca rooming house on cans of tuna and sardines along with carefully nurtured funds that allowed him, now and then, a hamburger at Bill's Diner, near the edge of what is still called Collegetown. Elliot, however, had had longstanding gastronomic ambitions of his own, or so he always insisted to me. Although no men in his family had ever seriously (or anyway, domestically) cooked—nor had his mother or her mother for that matter, since their gefilte fish, braised brisket, roast duck, and chicken soup with matzoh balls were always, in my memory, expertly produced by a large and charming black lady from Harlem named Mattie—he had started baking elaborate cakes as a boy of nine or ten, perhaps inspired by a chemistry set, perhaps by a fitful crush on Dionne Lucas, then one of England's and America's more popular and inspiring "gourmet" chefs. So maybe, who knows?, he was ripe for assimilation into my peculiar patrilineage.

Certainly, as Elliot also insisted to me, he had spent many happy hours of his boyhood watching his Uncle Jake, proprietor and manager of a hotel in the Catskills, getting "more slices out of a lemon than anyone would have thought possible." Nonetheless, when we were first married, it was I who resolved, in deference to my obsessive reading of "ladies' magazines" and Marynia Farnham, to do all the cooking, I who went to the local library and took out countless cello-wrapped books like *The Bride's Best Friend* and *The Newly Wed's Guide to Good Food*, along with a number of other rather more complex culinary tomes. When he was drafted and went to Germany, so did I and my cookbook collection (many volumes of which I still have, together with *ex libri* remarking that they are from the Jackson Heights local library). And there, in a strange bamboo-partitioned flat carved out of some former Graf's ballroom, I learned (or so I thought) to make roux and stew, puff pastry and—wonder of wonders, just like Grandpa!—*hors d'oeuvres variées*.

But my culinary karma was inescapable. To begin with, every time I set foot in the cozy little corner of the ballroom that we called a kitchen, I became even more anxious, dependent, clinging, and child-like than I was when, without much difficulty, I was learning from my husband how to drive a stick-shift car. I worried that I couldn't make the complex *pâté à choux* alone, that the roux would get all crumbly and crumply, that the Sicilian *arancini* to which I nobly aspired—magnificent golden rice balls deep fried in an incomprehensible batter—would fall apart, that the dilled shrimp would overcook. So Elliot, perforce (and from choice, too, of course), intervened. We learned together about the roux and the *pâté à choux* and the marvelous *arancini*—and perhaps more to the point, he learned so well that slowly he took over the cooking in our household.

Had I taught him about the *boeuf bourguignonne* that I learned (from Grandpa's mistakes) to stew properly from beef rump or chuck? He learned to do it better! Had I discovered a splendidly simple but elegant recipe for salmon mousse in my desperate perusals of the *New York Times* food section? He knew how to do it right—and fast! By the time we had returned to the States and were both settled back in jobs and school, he was the primary cook in our household, and, significantly, a cook who regularly exchanged recipes with his father-in-law and his grandfather-in-law. Did I crave creamy scrambled eggs like those I got in my grandparents' house? Elliot had learned to make them from his early studies of Dionne Lucas, but my family reinforced his proclivities. Did I want fabulous mashed potatoes, like the ones that circled the familial post-Easter shepherd's pie? He learned from Daddy and Grandpa how to make them. Stuffed mushrooms, marinated mushrooms, eggplant caviar? We both wrote down the recipes that Grandpa dictated, but my husband executed them—except, I must confide, in the case of eggplant, which he loathed. And as for stuffing—did we need stuffing for an occasional bird or two? Well, of course, there was Grandpa's stuffing, which my husband began to produce with style and skill.

Of course, we fought about Grandpa's stuffing. But we fought with me occupying what is ordinarily understood to be the place of the man. My friend Bob tells me that his father loved his mother's mother's stuffing and continually upbraided his mother for not replicating its moistness, its suavity. Well, that was the position I assumed, stuffing-wise. While Elliot labored to reproduce Grandpa's stuffing, I'd hang over him in the kitchen, complaining that he wasn't doing it right—it wasn't smooth enough, he didn't cuisse it enough, there weren't enough mushrooms or garlic in it, and so on. And I still protest like this to my son, who manfully carries on the family tradition.

As for my son, to be frank, he didn't take rapidly either to cooking or to eating. As a kid, he was skinny and finicky: for a while (when he was in nursery school!), his preferred foods were pickled green beans and Uncle Ben's curried rice; later, he graduated to more normal childhood fare—SpaghettiOs, hamburgers, hot dogs, and Kentucky Fried Chicken. His serious cooking, as I recall, began with, first, a suddenly strengthened adolescent appetite, and then a sometime close-up magician's interest in the technology of the kitchen.

When Roger was in his early teens, our family acquired a vacation place on the coast, and Bob gave us an electric ice cream maker as a house warming (cooling?) present. None of the rest of us could work this remarkable apparatus very well, but Roger took to the thing at once and soon became expert in churning out more flavors than Mr. Baskin or Mr. Robbins ever dreamed of. And when, a year or two later, somebody got me a pasta machine, his fate was sealed: within months he was manufacturing pastas that neither my grandmother nor my mother's Sicilian sisters-in-law had attempted in their long labors over flour, eggs, and pastry boards.

But of course pastas require sauces, and sauces entail recipes— recipes, in Roger's case, not only researched in countless cookbooks but inherited from grandfathers and great-grandfathers or exchanged with Dad or with Mom and Dad's friend Bob. And recipes for sauces lead to other recipes: for various curries, for French mousses and Chinese minces, Southwestern barbecues and Mexican moles. Inevitably, my son went the way of all (our family's) flesh. Since he cooked so avidly and expertly, he became the daily chef for his wife and son, masculine maven of breakfast as well as dinner, school lunches as well as *hors d'oeuvres variées*.

A few months after my husband quite horrifyingly and unexpectedly died following surgery in February of 1991, my son—on sabbatical from his teaching job at Cornell—came, along with his wife and child, to live with me in Berkeley for a few months. His plan, he told me, was to become the daily chef for me too, at least temporarily. When he got here, though, he discovered that there was already another man in the kitchen a good deal of the time. For as soon as it became clear to Bob (and it became clear almost at once) that in my state of shock and devastation I wouldn't eat unless I was fed, he not only organized a rotating "duty roster" of cooks and dinner companions, but also provided at least three-quarters of the food that was to be consumed by mourners and sympathizers. (As for the other quarter, a surprising lot of that was also produced by various men.)

Unfazed, Roger embarked on his usual drill of pasta-making, saucing, and spicing, while Bob and a few other male cooks energetically continued their labors with the unquenchable vitality of the broom and the bucket in *The Sorcerer's Apprentice*. Indeed, there were days during this period when my kitchen seemed to be crowded with men—men grating and grinding, steaming and stirring, baking and broiling. A man coming in with a great iron pot full of rabbit stew would pause to shake hands with another man bearing a huge wooden salad bowl, then both would turn to greet a third lugging a cassoulet and a fourth carrying a lemon cake—and all would salute Roger, already at the stove whisking a hollandaise.

To be sure, few, if any, of these men have the sort of culinary patrilineage to which Roger can point. Bob, the impresario of so many of these occasions, is a witty and courteous Southerner who can't remember any man in his family ever approaching a cooking fire except outdoors on the deck or patio. A bachelor existence together with an indomitable passion for good food, he explains, account for his gastronomic savoir faire. Nonetheless, considering the diverse male community that from time to time occupied my kitchen with, for the most part, brotherly amicability, he need never have felt in the least odd, even though his culinary proclivities are genealogically unprecedented. Indeed, as a virtuoso of soups and salads, mousses and cassoulets, he is regarded with profound respect by friends of both sexes, many of whom regularly appeal to him for advice, encouragement—and more recipes.

I speak of "brotherly amicability" but of course, like any other society, the community of male cooks that I've encountered, along with my own patrilineage, is marked by occasional flashes of Bloomian rivalry, hostility, or resentment. As I noted earlier, my husband and my grandfather could never agree about how long one should roast a turkey. My father refused to attempt many of his father's dishes. My son reproached my husband for disliking curries and for undercooking turkey. Bob considered some of Elliot's tastes stodgy, while Elliot thought Bob's were now and then outré. Elliot believed that Bob had once purloined his closely guarded (because embarrassingly simple) recipe for salmon mousse, while Bob swore that someone else had told him how to make that dish. Roger and Bob are now and then competitive about chutney, and I have heard Bob denounce the salad dressings produced by another man I know, and I have seen Roger scorn yet another man's puttanesca sauce.

By and large, however, all these men were and are as nurturing in their ways as women are (sometimes incorrectly) supposed to be. One example: when, during my early crisis of grief, Roger and Bob noticed that I couldn't swallow anything spicy or crunchy, each, quite separately, began making things blander, smoother, creamier, closer to the baby food I needed. Various recipes for mashed potatoes were recalled by both; tender potages were concocted; buttery noodles and couscouses appeared on the table. And when I nostalgically told Bob about the suavely slow-cooked scrambled eggs my grandmother and my husband used to make, he revealed that that is the way he makes such eggs too, and began to whip up Southern brunches featuring them, along with equally mild treats like grits simmered in chicken broth.

Interestingly, besides their nurturing qualities, Roger and Bob have in common a deeply scholarly interest in food, characterized not only by an almost theoretical fondness for cookbooks (which had been of little importance to my grandfather, my father, and my husband) but also by a mutual passion for the writings of M. F. K. Fisher. But then, as someone pointed out to me the other day, Fisher herself started out as virtually a culinary transvestite, since she evidently chose to write as "M. F. K." instead of as Mary Frances Kennedy because she aspired to a kind of gastronomic discourse that had long been associated with men like Brillat-Savarin (whose *The Physiology of Taste* she beautifully translated) rather than with women like Mrs. Beeton. Gender-bending in the kitchen, after all, takes many forms.

What, though, are the implications of such culinary sex-role fluidity? If my personal history is not just completely bizarre, does the ruminative introspection I have conducted here tell us something important about the gastronomic meanings of our historical moment? Does it, in addition, reveal a few points about ethnicity, class, and cookery? Does it at least partially subvert Ortner's claim about women as marginalized or subordinated because of their "lower-level conversions from nature to culture"? Does it, further, interrogate Chodorow's notions about the ways "the sexual sociology of adult life" reproduces "the structural situation of child-rearing"?

A few of these questions suggest that my mother—for most of her life the most emphatic non-cook in my family—may be somehow as crucial in this history as are the men who constitute my culinary patrilineage. All the women in my mother's Sicilian family did in fact cook: her mother, her sister, and her many sisters-in-law were as solely rulers of their kitchens as any of Ortner's or Chodorow's maternal figures. Stooped over triumphantly bubbling pots of marinara sauce or sauce Bolognese, they were makers of *lasagne, arancini, rolatini, scallopini, carciofi,* and holiday *salsizze.* No man touched so much as a wooden spoon in their households. No mere man ever opened the doors to their ovens, and few gazed upon their pastry boards. By many years the youngest and most Americanized of these simmering women, my mother grew up at what I guess was really the fabled "modernist" moment—her adolescence pretty much coincided with the teens and early twenties of this century—so that, both culturally and historically, she wanted *not* to be her mother or her sister or her sisters-in-law. She wanted to smoke in public, dance the Charleston, and argue politics with men. She wanted never to touch a wooden spoon, nor did it thrill her to gaze upon the pastry board. And during my childhood, she rarely did either of these things.

The consequences for me were probably both confusing and liberating. If my mother's yearning for Americanness and modernity was signaled by her refusal to cook, my own desire to be more American than my family paradoxically manifested itself in a temporary addiction to *Good Housekeeping*. Yet when it turned out that I was, for better or worse, not fated to be the culinary queen of all I surveyed, I never felt profoundly guilty about it: because my mother had nurtured me not with cookies but with words and kisses, I knew I could nurture my children too—and that they could be nurtured, as well, by their father's manly bosom, as I had been nurtured by my father's.

Lest this celebration of gastronomic role reversals sound too utopian, however, let me add one caveat, which significantly realigns my position with some of the views propounded in Ortner's essay. In my many experiences with cooking men, I have noticed that there is almost always *something they don't do*, even when they are most philosophically committed to the sharing of household and child-rearing tasks. My grandfather, for example, compulsively cleaned up after himself in the kitchen, but he didn't do laundry. My father did do laundry, but he didn't wash dishes. My husband washed dishes but didn't do laundry. My son does almost everything but won't bake. Bob does laundry and washes pots but hardly ever clears the table. I am reminded, therefore, of Ortner's remark that "ultimately the line is drawn" (70): perhaps, indeed, there is always some signal, albeit at times exquisitely subtle, that certain tasks are "women's work" and thus not to be performed by real men, not even by real men who eat quiche with enthusiasm.

But then, what is a "real man" anyway? Or a "real woman"? As we increasingly understand, such creatures are probably the supreme fictions of our culture, and of all others too. Not long ago, someone invented a kind of hollowed-out rubber contraption that new fathers could strap across their chests so they could suckle their infants just the way their wives do. Perhaps now, therefore, the psychoanalytically resonant breast can become a very different object of terror and desire from the one defined by, say, Melanie Klein. When juxtaposed with the concept of culinary transvestism, do these fake bosoms imply that I was nursed by falsies? Personally, I don't think so. Or, if I do, I think that from such a sex change we can learn that womanly bosoms may be falsies too. Or perhaps, rather, more extravagantly and abstrusely, we can learn that whatever is, is real.

WORKS CITED

Gallop, Jane. *Around 1981: Academic Feminist Literary Theory.* New York: Routledge, 1992.
Ortner, Sherry. "Is Female to Male as Nature Is to Culture?" In *Women, Culture, and Society,* edited by Michelle Zimbalist Rosaldo and Louise Lamphere. Stanford: Stanford University Press, 1984.

Islam in the Family

Leila Ahmed

I T IS EASY TO SEE NOW THAT OUR LIVES in the Alexandria house, and even at Zatoun, were lived in women's time, women's space. And in women's culture.

And the women had, too, I now believe, their own understanding of Islam, an understanding that was different from men's Islam, "official" Islam. For although in those days it was only Grandmother who performed all the regular formal prayers, for all the women of the house, religion was an essential part of how they made sense of and understood their own lives. It was through religion that one pondered the things that happened, why they had happened, and what one should make of them, how one should take them.

Islam, as I got it from them, was gentle, generous, pacifist, inclusive, somewhat mystical—just as they themselves were. Mother's pacifism was entirely of a piece with her sense of the religion. Being Muslim was about believing in a world in which life was meaningful and in which all events and happenings were permeated (although not always transparently to us) with meaning. Religion was above all about inner things. The outward signs of religiousness, such as prayer and fasting, might be signs of a true religiousness but equally well might not. They were certainly not what was important about being

Muslim. What was important was how you conducted yourself and how you were in yourself, and in your attitude toward others, and in your heart.

What it was to be Muslim was passed on not, of course, wordlessly but without elaborate sets of injunctions or threats or decrees or dictates as to what we should do and be and believe. What was passed on, besides the very general basic beliefs and moral ethos of Islam, which are also those of its sister monotheisms, was a way of being in the world. A way of holding oneself in the world—in relation to God, to existence, to other human beings. This the women passed on to us most of all through how they were and by their being and presence, by the way they were in the world, conveying their beliefs, ways, thoughts, and how we should be in the world by a touch, a glance, a word—prohibiting, for instance, or approving. Their mere responses in this or that situation—a word, a shrug, even just their postures—passed on to us, in the way that women (and also men) have forever passed on to their young, how we should be. And all of these ways of passing on attitudes, morals, beliefs, knowledge—through touch and the body and in words spoken in the living moment—are by their very nature subtle and evanescent. They profoundly shape the next generation, but they do not leave a record in the way that someone writing a text about how to live or what to believe leaves a record. Nevertheless, they leave a far more important and, literally, more vital living record. Beliefs, morals, attitudes passed on to and impressed on us through those fleeting words and gestures are written into our very lives, our bodies, our selves, even into our physical cells and into how we live out the script of our lives.

It was Grandmother who taught me the *fat-ha* (the opening verse of the Quran and the equivalent of the Christian Lord's Prayer) and who taught me two or three other short suras (Quranic verses). When she took me up onto the roof of the Alexandria house to watch for angels on the night of the twenty-seventh of Ramadan, she recited the sura about that special night, a sura that was also by implication about the miraculousness of night itself. Even now I remember its loveliness. It is still my favorite sura.

I remember receiving little other direct religious instruction, either from Grandmother or from anyone else. I have already described the most memorable exchange with my mother on the subject of religion—when, sitting in her room, the windows open behind her onto the garden, the curtain billowing, she quoted to me the verse in the Quran that she believed summed up the essence of Islam: "He who kills one being [*nafs*, "self," from the root *nafas*, "breath"] kills all of humanity, and he who revives, or gives life to, one being revives all of humanity." It was a verse that she quoted often, that came up in any important conversation about God, religion, those sorts of things. It represented for her the essence of Islam.

I happened to be reading, when I was thinking about all this, the autobiography of Zeinab al-Ghazali, one of the most prominent Muslim women leaders of our day. Al-Ghazali founded a Muslim Women's Society that she eventually merged with the Muslim Brotherhood, the "fundamentalist" association that was particularly active in the 1940s and 1950s. Throughout her life, she openly espoused a belief in the legitimacy of using violence in the cause of Islam. In her memoir, she writes of how in her childhood her father told her stories of the heroic women of early Islam who had written poetry eulogizing Muslim warriors and who themselves had gone to war on the battlefields of Islam and gained renown as fearless fighters. Musing about all this and about the difference between al-Ghazali's Islam and my mother's pacifist understanding of it, I found myself falling into a meditation on the seemingly trivial detail that I, unlike al-Ghazali, had never heard as a child or a young girl stories about the women of early Islam, heroic or otherwise. And it was then that I suddenly realized the difference between al-Ghazali and my mother, and between al-Ghazali's Islam and my mother's.

The reason I had not heard such stories as a child was quite simply that those sorts of stories (when I was young, anyway) were to be found only in the ancient classical texts of Islam, texts that only men who had studied the classical Islamic literary heritage could understand and decipher. The entire training at Islamic universities—the training, for example, that al-Ghazali's father, who had attended al-Azhar

University, had received—consisted precisely in studying those texts. Al-Ghazali had been initiated into Islam and had got her notions as to what a Muslim was from her father, whereas I had received my Islam from the mothers, as had my mother. So there are two quite different Islams, an Islam that is in some sense a women's Islam and an official, textual Islam, a "men's" Islam.

And indeed it is obvious that a far greater gulf must separate men's and women's ways of knowing, and the different ways in which men and women understand religion, in the segregated societies of the Middle East than in other societies—and we know that there are differences between women's and men's ways of knowing even in non-segregated societies such as America. For, beside the fact that women often could not read (or, if they were literate, could not decipher the Islamic texts, which require years of specialist training), women in Muslim societies did not attend mosques. Mosque-going was not part of the tradition for women at any class level (that is, attending mosque for congregational prayers was not part of the tradition, as distinct from visiting mosques privately and informally to offer personal prayers, which women have always done). Women therefore did not hear the sermons that men heard. And they did not get the official (male, of course) orthodox interpretations of religion that men (or some men) got every Friday. They did not have a man trained in the orthodox (male) literary heritage of Islam telling them week by week and month by month what it meant to be a Muslim, what the correct interpretation of this or that was, and what was or was not the essential message of Islam.

Rather, they figured these things out among themselves and in two ways. They figured them out as they tried to understand their own lives and how to behave and how to live, talking them over together among themselves, interacting with their men, and returning to talk them over in their communities of women. And they figured them out as they listened to the Quran and talked among themselves about what they heard. For this was a culture, at all levels of society and throughout most of the history of Islamic civilization, not of reading but of the common recitation of the Quran. It was recited by professional reciters, women as well as men, and listened to on all kinds of occasions—at funerals and births and celebratory events, in illness, and in ordinary life. There was merit in having the Quran chanted in your house and in listening to it being chanted wherever it was chanted, whereas for women there was no merit attached to attending mosque, an activity indeed prohibited to women for most of history. It was from these together, their own lives and from hearing the words of the Quran, that they formed their sense of the essence of Islam.

Nor did they feel, the women I knew, that they were missing anything by not hearing the exhortations of sheikhs, nor did they believe that the sheikhs had an understanding of Islam superior to theirs. On the contrary. They had little regard, the women I knew, for the reported views and opinions of most sheikhs. Although occasionally there might be a sheikh who was regarded as a man of genuine insight and wisdom, the women I knew ordinarily dismissed the views and opinions of the common run of sheikhs as mere superstition and bigotry. And these, I emphasize, were not Westernized women. Grandmother, who spoke only Arabic and Turkish, almost never set foot outside her home and never even listened to the radio. The dictum that "there is no priesthood in Islam"—meaning that there is no intermediary or interpreter, and no need for an intermediary or interpreter, between God and each individual Muslim and how that Muslim understands his or her religion—was something these women and many other Muslims took seriously and held on to as a declaration of their right to their own understanding of Islam.

No doubt particular backgrounds and subcultures give their own specific flavors and inflections and ways of seeing to their understanding of religion, and I expect that the Islam I received from the women among whom I lived was therefore part of their particular subculture. In this sense, then, there are not just two or three different kinds of Islam but many, many different ways of understanding and of being Muslim. But what is striking to me now is not how different or rare the Islam in which I was raised is but how ordinary and typical it seems to be in its base and fundamentals. Now, after a lifetime of meeting and talking with Muslims from all over the world, I find that this Islam is one of the common varieties—perhaps even *the* common or garden variety—of the religion. It is the Islam not only of women but of ordinary folk generally, as opposed to the Islam of sheikhs, ayatollahs, mullahs, and clerics. It is an Islam that may or may not place emphasis on ritual and formal religious practice but that certainly pays little or no attention to the utterances and exhortations of sheikhs or any sort of official figures. Rather, it is an Islam that stresses moral conduct and emphasizes Islam as a broad ethos and ethical code and as a way of understanding and reflecting on the meaning of one's life and of human life more generally.

This variety of Islam (or, more exactly perhaps, these familial varieties of Islam, existing in a continuum across the Muslim world) consists above all of Islam as essentially an aural and oral heritage and a way of living and being—and not a textual, written heritage, not something studied in books or learned from men who studied books. This latter Islam, the Islam of the texts, is a quite different, quite other Islam: it is the Islam of the arcane, mostly medieval written heritage in which sheikhs are trained, and it is "men's" Islam. More specifically still, it is the Islam erected by that minority of men who over the centuries have created and passed on to one another this particular textual heritage: men who, although they have always been a minority in society as a whole, have always been those who made the laws and wielded (like the ayatollahs of Iran today) enormous power in their societies. The Islam they developed in this textual heritage is very like the medieval Latinate textual heritage of Christianity. It is as abstruse and obscure and as dominated by medieval and exclusively male views of the world as are those Latin texts. Imagine believing that those medieval texts on Christianity represent today the only true and acceptable interpretation of Christianity. But that is exactly what the sheikhs and ayatollahs propound, and this is where things stand now in much of the Muslim world: most of the classic Islamic texts that still determine Muslim law in our day date from medieval times.

Aurally what remains when you listen to the Quran over a lifetime are its most recurring themes, ideas, words, and permeating spirit, reappearing now in this passage, now in that: mercy, justice, peace, compassion, humanity, fairness, kindness, truthfulness, charity. And yet it is exactly these recurring themes and this permeating spirit that are for the most part left out of the medieval texts or smothered and buried under a welter of obscure and abstruse "learning." One would scarcely believe, reading or hearing the laws these texts have yielded, particularly when it comes to women, that the words "justice," "fairness," "compassion," "truth," ever even occur in the Quran. No wonder non-Muslims think Islam is such a backward and oppressive religion: what these men made of it *is* largely oppressive. Still—to speak less judgmentally and, in fact, more accurately—the men who wrote the foundational texts of official Islam were living in societies and eras rife with chauvinism, eras when men believed as a matter of categorical certainty that God created them superior to women and fully intended them to have complete dominion over women. And yet, despite such beliefs and prejudices, here and there in the texts they created, in the details of this or that law, they wrote in some provision or condition that, astonishingly, does give justice to women. So, even in those bleak days, the Quran's recurring themes filtered through. They did so, however, only now and then in a body of law otherwise overwhelmingly skewed in favor of men.

I am sure, then, that my foremothers' lack of respect for the authority of sheikhs was not coincidental. Rather, I believe that this way of seeing and understanding was quite common among ordinary Muslims and that it was an understanding passed on from mothers and grandmothers to daughters and granddaughters. Generations of astute, thoughtful women, listening to the Quran, understood perfectly well its essential themes and its faith. And looking around them, they understood perfectly well, too, what a travesty men had made of it. This ingrained low opinion that they had of sheikhs, clerics, and ayatollahs stemmed from a perfectly just and astute understanding of their world, an understanding that they passed on to their daughters and, indeed, their sons.

Leaving no written legacy, written only on the body and into the scripts of our lives, this oral and aural tradition of Islam no doubt stretches back through generations and is as ancient as any written tradition.

One could even argue that an emphasis on an oral and aural Islam is intrinsic to Islam and to the Quran itself, and intrinsic even to the

Arabic language. Originally the Quran was an aural, and only an aural, text recited to the community by the Prophet Muhammad. And it remained throughout his life, and indeed for several years after his death, only an aural text. Moreover, a bias in favor of the heard word, the word given life and meaning by the human voice, the human breath (*nafas*) is there, one might say, in the very language itself. In Arabic (and also Hebrew) script, no vowels are set down, only consonants. A set of consonants can have several meanings and only acquires formal, specific, fixed meaning when given vocalized or silent utterance (unlike words in European script, which have the appearance, anyway, of being fixed in meaning). Until life is literally breathed into them, Arabic and Hebrew words on the page have no particular meaning. Indeed, until then they are not words but only potential words, a chaotic babble and possibility of meanings. It is as if they hold within them the scripts of those languages, marshaling their sets of bare consonants across the page, vast spaces in which meanings exist in a condition of whirling potentiality until the very moment that one is singled out and uttered. And so by their very scripts these two languages seem to announce the primacy of the spoken, literally living word, and to announce that meaning can only be here and now. Here and now in this body, this breath (*nafas*), this self (*nafs*) encountering the word, giving it life. Word that, without that encounter, has no life, no meaning. Meaning always only here and now, in this body, for this person. Truth only here and now, for this body, this person. Not something transcendent, overarching, larger, bigger, more important than life—but here and now and in this body and in this small and ordinary life.

We seem to be living through an era of the progressive, seemingly inexorable erasure of the oral and ethical traditions of lived Islam and, simultaneously, of the ever-greater dissemination of written Islam, textual, "men's" Islam (an Islam essentially not of the Book but of the Texts, the medieval texts) as the authoritative Islam. Worse still, this seems to be an era of the unstoppable spread of fundamentalist Islam, textual Islam's more narrow and more poorly informed modern descendant. It is a more ill-informed version of old-style official Islam in that the practitioners of that older Islam usually studied many texts and thus at least knew that even in these medieval texts there were disagreements among scholars and many possible interpretations of this or that verse. But today's fundamentalists, literate but often having read just a single text, take it to be definitive and the one and only "truth."

Ironically, therefore, literacy has played a baneful part both in spreading a particular form of Islam and in working to erase oral and living forms of the religion. For one thing, we all automatically assume that those who write and who put their knowledge down in texts have something more valuable to offer than those who simply live their knowledge and use it to inform their lives. And we assume that those who write and interpret texts in writing—in the Muslim context, the sheikhs and ayatollahs, who are the guardians and perpetuators (perpetrators) of this written version of Islam—must have a better, truer, deeper understanding of Islam than the non-specially trained Muslim. Whereas the fact is that the only Islam that they have a deeper understanding of is their own gloomy, medieval version of it.

Even the Western academic world is contributing to the greater visibility and legitimacy of textual Islam and to the gradual silencing and erasure of alternative oral forms of lived Islam. For we, too, in the West, and particularly in universities, honor, and give pride of place to, texts. Academic studies of Islam commonly focus on its textual heritage or on visible, official institutions such as mosques. Consequently it is this Islam—the Islam of texts and of mosques— that becomes visible and that is presented as in some sense legitimate, whereas most of the Muslims whom I know personally, both in the Middle East and in Europe and America, would never go near a mosque or willingly associate themselves with any form of official Islam. Throughout history, official Islam has been our enemy and our oppressor. We have learned to live with it and to survive it and have developed dictums such as "There is no priesthood in Islam" to protect ourselves from it; we're not now suddenly and even in these new lands going to befriend it easily. It is also a particular and bitter irony to me that the very fashionableness of Gender Studies is serving to disseminate and promote medieval men's Islam as the "true" and "authentic" Islam. (It is "true" and "authentic" because it is based on old texts and represents what the Muslim male powers have considered to be true for centuries.) Professors, for example, including a number who have no sympathy whatever for feminism, are now jumping on the bandwagon of Gender Studies and directing a plethora of dissertations on this or that medieval text with titles like "Islam and Menstruation." But such dissertations should more aptly have titles along the lines of "A Study of Medieval Male Beliefs about Menstruation." For what, after all, do these men's beliefs, and the rules that they laid down on the basis of their beliefs, have to do with Islam? Just because they were powerful, privileged men in their societies and knew how to write, does this mean they have the right forever to tell us what Islam is and what the rules should be?

Still, these are merely word wars, wars of ideas that, for the present anyway, are of the most minor significance compared with the devastation unloosed on Muslim societies in our day by fundamentalism. What we are living through now seems to be not merely the erasure of the living oral, ethical, and humane traditions of Islam but the literal destruction and annihilation of the Muslims who are the bearers of those traditions. In Algeria, Iran, Afghanistan, and, alas, in Egypt, this narrow, violent variant of Islam is ravaging its way through the land.

It has not been only women and simple, unlearned folk who have believed, like the women who raised me, that the ethical heart of Islam is also its core and essential message. Throughout Muslim history, philosophers, visionaries, mystics, and some of the civilization's greatest luminaries have held a similar belief. But throughout history, too, when they have announced their beliefs publicly, they have generally been hounded, persecuted, executed. Or, when they have held fast to their vision but also managed to refrain from overtly challenging the powers that be and thus avoided violent reprisal, they have been at best tolerated and marginalized— accepted as eccentrics outside the tradition of "true" Islam. From almost the earliest days, the Islam that has held sway and that has been supported and enforced by sheikhs, ayatollahs, rulers, states, and armies, has been official, textual Islam. This variant of Islam has wielded absolute power and has not hesitated to eradicate—often with the same brutality as fundamentalism today—all dissent, all differing views, all opposition.

There has never been a time when Muslims, in any significant number, have lived in a land in which freedom of thought and religion were accepted norms. Never, that is, until today. Now, in the wake of the migrations that came with the ending of the European empires, tens of thousands of Muslims are growing up in Europe and America, where they take for granted their right to think and believe whatever they wish and take for granted, most particularly, their right to speak and write openly of their thoughts, beliefs, and unbeliefs.

For Muslims this is, quite simply, a historically unprecedented state of affairs. Whatever Islam will become in this new age, surely it will be something quite other than the religion that has been officially forced on us through all these centuries.

All of this is true.

But the fact is that, however genuinely humane and gentle and pacifist my mother's and grandmother's Islam was, it left them and the women among whom they lived wholly accepting of the ways of their society in relation to women, even when those ways were profoundly destructive. They bowed their heads and acquiesced to them even when the people being crushed were their nearest and dearest. Tradition and the conviviality, warmth, companionship, and support of the women of the extended family were rich and fine and nourishing and wonderful so long as things went well and so long as these women were dealing with men whom they loved and who loved them. But when things went wrong, the women were powerless and acquiescent in a silence that seemed to me when I was young awfully like a guilty averting of the eyes, awfully like a kind of connivance.

This, in any case, seems to me to be what my aunt Aida's story points to.

Aida's marriage was absolutely miserable from the very start, but divorce, according to Grandfather, was simply not a permissible thing in his family. And yet his own niece Karima, my mother's cousin twice over (her parents were Grandmother's sister and Grandfather's brother), had divorced twice, and each time by her own volition. The difference was that Karima was an heiress, both her parents having died when she was young. Independent and wealthy, she had married on her own terms, ensuring always that the *'isma,* the right to divorce, was placed by contract in her own hands. (The Islamic legal provision permitting women to make such contracts is one of those details that I mentioned earlier that are written into and buried deep in what is otherwise a body of law overwhelmingly biased in favor of men. Generally, only rich women and women with knowledgeable, protective families are able to invoke these laws. Many people don't even know of their existence.) Aunt Aida had not inherited anything as yet and was financially dependent on her husband and her father.

Grandmother, grieving all her life over the cost of Grandfather's intransigence toward their son Fuad, was powerless to alter his decision about Aida. For all I know, Grandmother even acquiesced in the notion that divorce was so great a disgrace that, despite her daughter's misery, she could not bring herself to advocate that course or attempt to persuade Grandfather to relent. Karima, her own niece, who was always received, of course, with warmth and unconditional affection in their home, was nevertheless regarded by Grandmother and her daughters as somewhat scandalous, or at any rate as someone who was rather unconventional and living dangerously close to the edge of impropriety. Aunt Karima further added to her reputation for unconventionality when she founded an orphanage for illegitimate children. It was scandalous to men like Grandfather for respectable women even to mention such a subject, let alone to be founding a society and openly soliciting funds from him and his cronies to support an organization addressing the matter. She raised substantial funds for it over the course of her life as well as for another society, which she also founded, for the care and training of the blind. Both still flourish today and honor their founder. A bust of her stands in the front garden of the Society for the Blind.

Grandmother would not live to witness Aida's suicide. But she was witness to Aida's sufferings and unhappiness in her marriage, and the electric-shock treatment she underwent.

There is an irony to all this. In the circumstances in which Aida found herself, Islamic law would in fact have granted her the right to a divorce or an annulment. Had she been free to take her case to an Islamic court and had she not been constricted by the conventions of her people, she would have been granted, even by that male-created law, the release that she sought. Not by Grandfather and his customs or by Grandmother and her daughters and their conventions, steeped as they, too, were in the ways of their society, but by Islamic law, in another of those unexpected, startlingly just provisions of this otherwise male-biased construction.

Nor was this the only situation in the various family circumstances I've described when women would have been more justly treated at the hands of Islamic law than they were by the traditions of the society, traditions by which the women of the family, too, were evidently bound. Islamic law, for example, frowned on the practice, entirely accepted by cultural tradition, whereby a man repudiated a woman, as my dying uncle had done, because he doubted her virginity. Asked about such a case, a medieval Islamic judge responded that the man had no right to repudiate a woman by claiming she was not a virgin, since virginity could be lost in many ways—just by jumping about or any such thing. He could divorce her nevertheless, since men had the absolute right of divorce even in the absence of a good reason, but the woman was entitled to full compensation and could not be regarded or treated as guilty of anything.

And so we cannot simply conclude that what I have called women's Islam is invariably good and to be endorsed. And conversely, everything about what I've called men's Islam is not to be automatically rejected, either.

Foremothers

Gayatri Chakravorty Spivak

SOME YEARS AGO, CARL FRIEDMAN WAS looking for Frances Bartkowski and me at a bar called Polly's in Middletown, Connecticut. The bartender had called out, Carl reported, "Did anyone see two girls alone?" Two girls alone. I have been thinking about this—about when and indeed how women are not single—as I take hesitant steps toward older women in my family. But in stepping toward my great-grandmother, my shadowy paternal grandmother, my mother's aunts—women who were not single in the usual sense, except for one—I am moved to ask, When and indeed how are women not single? I respect that category, single. I respect women by themselves, making sense of their lives within a general culture of reproductive heteronormativity. And yet I wonder, do we need a special analytic category for female collectivities? For lesbian couples? For single lesbians? Is the antonym of single double? Multiple? Or, always, married?

These are the women who bred me. I am nobody's mother. The *Mahabharata* provides an answer: *nāthavati anāthavat*. My mother's aunt made me understand that phrase in a way that no one else has. My mother's aunt was single, but also singular. Singularity is a repetition of difference, repetition and difference, repetition with difference. Singularity is the universalizable. This is my relationship with her, and with my other foremothers. I am their repetition, with a difference. We are single, singular and together.

My biological mother, Sivani Chakravorty, was singular and in important senses, single. She lived as a widow for forty-eight years, and she did singular things on her own. With her recent death, I have lost an archive, and so for the first time, I have responded positively to writing my memoirs. In this hesitant decision, I have been helped by my niece, Medha Chandra, my sister Maitreyi Chandra, and most recently by one of the most eminent conventionally single women I know—Romila Thapar, historian of ancient India.

Confronted with the task of writing about the past, even my own past, I was planning to carve out time for research. Romila, a thoroughgoing social scientist who can be interdisciplinary with the humanities, dissuaded me. "It is your enriching memory," she said, "that will make your work worthy of readers." She restored me to my convictions and made my task more difficult. I dedicate this beginning to Romila.

My title comes from Assia Djebar, who is technically as un-single as I am—married a number of times. Romila turned me onto one of Djebar's grand lines: "If only one could occupy with desire that single spectator body that remains, and circle it more and more tightly in order to forget the defeat"—the defeat that is life (141). Assia is writing about pictures of insurgencies with women wailing on the side. Somehow, I seem to see the women in my family: Boronani; Thakuma; Taludidu; Pawto; Mother, gone so recently; and Didi, gone even more recently. I see them as part of some grand and distant picture, a field of singular women, my forewomen. And I sigh: if only I could "occupy with desire" their singular bodies, encircle them more and more tightly in order to forget the defeat.

The first in line is Barahini Debi, my mother's grandmother or Boronani—literally, the eldest grandmother. Yet *nani* is a maternal grandmother, and Barahini Debi was my mother's father's mother. Perhaps the detail means nothing. Perhaps there's a story there. It makes my heart twist for my mother, who knew the answer. Boronani died between 1929 and 1931, I think, but I want to catch the resonances

in the cavern of her living mind between the ages of five and eleven—
the probable years when she was married and widowed.

I can remember my own life, selectively but well, between five
and eleven. At five, I got my first double promotion into Kindergarten
Three and met Bharati Mukherjee. At eleven, I was in junior year of
high school and received my music degree (I was precocious). I was
developing a "nudge-nudge" interest in boys. Boronani went into my
making, and so I ask, how was it to live through an experience so
different from my own?

I must think of marriage differently in order to enter my great-
grandmother's normality. A tremendous and enviable party for a five-
year-old (or perhaps a seven-year-old; I do not remember exactly what
age she was at marriage, and Mother is not there to tell me). Her parents loved her. They had researched her husband's family painstakingly, attempting to assure their daughter's future social security. Did
the boy come to visit sometimes? Could she feel some version of that
"nudge-nudge" feeling toward this designated lover in the restricted
public sphere of her extended family? She would have been sent to the
home of her husband's parents' extended family after puberty but was
widowed before that could happen.

To be widowed in childhood was a terrible fate. I wrote, some years
ago, about the devastation of the caste Hindu widow, as an alternative
to the visible violence of sati. In that quaint, wordy prose that I fan-
cied twenty years ago, and for which I have been punished all around
from all political spectrums, I quote: "The woman as widow, by the
general law of sacred doctrine, must regress to an anteriority transformed into stasis." In other words, the widow's lot was stagnation
and a terrible feeling of self-hate. In that same essay that many people
seem to resent, I also congratulated the collaboration of Indian and
British reformers for criminalizing sati and commented on how it did
not necessarily rearrange the women's desires, as did the class-marked
access to colonial subjectship.

Rearranging desires. That is how I understand my task as a teacher.
I am no one's mother, but many people's teacher. This is my forty-fifth
year of full-time teaching. If you count when I started coaching at

seventeen, it's even longer: 1959. Like most of my readers, I am a paid teacher. A sort of servant, rearranging desires. That is how I understand the emptiness of mere reform. That allows me to see that widow remarriage is unevenly distributed across the caste divide.

If I were a Dalit intellectual, belonging to the Hindu out-castes, or an aboriginal, this part of the story would have no poignancy. Widow remarriage was customary among Dalits and apparently, at some remote date, even among caste Hindus. Apparently *devara*—the word for husband's younger brother in most North Indian languages—does also signify second husband.

Barahini's father, Biharilal Bhaduri, was a friend of Iswarchandra Vidyasagar, one of the chief proponents of widow remarriage among caste Hindus in nineteenth-century Bengal. (What goes unmentioned in most feminist accounts is the uneven relationship between reform, caste, and class mobility.) Vidyasagar's challenge to Thomas Babington Macaulay's infamous *Minute on Indian Education* (1842), as distinguished from his involvement in caste-Hindu women's liberation, has now been undone by class apartheid.

"The personal is the political" should not be reduced to "only the personal is political." My agent had said, "Don't make it too theoretical; this is a memoir." Here, Toni Morrison gave me courage. Sweet and wonderful Toni said to me, "Tell her it's Gayatri Spivak's memoir." Not just a memoir! These historical insertions are dedicated to her. I quote myself now: "Whereas Vidyasagar's literary activism, aware of the detail of rural education, applies to the subaltern classes even today—his feminist activism applied to the metropolitan middle class to which I belong."

Biharilal gave Barahini in marriage to Pratap Chandra Majumdar, my mother's grandfather, her Dadabhai. This appellation is also unusual. Why not the more common "Thakurda" instead of "Dadabhai"? Why didn't I ever ask Mother? It is of no importance to anyone, and even that seems an unutterable loss.

What was the second wedding like? There are accounts of such weddings in nineteenth-century male reformists' autobiographies. They are clandestine affairs on moral high ground. Some years ago, Dilip Basu from Santa Cruz sent me a bit of print memorabilia that he had found in the India Office Library in which my mother's grand-father, on being asked why he wanted to ruin his future by marrying a widow, is reported to have said that he considered his life fulfilled if he could provide a future for a young woman. I don't have the actual Bengali in front of me and so cannot give you an accurate translation, but it is a noble sentiment in its own way.

Majumdar was not a rich young man. He had put himself through medical college by cooking for a family—a cook in a domestic residence. My brother located his name in the records of the Royal College of Surgeons, London, as having eventually become a Licentiate of the Medical Faculty, an LMF degree holder. It is rather less than an MD or an FRCS (Fellow of the Royal College of Surgeons), of course, but still an achievement in 1865. Did the wedding take place before or after he received his degree, I wonder. How did he get to London? Was there an unofficial dowry?

(My own father did the unbelievable thing of refusing a dowry—a very poor man refusing a dowry in 1928. That story . . . all I can say here is that we were brought up to despise the rich.)

Was there, then, an unofficial dowry? As far as I know, Biharilal Bhaduri was not a rich man either. I must find answers to these questions, I say to Romila, in my mind. The question that I will not find an answer to, yet learn most from asking, is, How was it for her, the second-time bride? If only.

This is the difference between an historian, as it were—not that historians are not imaginative—and a literature person. We literary ones learn from the singular and the unverifiable, what is not there or is only imagined.

How was it for her? I can only try hard to imagine. She is, by the time of her second marriage, thirteen. Much less infantilized than a middle-class US teenager, yet undoubtedly sexually innocent. Was she completely an object of benevolence in the hands of reformist men? Or did she feel herself part, specifically, of a moral adventure? Remember, I was precocious. I entered college at thirteen. And this is my great-grandmother, after all. I must have gotten all that precocity from somewhere.

As I ask these questions, my mind shifts to the blithe lack of preparation with which an Afghan or Iraqi woman, for example, is constituted for Americans, and how easily her speech, relayed by an interpreter, is further reported as evidence. I sit at UNIFEM lunches, remembering the inaccessibility of Boronani. If only I could occupy with desire the single woman's body at that remote wedding, encircle it and hold on. But I have another rather contradictory question, as well. If, in the general sense, singularity is repeated difference in single humans before we are persons or individuals, and, in the general sense, universalizable, is singularity, in the narrow sense, exceptionalist? Subject to the law of the talented tenth? In other words, is Barahini Bhaduri Majumdar representative? Most of us, writing memoirs and looking back to the past, make those who come before us representative. They become evidence in a kind of social record. But is my mother's paternal grandmother representative? Is she at least representative of a narrative of class mobility?

Does the study of single singular women illustrate this law as well? Barahini wanted to do something independently. She opened a pawn shop in the back part of the house with an interior courtyard where I used to go for lunch when I took my BA exams. (Thirty-six hours of written exams for the English degree—honest. No wonder I learned the language.) Was this common, this opening up of a pawn shop by a middle-class woman in a good family? Mother didn't think so. Here, a social historian may be able to help me. All I know is that my Ma gave me a pair of earrings that were never redeemed from Boronani's pawn shop, saying to me, "Boronani wanted to be an independent woman. In this generation, you are the most independent woman. These are yours." I wear them sometimes, often on occasions that she could not have imagined.

I think now of my father's mother, Bimalasundari Debi, who died in 1928, just before my parents' marriage. The only photograph of her that was ever taken was when she was dying, held up by her two sons. I don't know where that photograph can now be found. She lived in a remote village in northeastern Bengal, in the shadow of the foothills of the Himalayas. She died of cancer of the uterus, which was discovered only when she could no longer stand. She literally could not speak of a disease in her genitals.

I think of her whenever I go to the doctor for a Pap smear, to the hospital for a mammogram. For I have the singularity of her body. I am tall like her. Big-boned. My father used to say, when I shot up like this at eleven, that when his mother was married at five or some such age, nobody knew she would be so much taller than her husband. And so all her life she walked round-shouldered. My dad would say, "Gayatri, the air is cleaner up there; people are jealous of you because you are so tall, you know that?" And this is where my posture comes from.

We would go out for walks at 5:30 in the morning in Calcutta. That's what middle-class families did in those days. And the cows would be out, because that was the milk service in my youth. And so, since I was constantly told, "Walk straight; don't walk like your grandmother," I was taller than everyone else. It irritated me—I was a preteen! I would walk bent backward, straighter than straight, and I would say, "Tell me if there is a cow in my way."

The only thing of my grandmother's that the family had, that lasted the move from the village of Dashahal-Andatia, via Dhaka, to Calcutta—a cataclysmic move related to the fact that my mother's grandmother was a remarried widow, rejected by the village—was a huge and wonderful quilt, now lost. There was also a metal waist ornament—gone. I was the only woman in the larger family who could wear that waist ornament because I repeated her frame. On everyone else, it just slid down to the floor. And yet shame killed her. I have her body, but shame killed her. I think of her in locker rooms all over the world, as I strip publicly. She was a woman of power and control, a manager of the many details of my grandfather's farm. Yet the weight of ideology killed her. This is why reform is not enough. We must rearrange desires.

She could read a bit, but could not write—I've heard. What can it mean to read and not to write? To have a half share of the right to dispose of the phenomenal world? I think of literacy differently because I learn of it as I approach my formidable foremothers. From my own experience over the last twenty-odd years, teaching the children of the poorest of the poor and training their teachers, I have consolidated that sense: that reading and writing do not just give access to the phenomenal world. It is of the right to dispose of the phenomenal world that we speak, when we speak of what reading and writing might bring.

In one of the rural schools where I used to train teachers, there was a student—Shamoli Sabar by name—who was, I think, my equal in intelligence. There was such a gap of cultural difference between her and me that I could not be absolutely sure of this. Shamoli was utterly reserved, but she had moved to the high school, to the girls' hostel that I also ran; and I thought I would get a little closer to her. But she died a few years ago of encephalitis. I bring her up here because she stood in the place of my village grandmother, although my grandmother might have found it peculiar to have been compared to a tribal girl. But can I be sure? Again, I think—if only.

The entire business of reading and writing is inhabited by my grandmother. A couple of years ago I was speaking in Toronto; George Steiner and Susan Sontag were sitting in the audience. That I was speaking of my mother was audacious enough. They could not have known that in my thoughts was my grandmother of the village. I said that we betray contempt when we think of literacy merely as a primary vocational skill, although it is that, too. We betray contempt also if we think employability is identical with freedom, although employability is indeed necessary for legitimate social mobility.

I speak from experience. My mother was an indefatigable social worker. At age eleven, I learned how to grade papers. Precocious, right? Because my mother worked day and night to make destitute widows employable, my mother and I talked about what employability meant since I was a preteen. I do believe that although employability is necessary for legitimate social mobility, to equate it with freedom is a major mistake. Have we ever known what it is to read and to write, two separate but related activities—performances that transform ourselves and the world? It is not just learning to read and to write, but learning to read and write ourselves, in every sense of that phrase, that I encounter every day in the work of teacher training. Yet reading also allows us to privatize the public sphere and to contextualize and decontextualize the other; at the same time, all reading transforms and holds the key to making public our most private being.

The stories I know of this village grandmother—my Thakuma— I heard from Jyotsna Chakravarty, my second cousin, my Pholindi, about twenty years older than I. She had been hit so badly by her violent father that her reproductive system had been damaged. She had lived with my grandmother because she came from my father's side of the family. Her family left the village at the time of the partition of Bengal into West Bengal and East Pakistan in 1947. (My father had left as a student in 1917.) Jyotsna's was a peculiar singularity. Her wedding was arranged while she was still in the village, but her new husband took off the day after the wedding, never to be seen again. She insisted all her life that she was not single and remained carnivorous, refusing to go on the Bengali widow's vegetarian diet.

It was, once again, my indefatigable mother who recognized Pholindi's singularity in the 1950s. Just after my father's death, my mother organized and started running the only working women's boarding house in Calcutta. It was called the Sarada Sangha Mohila Nivas. She ran it with such efficiency that even people from the state government marveled at her success where they had failed. And much of the success of the undertaking came from my mother's choice of the superintendent, Jyotsna Chakravarty, our Pholindi. She was not institutionally educated but knew how to read and write. Steel in the flower personality at once—gentle and firm. Stern and kind. Looking after women who were "single" in the strict sense, during the early years of lower-middle-class female economic independence in West Bengal.

I will skip a bit to consider the foremother who opened up my intellectual world. Boronani was my mother's father's mother. Thakuma was my father's mother. Now I come to my mother's mother's side. My maternal grandmother, Raseswari Debi, had two sisters, Saileswari and Bhubaneshwari. Bhubaneshwari, the youngest one, killed herself at seventeen. It is her story I tell in "Can the Subaltern Speak?" in order to show that whereas the British Indian reform of sati is much celebrated, when a young, single girl attempted to write resistance in her very body, she could not be read.

If only I could occupy with desire that singular inscribed body. I have tried to understand how Bhubaneshwari felt as she waited for her periods to begin, so she could disprove what she knew would be the conclusion drawn from her hanged body: illicit pregnancy.

My modest reputation rests on two items: my introduction to Derrida, and my commentary on Bhubaneshwari Bhaduri's suicide. I am following that track still. Why did I not mention my relationship to her when I wrote of her? I wanted to see what would happen if she didn't have that certificate of authenticity which would reflect more on the people's approval of me than on her. And I learned a lesson from people's complete neglect of her, except for Abena Busia. Most people did not understand that I spoke on her behalf.

An extreme reaction came when my dear friend Raji, kindly commemorating the twentieth anniversary of the speech that became "Can the Subaltern Speak?," said in public that had Bhubaneshwari lived, she would have grown into a fascist, nationalist grandmother, like some character in an Amitav Ghosh novel. Now, Raji would never have expressed herself so if she had known the family connection. I was cut to the quick, of course.

But the defense I offered was reasonable. Ghosh represented a woman in fiction who had wanted to stand by the "self-styled terrorist freedom fighters." Bhubaneshwari had joined such a group. She supported armed struggle. Yet I would like to think that my pacifism resonates with her inability to kill. When recently, in a public conversation with Judith Butler, I said in answer to a question from the audience as to how I could be a pacifist in the face of Palestine, that the problem with the situation in Palestine was that politics would not allow me to be ethical, no one in the audience knew that I was thinking, in my heart, that it was a lesson I had learned from Bhubaneshwari, who was only seventeen when she died. She was four years older than my mum. And it was my mother who told me the story. What kind of flip is given to a mother's testimony, in terms of veridicality? One doesn't know.

In this essay, I cannot tell how it was Bhubaneshwari who opened up for me a line from the *Mahabharata*, a description of Queen Draupadi dressed in a single cloth stained with menstrual blood and dragged into the royal court. But I can say that it is perhaps from this single woman, a girl of seventeen who engendered my intellectual trajectory, that I get my sense of singularity. I repeat in difference these singular women who are mothers in many different ways, who teach me that reproductive heteronormativity is simply one case among many—like a stopped clock giving the correct time twice a day, rather than a norm that we persistently legitimize, even by reversal.

The entire epic of the *Mahabharata* is about this particular insult to Queen Draupadi, who had five husbands. Because the *Mahabharata* was an oral formulaic epic and each bard had to know the whole story, the entire story of the epic is given in the form of a young boy telling it to the blind king. Again and again throughout that recounting, we hear that disaster happened because a woman was brought into public while she was menstruating, while she was in her feminine nature, *stridharma*.

Draupadi was a queen, and the queens, when they menstruated, were taken to a lower chamber and wore only one piece of cloth until the menstruation was over. Then they took their bath, a healing bath, I suppose, because they were unclean. This is the story behind Bhubaneshwari also, the story I'm asking you to remember. She used menstrual blood as a way to inscribe her message and was not heard.

But the story continues. When the eldest of the five husbands in the *Mahabharata* is playing dice in the main court, he keeps losing until finally, he wagers Draupadi. He loses, and Draupadi is dragged from that chamber. The queen comes wearing nothing but one white cloth, smeared with menstrual blood. This insult leads to the great fight.

Now, how a feminist might read this is something else. This is not a presentation of a feminist reading of the *Mahabharata*. I'm saying only that because my grandmother's sister dragged herself into the open court of death menstruating, I was met with opprobrium from people who read quickly and said, "Spivak refuses voice to subaltern resistance." I see women every day saying, "The subaltern is speaking because I am," and I say to myself, "My mother was wrong." She had said, "You are using Bhubaneshwari's name?" And I had said, "Ma, no one will pay any attention to her." And I was right.

So Queen Draupadi is dragged up. She asks the oldest member of the court, who also has a marriage story, "Am I a piece of property that can be wagered?" And Bhishma, the oldest member of the court, is not able to answer her. This is not a bit from the *Mahabharata* that's given much popularity. If you have seen Peter Brook's version, you certainly have not noticed this. But there are female versions of the epics, *Stri-Mahabharata*, which are very different, and in the best-known of them, the entire epic ends not with the five husbands of Queen Draupadi climbing the hill to heaven, but with Draupadi laughing in the devastated field of war. Draupadi's laughter ends the women's epic.

The boy relating the story in the main *Mahabharata* describes Queen Draupadi as *nāthavati anāthavat*. Generally, this is translated as "someone with husbands, as if an orphan." But *nātha* actually means "lord," so I translate this differently. As I said, I am the object of opprobrium from traditionalists, who fault me for being too European, and from racists, as well as from those resenters of theory, the activists. But on the other hand, the folks in disciplinary Sanskrit fault me for daring to offer new translations of these kinds of ancient texts. It's hard, but I persist in translating *nāthavati anāthavat* as "Lorded, and yet, as if not lorded." In my reading, each time the woman menstruates, lording has misfired in the suspension of reproductive heteronormativity. And I believe that's why, again and again and again, in the opening conversation that is the entire story of the *Mahabharata*, what is told is, "Queen Draupadi is in her feminine nature," in her *stridharma*, suspended.

A suicide at age seventeen and a disgrace in the family made me understand how the message in this ancient text was transactional. She became my allegory of reading of a powerful woman-moment in my past. And in fact, that way of reading is what allows us to be responsible to our students. My foremothers teach me in more ways than I know.

WORKS CITED

Djebar, Assia. *Women of Algiers in Their Apartment*, trans. Marjolijn de Yager. Charlottesville: University of Virginia Press, 1992.

Lost (and Found?) in Translation

Hazel Carby

"Every story is, by definition, unfaithful. Reality . . . can't be told or repeated. The only thing that can be done with reality is to invent it again."

—TOMÁS ELOY MARTÍNEZ, *Santa Evita*

MY EDUCATION IS AND ISN'T A PROD-uct of the "disorderly year" of 1968, a year fissured by contradictions that have long since been paved under a seamless cultural mythology of student rebellion. I was an undergraduate between 1967 and 1970, reading for a degree in English and history, steeped in Marxist theory, with a talented, progressive faculty at what was then Portsmouth Polytechnic and is now Portsmouth University. I was an eager student in 1967, a successful student, if exam results are the measure of success, but my schooling so far had "filled me with questions that were not answered" (Kincaid 79). I was remarkably unaware that most of what I thought I already knew, information I could regurgitate at a moment's notice, I was going to have to unlearn if I was going to know anything.

The city of Portsmouth, on the south coast of England, was not a university town; it suffered from neglect and was decaying. In the late 1960s, bomb damage from World War II was still evident, and unex-

ploded ordnance was frequently uncovered whenever repairs to buildings or roads were undertaken. Portsmouth could not survive on the
paltry commerce produced by the seasonal cycle of poverty-stricken
renters and tourists: students who arrived each October were replaced
each July by coach-loads of octogenarians in floral prints hoping for
an inexpensive holiday by the sea. During the last three weeks of each
spring term, our landladies would be eager for us to be gone, willing
us away with uncharacteristic impatience because the senior citizens
paid twice as much for a room as we did.

Portsmouth was dependent for its economic health and for the
employment of its residents upon the Portsmouth Naval Base, which
had been an integral part of the city since 1194. The Royal Naval eventually occupied three miles of its waterfront and more than 296 acres
of the city center. From the windows of our lecture halls, we could
cast our minds adrift and gaze across the acres of destroyers, frigates,
and minesweepers of the Royal Navy. I saw the ships, I saw the city, but
I did not see anything. As Jamaica Kincaid puts it, "I did not yet know
the history of events, I did not know their antecedents" (15).

I had been schooled in the history of the heroes of the Royal Navy.
I knew that Sir Francis Drake, 1540–96, born, as I was, in the county of
Devon, was a revered British hero, a "founding father" of British naval
might, the most famous Vice Admiral of the Fleet who led the attack
on the Spanish Armada in 1588. I knew nothing about the Francis
Drake who, along with Sir John Hawkins, led the first slave-trading
expeditions and then later supplemented his wealth through acts of
piracy, plundering throughout the West Indies and South America.
Both were knighted for their exploits. I did not know that at least eight
slave ships left Portsmouth between 1699 and 1711.

While I studied literature and history in a city whose history I
could not access, my education took place on streets that became very
familiar to me. I learned about the power of the state, not in my college classrooms, but in confrontation with the British riot police sent
to guard the US Embassy at 24 Grosvenor Square, London. I was the
first in my family to go to college, or to regard the United States as
anything other than the saviors of the "free" world. However, what I
was learning during the protests against the Vietnam War had little,

if anything, to do with American power and everything to do with confronting the friendly British bobby whose mission was smiling and helping lost children, dogs, and the elderly, or so I had been taught.

My brother and I were very young when we learned that bobbies did not help "nigger kids," "black bastards," or "half-caste scum." But my parents did not know this; my parents could not imagine that anyone, let alone bobbies, saw my brother and I as "half-caste scum." My respectable parents believed in teaching their respectable children, "If you are ever lost or in trouble, find a policeman." Anyone who was afraid of the police, in their eyes, was not respectable and must have a reason to fear authority, presumably because they misbehaved. My parents had never witnessed a riot squad of bobbies on horseback unleashed on people taking part in a peaceful protest. But, if they had witnessed this, if they had seen the swinging batons breaking heads, I do not know that they would have thought the police action wrong. My parents regarded what they called my "antics" outside the American Embassy as more than foolish. My mother, in particular, felt that I was being disloyal and that I was disloyal because my education was sorely lacking. I did not know, she said, what the British nation (and, by implication, I as an individual) owed to the people of the United States of America. "The Americans didn't have to come all the way over here and put their lives at risk to help us during the war," she repeated over and over again. These words were more than a reminder; they were issued as a warning, as if to say that when "we" needed the Americans again they might not come next time because of the behavior of ungrateful people like me. When I was in college, I actually worried about this.

During World War II, my mother was a civil servant in the Air Ministry, and my dad was a flight sergeant and navigator in the RAF. Persecuted and ostracized as a "multiracial" couple and having only meager financial resources, my parents believed their primary investment as a material legacy for their two children was education. Education was not just a path to financial security and social mobility; it was armor for their children. "Sticks and stones will break your bones, but words will never harm you," and "Just be the best, be the first in your class, and they will leave you alone," were the phrases that resonated in the background of our school years. Were these word offered in comfort? Were these words offered as a protection? Did these words originate from the depths of my parents' bewilderment and frustration, from a profound ignorance of what to do? Or do these words, offered as wisdom, signal denial, a denial of how deeply racism was shaping postwar Britain?

My brother and I knew from first-hand experience the limited value of these offerings, of course: words of hatred signaled imminent danger, often immediately preceding the sticks and stones that broke bones, or in my case, teeth. But when we were hurt, we told our parents that we had had an "accident," for admitting that we had been beaten meant that we were not trying hard enough, were not good enough and, thus, had let *them* down in some unfathomable way. My brother and I were always having "accidents."

Education, in my family, demanded endless sacrifice. We were removed from the local schools and sent to private schools. Was this move an unspoken recognition that we were suffering more than accidents? I do not know. My brother had a partial scholarship to his school, but my mother still had to work multiple jobs, day and night, for years to pay the fees. I am convinced that my parents' belief in the promise and transformative power of a British education was a measure of the depth of their faith in Britishness. My brother and I never witnessed the wavering of this faith, not even when my father had to go to the Tottenham Court Road police station to obtain the release of my Dulwich Prep and Alleyns-educated brother, who had been arrested and detained under the notorious "sus" laws (stop and search on "sus"picion alone) for walking along Oxford Street with a checkbook (assumed stolen but actually his own) in his hand.

You could say that I inherited an obsession with education, but I translated it into an entirely different political and intellectual agenda, or did I? I certainly didn't have faith, but I retained my grasp on an endless list of questions. I registered for a postgraduate degree in education at the Institute of Education, London University, because I wanted to understand why the British educational system, instead of challenging inequalities of class, gender, and race, actually preserved, reproduced, and promoted institutional racism alongside class and gender divisions. At the end of the year, in my final examination, instead of responding to the questions asked, I wrote what I considered to be a devastating analysis of the Institute's postgraduate program—a program that completely ignored the issue of racism. I graduated with even more questions about the education system than when I had begun, but now I was certified as an integral part of it.

Who knows what happened to that paper after I literally stormed out of the exam room? The next thing I knew, I was contacted by the chief education officer of the London Borough of Newham and recruited to be part of an educational experiment in a newly formed high school in a sector of London with extremely low income and high unemployment. A single-sex school system was going coed for the first time, neo-Nazi gangs and the Kray brothers ruled the streets, and the area had a substantial Afro-Caribbean and black British population. As I prepared for my first teaching job in August 1972, Idi Amin expelled British Asians from Uganda. Shocked and stunned, many of them found themselves in Newham, and I met their traumatized teenage sons and daughters in my classroom.

My mother drove me to my first teaching job at Eastlea High School in the East End of London, and she wept copious tears as she helped me move into what she regarded as the "slums." If this was the result of private schools and college degrees, if the fruit of her sacrifice was depositing me in an area of even deeper poverty than the poverty she had struggled so hard to climb out of and move away from, my mother wanted no part of it. I had accepted the position as an English teacher in Newham because I naïvely thought I could be part of fixing what was so obviously broken. I guess going to the Centre for Contemporary Cultural Studies at Birmingham University was another step in the same direction.

I arrived at the Centre an obnoxiously self-righteous, anti-racist activist, in my seventh year as a high school teacher of English on a fully paid sabbatical funded by Newham. Into the corridors of CCCS, I carried the baggage of those years: a politics of the classroom forged in defense of the tenets and practices of progressive education against the insidious incursions of the Department of Education under "Maggie Thatcher the Milk Snatcher," and a politics of the street honed in anti-racist battles waged against fascist gangs and their racist cousins in police uniform who patrolled our neighborhood. While I learned much from each of those struggles, they cost me little. However, I riffed upon them brazenly, elaborating them as "street cred," to disguise how terrified and insecure I actually felt about being back and black in graduate school.

I had taught in the vibrant and turbulent multiracial, multiethnic, un-streamed classrooms of a comprehensive school where a handful of us worked collectively in the hope that our pupils could be equal partners in the learning process. I saw how young minds and bodies opened under progressive, creative, and imaginative educational practices supported by generous resources. But in the midst of possibility, I also saw my black and brown students terrorized by violence and the threat of violence: bricks were thrown through their windows as they slept; feces and flaming bottles full of petrol were pushed through their letterboxes; and going to and from school, or the shops, they were pushed and shoved, or punched and beaten as they passed by the racist slogans daubed all over the walls, doors, and streets of our neighborhood. At any hour of any day, they could be subject to physical and mental abuse, in or out of school, from their peers, from shopkeepers, from the police, and from the social service workers appointed to assist them. To be of any use to these students, my classroom had to be transformed into a safe place: a laboratory for the forensic examination of racist encounters and for the translation of analysis into practical strategies for countering and overcoming the effects of institutional racism.

When I applied to attend the Centre, I had a much-thumbed copy of Paolo Freire's *Pedagogy of the Oppressed* on my bedside table, a text which informed my practice in my high school and in the adult literacy program that I ran two evenings a week in the same building. I had also assembled a growing library of books and papers published by CCCS, including *Resistance Through Rituals* and *On Ideology*. Exhausted at the end of the day, in moments stolen from grading papers or working on lesson plans, or during a weekend when I wasn't taking my class on a camping trip or to the theater, I read with diligence and care what was being written at the Centre. I was eager for an intellectual challenge, though I sometimes found the reading difficult and, occasionally, impenetrable. But I never doubted that the effort was worth it.

Even though I hadn't yet met any of the members of CCCS, I regarded them as allies in the fight against the increasingly authoritarian and conservative forces being mobilized against the poor, the working class, the black, and the immigrant—in short, against everyone in my world. I devoured the insights that addressed our condition in an area with high levels of unemployment, imprisonment, immigration, and racism, inadequate housing, and very low income levels. CCCS publications, I thought, contained analyses with which one could begin to develop defensive strategies and to imagine the construction of paths to a just and equitable world. The interview which followed my application to the Centre terrified me, but the letter offering me a place terrified me even more. I was afraid that I would be unable to translate the knowledge I carried with me into what I regarded as the theoretically sophisticated world of CCCS.

Before I left Newham, I carefully explained to my students that I was going to the Centre for Contemporary Cultural Studies for a year to study in order to get a master's degree, and they all seemed to understand and applaud my reasons and motives. When I met five or six of them outside the butcher's shop around the corner from my flat in Forest Gate, after my first term in Birmingham, they were very pleased to see me, and we chatted for ages. But gradually they revealed some doubts about my rate of progress, were curious as to exactly how hard I had been studying, and asked if I was sure that I could pass my exams at the end of the year. Eventually it dawned on me that the cause of their concern derived from the fact that my manner of speaking had not "improved" in their eyes, despite the months that had been spent studying culture. Only gradually did I understand the terms of their equation: for my students, "cultural studies" translated into becoming "cultured," and being "cultured" meant sounding like a BBC broadcaster. Culture, then, was the means by which I was to acquire class mobility, class position in Britain being recognized and confirmed through accent. My failure to make "progress" was registered in my voice, and much was at stake in my evident lack of success. If I hadn't learned to speak "properly," how on earth was I going to be able to return to teach them, or their children, how to be cultured and thus upwardly mobile? If I didn't make it, they didn't either.

The year before this conversation, during my last year as their teacher, we had taken a class trip—not one of our major expeditions, just a walk down the road to the office of the London Docklands Development Corporation in the last class period of the day. There we walked around and between tables on which lay detailed models of the future of the area in which we lived. Gone were the familiar shabby streets, decaying high rises, and council flats. The voices of my pupils, usually loud, energetic, and buoyant, were hushed, their almost-whispers a measure of a certain awe and respect, if not of comprehension. I stood apart from them, leaning against the wall, strictly an observer, for I had visited this office before. I had seen the display, and I was aware of what the development plans meant for the residents of the area. I didn't have the heart to translate it for them; I wanted them to see and understand for themselves what was coming. One conversation will stay with me always: "It's beautiful," I heard one say, followed by, "Which of these houses do you want?"

"I want this one right on this canal."

"I don't; it's too close to the water." Pause. "Why does the water go right under the side of these houses?"

"So you can keep your boat in there, stupid."

"But my mum doesn't have a boat."

Silence was followed by gradual realization. First, they understood that these houses were not for people who didn't have boats, especially not for people who couldn't even imagine owning a boat. Then they saw that redevelopment was not for them, that people like them were not to be included in the rosy images of the future docklands. How many of them knew that people like them were expendable and would, inevitably, be displaced, I don't know. The volume of their voices rose to their normal levels; they glanced out of the corner of their eyes, trying not to read in my face explanations they didn't want to hear. Without being prompted, they collectively turned their backs on the tables, gathered their jackets and bags, and moved to the door, ready to leave. In a discordant chorus of voices, each of them announced other places they had to be. A year later, outside the butcher's, as my students searched my face, another hope, the one they had eagerly placed in their teacher, bit the dust.

1978–84, the years I was associated with CCCS, completing first an MA and then the PhD which produced the study *Reconstructing Woman-hood*, were years of seemingly inexhaustible intellectual energy, passionate commitment, and political vision. Pessimism of the intellect, a response to a rapidly increasing state authoritarianism, the brutal effects of everyday racism and gender inequality, and what appeared to be the continual defeat of left and progressive agendas was countered by an optimism of the will exercised in intellectual activity in the service of social, political, and economic transformation. But I am to this day haunted by the loss of the students I left behind.

WORKS CITED

Kincaid, Jamaica. *The Autobiography of My Mother.* New York: Penguin, 1997.
Martínez, Tomás E. *Santa Evita.* New York: Knopf, 1996.

Unreconciled Lives

Neferti Tadiar

A T THE AGE OF FIVE I SAW ONLY glimpses of the worlds in which my own was enmeshed. Some were hidden; some quietly, enigmatically felt; some wholly expressed elsewhere, while here barely known. Yet some of these worlds made an occasional appearance in the intimate domicile made up of children and maids that was my early world.

They were *katulong*, "helpers," as the mostly young women who enter other households as domestic workers were and continue to be called. They cooked, cleaned, laundered, and took care of the small children of the families they worked for. Often these young women did this work for a few years before they married and settled into households of their own. A few stayed with the families they worked for for the rest of their lives. Some were daughters of the helpers of one's parents. Some were daughters of one's own relatives who needed work. I knew the women who were my parents' helpers as my *manangs*, or "older sisters," the honorific in Ilocano for females older than oneself. In turn, they called my parents *tata* and *nana*, or "uncle" and "auntie." They lived with my family in a newly constructed, modern concrete house on Rizal Avenue, the major cross street of the one highway that connected our small but central provincial town, San Fernando, to all the other provincial towns along the hilly northern coastline and through the provinces in the central plains south and finally to the nation's capital, Manila.

Having plied that highway many times during their schooling, my parents appeared distinctly modern, as members of their generation of young professionals fashioned themselves in those heady years of nationalized development two decades after the harrowing devastation of World War II, a war in which all the men in my father's family were killed. In photographs, my parents are beautiful, stylish and cosmopolitan, seemingly unencumbered by their provincial surroundings or the taint of backwardness that inevitably adheres to a formerly colonial people. In their stories, they are forward-looking and independent-minded, refusing the obligations of social custom and the collective and individual humiliations of our shared history. Even the tale of their romance bears incidents of small yet significant acts of defiance against the older generations' hierarchical ways—my mother catching my father's eye as she raises her voice against an elder aunt, my father impulsively asking her father for her hand without his mother's intercession. As they pursue their own promising individual careers in law and medicine, while raising their own family, and become involved in civic-minded enterprises innovated in the first world—family planning, life insurance, and the Rotary Club—they contribute to the very modernization and development of the nation which they believe is already the most advanced among its neighbors. In those early years of their marriage, which was also the beginning of my life, they were the very image of progress.

My parents built a new house made of gleaming light-colored, painted concrete, with a galvanized, corrugated iron roof and louvered glass windows. It stood in striking contrast to the old, bamboo-thatched and wood, *capiz*-shell-windowpaned house of my aunt's family, which sat right next to it on the other side of the shared family lot, the last remaining inheritance from my paternal great-grandfather. In this house my grandmother and her "playmates" played mah-jongg on the porch every afternoon, smoking thin tobacco cigars in their long skirts and embroidered sheer fiber blouses, the dress that native women had worn since Spanish colonial times.

Manang Masa, my aunt's lifelong helper and cook, oversaw the mah-jongg game, providing *merienda* of sponge cake and Coca-Cola along with prizes of cans of Liberty condensed milk and boxes of Tide detergent, which she bought with the *tong* the old women paid with each game. This daily afternoon mah-jongg game was a business Manang Masa ran on the side of her main living, which was to cook and keep house for my aunt's family as my aunt devoted herself to educational projects and church work, and her husband, my uncle, made alternately failed and profitable shady deals with men with glassy eyes and faces reddened with drink, who would show up in the evenings to plot, confer, debate, and drink some more.

Though it was undoubtedly my aunt's house, Manang Masa was her steadfast right hand, and to my mind she, along with my aunt and grandmother, defined that other household, in which my older sister and brother and I spent almost as much time as in our own, playing with our older cousins, eating the food she prepared. It was a place where unsavory worldly affairs and spiritual and intellectual pursuits crossed paths, a mixed household whose economic management and daily work of provisioning were in the steady and sure hands of these women. At the back of the house, they kept various domestic animals, almost adjacent to the rooms in which they slept. Sometimes I would watch Manang Masa take a chicken from the back to butcher it for dinner, the bird shrieking, its wings flapping wildly, her unflinching hand gripping its neck as she drained its blood into a bucket before she pulled its feathers off.

In our house, there were no live animals except the ubiquitous lizards on the ceiling and our pet dog, Spot. Screened windows and doors, a sealed floor of polished concrete and a picture-book imagination of home vigilantly kept non-human life, unseemly relations and activities—all that should remain outside—outside. And yet other worlds nevertheless entered and pervaded, most never after all having really been let go or left behind. From the perspective of a foretold future, we lived as much in a time of lingering pasts and outmoded practices and beliefs as in a place still at a disabling distance from the developed world, lacking the everyday conveniences of modern life— dressed chicken, prepared foods, ready-made clothes, electric irons, washing machines—and the liberation and enlightenment that modern life would bring. Old ways continued, such as the domestication of servitude and exploitation and the extension of both one's bounty and one's hardship through relations of kinship, the organizing principle of all social life, power, and happiness. Repeated stories brought to life unseen forces of malevolence and beneficence that permeated our landscape and mapped the vital connections across time and space between persons, living and dead. Gatherings instilled those connections and gave ceremony to the uncontrolled spilling over of lives into one another that took place on all the other days. Through these habits of making collective life, intangible kinds of inheritance, including immanent worlds, were passed on. Indeed, despite all aspiration on my behalf to the contrary, I grew as much on the strength and influence of these other worlds as on the promises and ideals of that more powerful, distant world that captivated us all.

Brought up with the liberal, egalitarian convictions of my father, whose own Mason-turned-Protestant father had gone against the wishes of *his* father by deciding to bury his dead nine-year-old daughter in accordance with his chosen faith without the proper blessings and sacraments of the Catholic Church, I never called my older sister and brother by the honorific *manang* or *manong*, as both my parents did with their own older siblings. A strange honor that *manang* should be confined to our helpers and other people and relatives outside of the nuclear home, as if this form of deferential respect was to be reserved for older ways of life that my own family was intending to leave behind, even while we were cared for and maintained by those very ways that we were supposed to transcend or eventually become estranged from.

But childhood allows a blurring of boundaries that may later be more firmly drawn. From the time of my earliest memories, my comforts, fears, and dreams of what was possible, of elsewheres and unknowns, were tied up with our *manangs* and the small universe I shared with them. Without doubt, from this intimate world I learned hierarchy—graduated orders of families and clans, of languages written and spoken, of villages and their relative proximity to the center of town or to the mountains, of ethnic lineages, and of opportunity and employment—objective social orders that would also shape the proper form and propriety of our deepest sentiments and most loyal attachments. Our *manangs* not only exemplified these orders in relation to my family, but also came to be the very means for instilling them. From them, my siblings and I learned to speak and make authorized sense of the world in English, the valued language of reading, school, and government, at the same time that we learned to understand and relate to people in Ilocano, the commonplace language of all domestic and social life, of personal confidences as well as easy and heated exchanges in the plaza and in the market. It took me a long time to learn to keep these languages separate, to know which words belonged where, especially when I had in addition to learn the national language as everyone had to in school. But the differences, in languages as well as in the people who used them, had been established and our selves took shape around them.

Even as they helped to rear us on these differences that were already directing our divergent fates, our *manangs* also provided us that primordial comfort in which such differences could be dissolved. In their care and in our shared dwelling I experienced love and joy and the unspoken connections of feeling between people. In the small bedroom by the side of the kitchen and next to the carport where I sometimes slept with my *manangs*, I have pleasurable memories of our bouts of raucous laughter and boisterous play. I liked how my *manangs* combed my hair and picked my head for lice eggs with their gently rummaging fingers as I sat idly between their legs and they chatted among themselves. I always enjoyed the sensuous feeling of comfort and excitement it gave when they would use their thumbnails to split the tiny eggs on my scalp and pull the pieces down the shaft of a strand of hair. They brushed, braided, and played with my hair, the way they tickled and teased and played with us in moments of carefree indulgence. Simple bodily pleasures but also forms of tenderness and care that I knew, when I began to brush and play with my own daughter's hair almost three decades later, had become an instinctive way of loving now mine to transmit.

As a small child, I learned from my *manangs* a fear of ghosts, in particular of a white lady appearing on the chico tree, beneath the roots of which my and my brother's placentas lay buried, as well as a fear of other spirits, human and nonhuman, that inhabited and moved through the world we lived in; a fear of swallowed santol seeds growing into seedlings in one's stomach, for despite all warnings, the sweet sour succulence of their pulpy juices, which we children sucked by passing them over and over again through our teeth, made them impossible to resist swallowing; a fear of drunks sometimes glimpsed in broad daylight silently wending their way down the road, who, we were given to understand, harbored underneath the languorous placidity of their comportment a hidden and unpredictably explosive capacity for violence. The experience of ambient threats to our safety and well-being prepared us for later fears. A few years later, after martial law had been declared, inaugurating a dictatorship that would outlast our youth, a new fear gripped us, absorbed like almost all our fears from a current of rumors and tales for which our *manangs* served as an important channel—a fear of soldiers on the streets forcibly cutting the fashionably long hair of young men and harassing young women for their fashionably short skirts, treatment which we were led to intuit augured only worse things that we could not yet even imagine.

There were many things to fear in the outside world, things in the shadows of our gleaming, clean, and pressed lives that it was the duty of our *manangs* to shield us from. But our *manangs* were themselves of the outside world, and they brought with them traces of the unfamiliar worlds and lives they lived elsewhere. Our laundress, Manang Aning, we knew was an alcoholic, and I at least viewed her with some trepidation. I do not remember her ever being intoxicated during the day when she worked, but I kept my distance, watching her only from behind the screened door of the kitchen. She worked quietly and did not seem to socialize much with the other *manangs*. She was an older woman, bone thin, with hair cut unusually and severely short. Her hands looked surprisingly smooth, the extremely taut skin on them no doubt the result of washing thousands of clothes by hand. Although my parents generally knew something of the lives of our *manangs*, often knowing their personal predicaments and even their families, for in a small town such as ours all relationships were personal and my parents' role with respect to their helpers was as patrons and temporary kin, we children knew little if anything at all of our *manangs'* lives outside. And so Manang Aning's life, her unhappiness or sorrow, palpable as it was in our shared everyday life, remained mysterious to us.

One day while my parents were away in Manila, Manang Aning got hold of some liquor and drank to the point where she reached some kind of end, and she began to run amok. My siblings and I knew what to do: my older brother gathered all the kitchen knives and we locked ourselves in our grandmother's room, huddling by her bed while we waited and listened for something to come to pass. We took comfort in the thought that our other *manang*, my brother's nanny, Manang Annie, who was Igorot (the term lowland Christianized people like ourselves used for the minority tribal communities of the mountain provinces), was brave and strong like her people and would protect us. And she did. Though it is unlikely that I actually saw this, I have a distinct memory of Manang Annie chasing Manang Aning through the two houses to subdue her, her strong bare feet running across the wide wooden planks of my aunt's house with the formidable power they impressed upon me when she once performed an Ifugao ritual dance in our home.

The night Manang Aning ran amok, Manang Annie was the hero and Manang Aning the tragic victim in a drama that we were somehow a part of but did not really grasp. For many years afterwards, I imagined Manang Annie had drawn on resources and capacities from the cultural commons of her tribe, a distant world that to me was as enigmatic and exciting as the sources of Manang Aning's angry pain were mysterious and frightening. As in many of the dramas that would unfold in our midst, it was for me as much the other social worlds summoned by or entangled in the immediate conflict as the conflict itself that left a lasting imprint. Both Manang Annie's and Manang Aning's bodily enactments of the power and violence of worlds seemingly beyond yet intimately intertwined with ours stirred my senses, and the memory of this stirring is still as vivid as the trickle of blood that the knives drew from my brother's safeguarding arms.

Those worlds were not only objects of fear and awe but also the sources of dreams. My nanny, Manang Perlita, was a tomboy who owned and rode a motorcycle in a place-time when horse-drawn carriages still plied the roads and all vehicles were driven by men. To me, she was someone who could ride away from everything at a moment's notice. In fits of child fury and fancy, I would declare my intention of getting on that bike with my *manang* to ride away with her. Whatever her intent, Manang Perlita brought with her that bold possibility of flight. Perhaps all our *manangs* did, for were they not to some degree all testaments to such flight, to leaving home and being on one's own?

When I was the first in the family to leave home on a lone adventure abroad, I did not think about Manang Perlita or the possibility of riding away to I knew not where, which she enabled me to imagine and which I never forgot. I ended up very far from home, though no farther than my aunt who, almost three decades earlier, one day suddenly told her husband that she was leaving for the US the very next day and that he could follow her or not. She could no longer bear her stifling parochial life in the middle-of-nowhere town where he had taken up a comfortable position as a doctor, content to while away the evenings playing poker with his friends. So she worked on her travel papers in secret until that day when she showed him her passport to announce her departure, and the very next day she left.

I only learned this story of my aunt as an adult, though I had known her since I was a child. By then the theme of women leaving home had become a national story, an official lament, as millions of Filipina women left the country every year to work as nurses, caregivers, and domestic workers elsewhere. My aunt herself was a nurse, and that is how she made her way to the US. Some of these women had been "helpers" before. Many years after she had worked for us, my mother received a Christmas card from Manang Annie. She was working in Hong Kong, now a professional domestic worker among the tens of thousands of others there on several-year contracts, which despite widespread reports of abusive treatment, most renew more than once. Others became "helpers" for the first time. As I was nearing a decade in my own prolonged sojourn away from home, I learned that my older female cousins, whom I also call *manang*, one married to a doctor, the other to a businessman, each with businesses, families, and "helpers" of their own, both abandoned their lives of privilege to work as nannies in New York. They were now part of the growing statistic of overseas Filipina domestic workers, who en masse had become and remain the object of sensationalist media attention, steady scholarly interest, and urgent feminist concern. For national and transnational feminists, these women continue to serve as a prominent symbol of globalization and its symptomatic dependence on the devalued reproductive labor of disenfranchised women from the former third world.

I, too, have written on Filipina domestic workers in terms of the exploitation and devaluation of their gendered and racialized labor and the debased forms of personhood, even thinghood, that they, as the objectified embodiment of this labor, are often socialized into and sometimes forced to occupy. The feminist perspective I brought to the phenomenon of overseas Filipina domestic workers emerged out of my grappling with the violent conditions of the Philippines' authoritarian state–promoted national prostitution economy, conditions that a vigorous movement of Filipina women activists and journalists had brought to public consciousness through years and years of relentless, courageous criticism and protest. Like me, many of these Filipina activists and journalists from whom I learned to see the world in a radically critical light were raised on the strength and power and care of other women who were our "helpers." Few of us write about these women who helped in our making as individual persons and social subjects; whose effect on our lives may have exceeded the labor they expended to maintain us; with whom we may have shared more than the relations that defined and differentiated us or the social categories through which we might now claim and experience political identity and solidarity. As we comprehend and struggle to transform the conditions of our own making, we tend to stand apart from these women, as well as men (including transgender men, like our "*manang*" Jun who did "women's work" in our home later in my childhood), who now only stand for the structures we critique, whose unaccounted part in our own lives can only appear as an irreconcilable contradiction to our politics, a contradiction that can be resolved only through radical change.

Many of us long for this radical change, for the release and flourishing of people, possibilities, and futures that have been impeded and
destroyed by the unjust and rapacious forms of social life, which have
become global human norms. Yet how can we realize the worlds and
lives we long for if we do not reckon with the experiences to which we
owe the nurturing of this longing? It is difficult to try to remember
these almost forgotten times of my own making without nostalgia or
disavowal, redemption or apology. Writing in the US, I face the collective habit of portraying the third world as a place of despots and their
victims, humanitarian images of third world life under incorrigible
regimes of violence, squalor, and elite indulgence. Such images can
only render us in terms of complicit enjoyment or pathetic abjection,
while the place from which we are judged is vindicated of the crimes
that were the making of the third world. Our own outrage at the violent conditions of human life is viewed as the result of our exposure
and assimilation to a world from which a humanitarian concern for
the plight of others is understood to have originally issued, even as
that same world defined the very condition of inhumanity to which it
condemned others. Our narratives are limited by the direction toward
a change already known or decided, their lessons and value determined by the measure of a shared political morality that we have perhaps too easily acceded to or not sufficiently questioned. We view the
world outside us with critical reason, and when we look at ourselves,
we see only the reflection of that world we apprehend and convict. Its
truths become our truths, eclipsing all the other fictions that sustain
our sensuous and feeling lifeworlds, fictions that might still be the
source of our endurance, the form of our immanent strengths and
hopes.

The worldly power of many Filipina women—whether as presidents or as activists fighting those presidents—depends on the hidden
and exploited labor of other Filipina women. We often fail to acknowledge this contradiction, to grasp the fact that our capacities, including that of critique, depend on a world economy of such relations,
i.e., on the very world that we critique. But more than this, we fail to
fathom what contradiction cannot fully encapsulate. For while vast
social differences divide us, it is also true that the formidable capacities

Filipina women exercise across these differences issue out of shared and entangled, as much as opposed, ways of life, ways of being in the world, of being women, that cleave but also coincide.

Like my aunt, my cousins abruptly left lives to which they had not, perhaps never, been reconciled. I think about my own leaving, a flight like so many others from a too familiar life, and I find that I, too, was and am unreconciled, both to the present and to what has become my past in the easily told stories of my departure and settlement. In those stories, lives and lifeworlds left can only appear in conflict with the life now lived or sought. Or they become merely interpretative keys to a later unfolding, a storehouse of lessons for lives that will have already surpassed them. *Just as my present life is surpassing and making fodder of these lives past.*

When I was around nine, a young girl a few years older than me whose name was Teresa became part of our household. She had run away from the house of the man to whom her parents had sold her and her siblings for a few sacks of rice. After years of regularly taking and fighting back his abusive blows to shield her younger brother and sister, she had had enough and decided to report the man to the police, who took her to the judge, my father. Fierce and indomitable, Teresa nevertheless consented to come live with us, while my father looked for other families to take in her siblings. My parents put her through school, and she did some work in the house in exchange. It was an awkward relationship. Teresa was not my *manang*, not really a helper, not my sibling. The line dividing us was drawn, lifted, drawn again. We played together, we ate apart. I was not always kind. At nine, I felt threatened by the blurring of the differences between us and I would sometimes try to cement them. One day, while my siblings and I were playing "market" among ourselves with leaves, stones, and sticks for our wares and currency, Teresa drew us to her, showing us how to make birds, grasshoppers, bracelets, and rings out of the leaves of coconut trees, and at least for an afternoon of wondrous play, perhaps forever, I relented. I cannot say we ever became real friends, but we did share part of our childhood and perhaps something of ourselves.

After Teresa had left us, my spinster aunt decided to adopt Teresa's younger sister, Dalisay, who appeared unscathed by the brutalities that had hardened and coarsened her older sister's looks and ways. I occasionally saw Dalisay at family events and in visits to my aunt, but I did not meet Teresa again until more than twenty years had passed. My family had long moved to Manila, and I had long left the Philippines, having made another life for myself, including a family life, in a country I had once vowed never to settle in. I was now a scholar and teacher at a university in California, a place that was the epitome of the future-driven world from whose vantage point the world I grew up in was a cheap version of the pre-industrial stage. It seemed like several lifetimes had taken place in the great span of worlds that I had traversed. My American husband, daughter, and I were visiting with my family in Manila, and together we all made a trip to my hometown. Hearing of our visit, my aunt invited us to drop by, as Teresa and her husband were also visiting and Teresa had asked about me in particular. We approached the house, and Teresa came out to greet us, her own American husband in tow. She and I looked at each other with a mix of curiosity and recognition. When we were children, I remember such looks between us through which passed many unspoken thoughts and feelings. Now we exchanged no more than a few friendly words, constrained as we were by the awkwardness of our relationship and perhaps by the daunting immensity of life contents that filled the great breadth of time since we last saw each other. *It was I who could not speak, was embarrassed, ill at ease.*

My aunt and my mother did most of the talking, and we learned that Teresa had been a singer in a nightclub near the US military base before she got married and migrated to the US. Our elders prevailed upon her to give us a song on the piano, and she complied with an ease greater than that of simply an experienced performer. Her voice was warm and melodious, strangely out of sync with the harshness of the life I remembered her having lived and imagined her continuing to live after she left us. In between her singing, she exchanged both light and aggressive banter with her husband, whose bored, cruel amusement in taunting her seemed to me characteristic of a certain underclass of white men relishing their found power over an underclass people, examples of which I had seen plenty of in the tourism- and military-dominated areas of the country. But Teresa was unfazed and unintimidated by this abuse. She seemed at least equal to it, able to check or send back every barb that came her way. I recalled the young girl I knew, the young girl I was.

I could see the aspects of Teresa's life that as a feminist I knew well—the conditions that disenfranchised third world women face and that we deplore, the devalued roles that are their options in a world economy in which their role is to service the lives of others. I do not know what Teresa saw about me and my life. I could certainly see what I might have seen and known of many others like her, and of many others like me. And yet, the things that I knew and could see were not the things I felt and experienced on that day we met again. While I could hardly ignore and would not want to belittle the obvious, objective chasm between our lives, I remember feeling the semblance and parallelism of our trajectories, the kindred turn of our respective fates shaped by unconscious covenants, potentials, and qualities provoked and animated in each other's witnessing company. *Before her once again I felt I had somehow fallen short of an expectation I could only surmise. How was it that I was found wanting?* It was not only that we had both embarked on paths well-trodden by other Filipina women, paths of flight that had turned into forms of life, so familiar as to become national types. It was also that we were related—not by blood or law or even sentiment, but rather by a shared passage in a world we had together lived and made as children, a world we were still carrying forth and leaving behind long after the parting of our individual lives. We had once been companions in a world in whose survival and passing, as much as in our own, we were now also accomplices.

My cousins had become other people's helpers; our "helper" had become my cousin. More than the fungibility of our places or the social logics that make for that fungibility, more than the precariousness of the distinctions we take pains to make the ramparts of our souls, a precariousness heightened by the unmooring, wantonly ruinous consequences of machines of war and capital on the petty fates of supplemental humans—more than these facts, which figure in the rational account I reach for, are the untold ways we, in whose lives we had once been intimately involved, have made each other—ways we have swayed each other's life acts, curtailed or fostered each other's longings, cultivated and passed on intangible capacities and strengths, including the capacity to bear with the losses our own dreams might entail and the strength to remain nonetheless unresigned.

If I write only of early memories and such fleeting encounters, it is because they are what are most easily consigned to irrelevance and triviality compared to later events and friendships that would fit a proper narrative of political awakening. Yet these early experiences and the insoluble feelings they give rise to, even now, were openings through which I received the people and events that could be said to have politicized my understanding of the world, openings through which I came to those passions that continue to fuel my deepest political commitments and hopes, even commitments and hopes that I have yet to know and understand.

My daughter's name is Luna. It is easy to tell people about the famous Luna brothers to account for her name. Juan and Antonio Luna were Filipino revolutionaries who fought against the colonial power of Spain, one a painter, the other a general. Like many nationalists, their heroism was not without compromise, their valor and vision sullied by ignominious acts. It is easy to mention the first letter shared with her Jewish great-grandmother, on her father's side, who died shortly before my daughter was conceived and whose memory we wanted the letter to trace. But Luna is also the name of the town that Manang Masa was from, a town known for its stones—smooth, silvery flat disks and colored, egg-like stones on the coastal shore, like the stones that lay on the dry riverbeds, which became drier and drier for longer spells through the years, the once raging rivers of our province now mere trickles into the sea. It seems too far-fetched, this connection to a town I had only been to perhaps once or twice as a small child at a picnic by Manang Masa's childhood home. Manang Masa herself was unaware of the connection. When my partner and I brought our newborn to visit, she found the name we had chosen for our daughter strange. To name one's child is to utter a wish and a promise, to preserve a past and to will a future, and I could not say to Manang Masa, who had lived all her life not with us but with my aunt in the house beside ours, how or why this wish and promise bore the remembrance of her hometown and its stones, and her.

We cannot want to transform a world or a life to which we are reconciled. No day passes that does not offer evidence of the great and small degradations that we inflict upon others or that we suffer at the hands of others according to a grossly inequitable order of allocation of human value. We see this order reflected in the division between helpers and those whose lives they help, between supplementary actions and real deeds, between formative forces and experiences and true subjects and events, which our own stories of struggle seem destined to repeat, which this essay, with its circumspect equanimity of self shored up by experiences it cannot fully command or possess, unwillingly reproduces. Yet within this stringent domestic order, there can be found enactments of worlds that escape it, ways of living and acting, drives and capacities impossible to bind to the house rules of proper personhood, that are shared and passed on in unaccounted ways among the unreconciled.

At the age of five, I burned half my house down. No one knew how the fire had started. But I remember lighting the match in the room I shared with my *manangs* that set the house ablaze one Sunday morning. Weeks later, as the carpenters began rebuilding the house, my mother overheard me say, "They can build it up, but I will burn it down again!" My family and friends laugh at this story, which to them is all about me. But like all enabling fictions of the self, it is also about other people and other lives.

Feminism, Black and Blue

Ann duCille

I WAS NOT BORN A FEMINIST, BUT I will die one. And it may be feminism that kills me. Not literally, I hope. This is not another essay about feminists stabbing each other in the back or about what white feminists have done to women of color and vice versa. Nor is it meant to be a black female rendition of *Portnoy's Complaint*, although I certainly have my own set of frustrations and longings ripe for psychoanalysis. Rather, I want to use the occasion of having arrived at the age of sixty to reflect on the benefits and bruises of living gender-wise and race-conscious.

Those of us who reside at the intersection of race and gender difference have often been spoken and written of as doubly burdened. All subject positions are fraught in one way or another, but for the most part, I have refused to think of either aspect of my black female identity as a burden. I would gladly trade Michelle Obama's svelte figure for my own, but beyond wishing away some too, too solid flesh, I would not choose to be other than who I am: a black woman of a certain age, experience, and education. I am painfully aware, however, that what I mostly think of as the great good gift of a black feminist consciousness, as well as a black female body, carries with it certain stresses and strains that have conspired to make black women academics a kind of endangered species.

We are endangered not because ours is a profession that throws us in the path of bodily harm as combat soldiers are thrust into the line of fire, but because we live by and through our minds and therefore run the risk of thinking ourselves to death. As black feminist critics, scholars, and theorists, we are by definition, if not by nature, critical, contrary, oppositional. Finding fault lines in the bedrock of American society is our job. Our contrary points of view often leave us out on a limb, alone.

We have a long line of black female ancestors whom it has been our life's work to claim. At the same time, we are autogeneric: having been erased and excluded from the historical record, we have invented and inserted ourselves into the national romance and the global narrative. We have made a profession out of studying ourselves and have carried that study out into the universe and—more importantly in terms of what I want to explore here—the university. That is to say, the academy in which we work today looks very different from the one we came into as students and as teachers thirty or forty years ago, at a time when black women like us were nowhere to be found in the halls of academe—not in the volumes that lined the library shelves and certainly not on the syllabi of the mostly white male professors who schooled us in the great books and natural wonders of the Western world.

We absorbed but did not accept as normative the wisdom of the ages. For us as black feminists, nothing ever was or is neutral, natural, normative, or universal; no one is ever innocent; objective truth is a falsehood we live to expose. We labor at the margins and read between the lines. Everything around us is a text—a text which not only must be read but which must be read against the grains of patriarchy and Western civilization. "The master's tools will never dismantle the master's house," we say, even as we use the King's English to do precisely that: to deconstruct the very house in which we live and work. Doing our job even remotely well can leave us not merely alone but also homeless, expatriates in our native land, or, worse still, outsiders in our own families and communities.

The familial estrangements are particularly wrenching. It's not that family and friends are uninterested in our careers but rather that much of what we say and do as feminist scholars falls outside the pressures and priorities of their daily lives. That is, our advanced degrees and tenured professorships—and the class privileges they afford us— may distance us from friends and relatives who not only lead very different lives but who also figuratively and sometimes literally speak a different language. I do not necessarily mean here the "yo-baby" Ebonics of the street versus the standard English of the academy— although that may be the case in some instances—but, rather, that the discourse of our profession is not plain talk by any standard other than our own.

Even within our field, the debate over the nature and level of discourse—over high theory and low culture (discourse versus dat course, I once suggested playfully)—has been hot and heavy, despite the dream of a common black female language. If we as critics, scholars, and theorists cannot agree on how to talk the talk of our discipline, how can we expect our parents, siblings, and childhood friends to know or care what the heck we are pontificating about when we lapse into our black feminist critique of, say, Halle Berry's Academy Award–winning performance in *Monster's Ball* or the problematic race and gender politics of Tyler Perry's latest drag send-up of black womanhood?

Still, there is irony in the distance and disconnect between critic and community, because whether a real fact or a rationalized fiction, many of us who write about race and gender—who attempt to expose and dismantle the deep structures of racial, gender, and class oppression—tell ourselves that we do what we do for our people. That our words often go unread by those on whose behalf we have written them enhances our sense of alienation and aloneness.

Thus far I have been saying "we," "us," "our," but while I know I am not unique in laboring over and under this sense of separation, I am really talking about myself, about my own experience. I'm not particularly fond of the confessional mode when it comes to my own writing, except perhaps as a jumping-off point from which to theorize. Why should anyone care what I have to say about myself? But I herein own up to the aloneness that I am suggesting is a part of the black feminist condition. Not universally so, of course—we, I, eschew universals—but widely enough felt to be a topic of constant concern and ongoing conversation among black women academics across disciplines and age groups.

Some years ago, I wrote of what I called the crisis of black female intellectuals: the hyper-visibility, super-isolation, emotional quarantine, and psychic violence of our precarious positions in academia. I noted that black feminist scholars had played a pivotal role in bringing the work of generations of African American women from the depths of obscurity into the ranks of the academy, but I also suggested that we had paid a heavy price for this labor—in exhaustion, depression, loneliness, and a higher incidence of cancer and other killing diseases. Fifteen years later, I am, frankly, frightened by the extent to which these words seem even truer now than they were when I wrote them in 1994. I don't know how the statistics on professorial mortality stack up against other occupations, but black women in and around the academy seem to me to be dying at an alarming rate. And the evidence I'm drawing on is not anecdotal but personal and too close to home for any black woman scholar's comfort.

In May 1998, more than two hundred teachers, scholars, critics, artists, and performers gathered at the University of California, San Diego, to honor and celebrate the work of the poet, novelist, critic, and UCSD literature professor Sherley Anne Williams. The three-day conference—"Black Women Writers and the 'High Art' of Afro-American Letters"—was occasioned by the twelfth anniversary of the publication of Williams's Pulitzer Prize–nominated novel *Dessa Rose* (1986). From the keynote address by Angela Davis to a stirring staged reading of *Dessa Rose* and an array of performances, papers, panels, workshops, banquets, and barbecues, the conference was an unusually full and moving event. But for me, the most poignant moment came at the very end when Sherley Anne Williams stood up and said tearfully to the conference organizers and participants, "Thank you for giving me back my work."

None of us knew then—least of all Sherley Anne—that a year later we would again gather in her honor, but this time for her funeral. She was diagnosed with cancer the following April and died just three months later, on July 6, 1999, six weeks shy of her fifty-fifth birthday. As shocking, tragic, and untimely as her death is the sobering fact that several other black feminist writers and scholars who attended the conference in May 1998 have since also died of cancer: Barbara Christian in 2000, June Jordan and Claudia Tate in 2002 (Claudia was with us at the conference in spirit; she was already too ill from lung cancer in 1998 to make the cross-country journey from Princeton), Nellie McKay in 2006, VèVè Clark in 2007. These are the names I know; I fear there may be others from among the roster of conference participants. I do know that there are others—too many others—from among the general ranks of the black female professoriate. Most of these women, like almost all of those named above, were in their mid-fifties, although Sylvia Boone, the first black woman to be tenured at Yale, was just fifty-two when she died of heart failure in 1993. All of these women began their academic careers in the late 1960s or early 1970s as part of that pioneering generation of black women who helped open the doors of the academy to other underrepresented groups. All of them trained legions of graduate students who have become a kind of black feminist diaspora spreading across the academy.

Because we were colleagues at UCSD, I knew Sherley Anne better than I knew most of the other black women academics who have been snatched from us. I know that she worked hard and worried a lot. I know she felt bruised and battered by decades of doing battle in the master's house and that in what turned out to be the last years of her life, the weary blues hovered over her like a thundercloud. She had begun a new project, though, a sequel to *Dessa Rose*; that and the conference had raised her spirits. Still, knowing that the marginalization, the isolation, the exhaustion were not hers alone but are shared conditions many of us have talked and written about, I have to wonder at the toll it takes—this life of the mind and imagination lived in the lion's den.

Don Imus, the controversial talk-jock whose radio show was canceled after he called the Rutgers women's basketball team "hard-core, nappy-headed hos," announced in March 2009 that he has prostate cancer, caused, he speculated, by "all the stress." I was sorry to hear the diagnosis, but I thought at the time that if Imus, a member of the most privileged of the species—moneyed white male—thinks stress brought on his cancer, he should try living as a member of a disparaged group—as a black woman, for example—so that he could experience the psychic trauma of knowing that no matter what you accomplish, what you achieve, you are always reducible to a nigger or a "nappy-headed ho."

Within medicine, stress—both mental and physical—is widely acknowledged to be one of several significant risk factors for killing conditions such as cancer, heart disease, hypertension, and diabetes, although the exact causal relationships are matters of ongoing study. But black women academics would do well, I think, to take seriously Imus's claim that stress caused his cancer and to consider the ways in which our work environments and intellectual lives may be toxic, hazardous to our health. As if being black and female in America were not challenging enough, our critical, oppositional standpoints as feminists may be killing us. One recent study suggests, in fact, that pessimism is as much a risk factor for cardiovascular disease as high blood pressure. I am not suggesting that an oppositional critical perspective is the same thing as a pessimistic outlook, but I am saying that we need to see ourselves as an at-risk population—an endangered species, if you will—and to consider our own health a matter of life and death.

All of that said, looking back at my own career, I do not have to put on rose-colored glasses to see the bright side of my gender-wise, race-conscious life. In many ways, I feel that I have had the best of all possible jobs. I am proud and honored to know and to have worked among the black women scholars who helped to change the course of literary and historical studies and the composition of the academy. Thinking back thirty-five years to my first tenure-track teaching job at Hamilton College, I remember that in order to teach *Their Eyes Were Watching God* in my intersession seminar on African American literature (the first course of its kind at Hamilton), I had to Xerox copies of the novel by hand and distribute them to students, none of whom had heard of Zora Neale Hurston. Photocopying out-of-print volumes of African American literary texts was standard practice in the 1970s—a form of illicit book-making that first brought the work of forgotten, out-of-print authors like Hurston into literary and historical studies at the university level. The Hamilton students and I made our way through *Their Eyes* that fall largely without benefit of critical interpretations other than our own, since what little secondary material there was on Hurston at the time, with few exceptions, did not do justice to her or her oeuvre.

I recently Googled Hurston for the fun of it and found that there are upward of 540,000 entries relating to her and her work. Some of these are duplicates, of course, but still: 540,000 entries for a black woman writer whose work was little known and completely out of print when I attempted to teach it in 1974. I also consulted Amazon .com while I was looking for Zora, and found that there are more than 6,000 Hurston-related titles in the book category alone. Again, many of these are repeats, but I know from sources other than Google and Amazon that pretty much all of Hurston's known work, including posthumously published collections of her short stories, essays, folktales, and plays, is readily available in multiple languages. The difficulty one encounters today in teaching *Their Eyes Were Watching God* is deciding which of the numerous editions of the novel to order and how much of the rich body of criticism to assign. And the difference between then and now—between zero and 540,000—is one wrought largely, though by no mean solely, by black feminist scholars and critics.

Lest we get too cocky about our accomplishments, however, there are about 11,600,000 Google entries for Mark Twain. More to my final point—and harkening back to what I said earlier about the disconnect between the black feminist critic and her community—a few years ago, when I confided to a helpful sales clerk, a young black woman, that I was shopping for something to wear to Toni Morrison's retirement party, she replied: "Toni Morrison? Who's he?"

We have work to do.

PART TWO

Professional Vistas

"Don't Smile So Much":
Philosophy and Women
in the 1970s

Martha C. Nussbaum

IN ONE OF THE PHOTO ALBUMS THAT I used to fill when I still thought it important to put photos into albums, I see myself in the late summer of 1972, the beginning of my fourth year of graduate school. I am standing in our little garden in the backyard of the Peabody Terrace apartments for married students at Harvard University, a garden that always looked more like a jungle, where our cat Pamina used to play at being a great cat of the wilds. I am wearing a sleeveless navy dress with a spotless white bib. The skirt is very short, but in all other respects the look is one of Doris Day respectability. I have well-cut short light brown hair. (Blondeness came later.) I am smiling. I am seven months pregnant.

Three years before, when I was a senior at NYU and about to go for my final interview for the Danforth Graduate Fellowship—which I won—my dean at NYU, a round old-fashioned-looking Latinist named Cooley, who wore three-piece suits and taught the *Aeneid* without giving the appearance of understanding anything about either *amor* or *ira*, gave me some advice that shocked me. Don't smile so much, he said, because it gives an impression of subservience. This shocking and memorable advice was one of my first moments of feminist consciousness-raising, from a most unlikely source. At first, Cooley's suggestion offended me, for I had been brought up to think a smile an essential gesture of politeness. And yet, as I reflected, I did notice that I was smiling all the time, even when there was nothing particular to smile at. And I began to wonder, from time to time, whether that smile was not, indeed, a gesture of submission. Still, in 1972, even after three years of Harvard, I am still smiling, standing in the little garden of our married student dwelling, in my dress-for-success maternity dress, with a small additional female person pounding away inside me.

There was a lot of radicalism at Harvard in those days, particularly in the philosophy department, but I was not a part of it. For one thing, I was just too busy doing my work and having a baby. But there were other reasons. I had left my elitist WASP background to marry into a liberal Jewish family who read I. F. Stone and the *Nation*, and I had left my high-school Goldwater libertarianism to join the Democrats. But the left-wing groups of the 1970s had little appeal for me. At heart I suppose I have always been a liberal, attached to free speech, respectful debate, individual choice, and other Enlightenment values. I have always had extreme suspicion of cults and their leaders. The Progressive Labor Party, the part of the SDS that was prominent at Harvard, always struck me as a corporatist and totalitarian movement, a cult in all but name. People I knew were ordered to marry (or, as the case may be, to leave their marriages) for the sake of correct political values. They would say, quite seriously, absurd things such as, "We are getting married to emulate the lifestyle of the workers." Children were suddenly told not to talk to some adult they loved, because that person had the wrong view on some micro-sliver of revolutionary politics. Every petition that began with a perfectly reasonable demand ended with a list of further demands that were not entailed by the first, and with at least one of which I always disagreed.

In other ways, too, I was not of my generation. I got married young, while most of my fellow graduate students were living in communes and having sex without commitment. The daughter of an alcoholic mother, I have always had a horror of chemical intoxication, and I am in the very small minority of people my age who have never used marijuana even once. I always was obsessed with fitness, for related reasons, and was running several miles a day even during my pregnancy. When the young interns came into the delivery room to interview me about the evident success of the Lamaze childbirth classes I had been taking (for I was lucky enough to have a fast, easy delivery with no anesthesia), I told them that Lamaze was for wimps, and running was the key. So I have always been something of an outsider, and, like most runners, a loner. The world of radical left-wing solidarity was, in so many ways, not made for me, nor I for it.

Feminist movements came along somewhat later than the SDS, but, although they were often reacting against the sexism of left-wing men, they often struck me as equally dictatorial. People were told what clothes were correct and what were not. (Skirts were out, pants were in, even if the pants were extremely tight and revealing, and worn with a halter top.) They were told what sort of teaching was compatible with correct values and what was not. Although it was at one time a common view in SWIP (Society for Women in Philosophy) that women would do philosophy differently from the way men did it, more cooperatively and less destructively, the women of SWIP could be extremely destructive. My friend and fellow graduate student Eunice Belgum came to Harvard from St. Olaf College in Minnesota, and from a conservative clerical family. Dazzled by the brilliance of fast-talking East Coast graduate students and eager to join their bohemian, radical way of life, she came to depend too much on the approval of SWIP. One day around 1975, while teaching at William and Mary College, and depressed for many reasons, Eunice killed herself. Shortly before, she had been denounced in a SWIP meeting for co-teaching a course on the philosophy of sex roles with a male colleague. Her parents followed up the phone calls listed as having been made on the day of her death. They found that the calls were all to students in that course, apologizing for having corrupted their consciousness by teaching with a man. I wrote the last chapter of *The Fragility of Goodness* thinking about Eunice and gave it as a lecture in her memory at St. Olaf. I used Euripides' *Hecuba* to argue that the possibility of trust is an essential prerequisite of any political community, and indeed of decent human relations. In that way, too, I have always been a liberal.

So, out of my mistrust of the radical left, I came more slowly than some to feminism. But Harvard, in the vanguard of sexism then as now, did a lot to prod me. As I recorded in *Cultivating Humanity*, my career as a graduate student (in Classics) at Harvard began when a noted Roman historian took all us new graduate students up to the roof of Widener Library and, with a broad sweep of his aristocratic arm, showed us all the Episcopal churches that could be seen from that vantage point. I learned the anti-Semitism of the Classics department very quickly, from the snide comments about my change of name from Craven (on my application) to Nussbaum (at the time of arrival), and by the rude treatment typically given my husband, a graduate student in linguistics. Its sexism I learned more slowly, watching how women were never recommended to jobs at the top universities, even though they sometimes got those jobs anyway, proving that it was false that "Yale would not hire a woman"; watching how Emily Vermeule, hired to fill Radcliffe's one tenured faculty position, a chair reserved for a woman, was treated rudely by her colleagues; learning that women could eat lunch in the Harvard Faculty Club only if they used the side dining room; watching the vilification and the firing of Caroline Bynum and Janet Martin, two first-rate female scholars who formed the first faculty women's group at Harvard. But a big moment in my transition came right around the time of that smiling photo.

In 1972, I became the first woman to be a Junior Fellow in the Society of Fellows, an organization modeled on the Prize Fellowships at Trinity College, Cambridge; it gives young people three years at good pay to embark on interdisciplinary careers, free of any further official degree requirements. The society had a long tradition of misogyny, going back to one of its leading figures, the classicist Arthur Darby Nock, who refused even to allow women to be invited as guests. As the first woman to breach the tradition in the sense of full inclusion, I was welcomed with both respect and warmth by Nobel Prize–winning economist Wassily Leontief, a true feminist, who also created a child care stipend for me, promising me that the same support would be given to male fellows who did child care. (Leontief left Harvard shortly after, in protest over its denial of tenure to two left-wing economists.) Right after my election, I got a letter of "congratulation" from a leading Latinist in the Harvard department, one of my teachers. He said that it was difficult to know what to call a female fellow, since "fellowess" was such an awkward term. Perhaps, he opined, the Greek language could solve the problem: since the Greek for "fellow" is *hetairos*, I could be called a *hetaira*. *Hetaira*, however, as both he and I well knew, was the Greek term for courtesan, or high-class prostitute.

Here we see the real difficulty of feminism in the academy. It is the difficulty that John Stuart Mill long ago correctly identified: most men are simply not prepared to live with women on a basis of equality. They may think and maintain that they are, but their human development is paltry and does not sustain such good intentions as they may have. They have learned deviously infantile ways of perceiving women, and these ways always inflect their dealings with women as graduate students and colleagues. Men's ways of being infantile vary. Some are flirtatious and silly in a relatively harmless way. Some fear old age dreadfully, and believe that continual exercises in seduction will produce something like erotic immortality. Some long to tell you in no uncertain terms that you are a whore, because it makes them feel power. Some hate themselves and have contempt for any woman who is nice to them. Some—and these are the worst, I think—are satanic, by which I mean that they have an emptiness at their core that they fill with exercises in domination, which they market with a frequently dazzling charm. (For many years, philosophical life at Harvard was dominated by such a man, despite the utter paltriness of his philosophical contribution.) Some take no stand on any of these issues, like Dante's souls in the vestibule of hell, waving their banner now this way and now that. They don't really like what Satan does, but it seems to them excessive to say that he is bad.

There are also the good and decent men. I have the good luck in life to be drawn romantically to these types and not to the others, no doubt because of the formative influence of a father who was strong and daring but also kind and devoted, and who sought equal strength and daring in me. I also prefer decent men as friends; I find the other types exceedingly boring. Among the good and decent men, some are unprepared for the surprises of life, and their good intentions run aground when confronted with issues like child care, housework, and women's fame. These men do better as friends than as spouses. (My husband, whom I deeply loved, and who is still one of my greatest friends, was such a man, at that time; after the birth of our child, our marriage gradually became an unhappy one.) A few, like my dear friend John Stuart Mill (for I cannot help thinking of Mill as my friend when I read his surprising letters and works), are ready to think in truly unconventional ways and to be a different sort of man.

I got my PhD in Classics, and thus, although I spent a lot of time in the philosophy department, I was there primarily to work with my thesis advisor, of whom more later. I believe that the sexism of that department at that time was less extreme and less universal than that of the classics department, but real all the same. More generally, the philosophical academy contains all the types of men that life contains, with the qualification that philosophy selects for proud, quick-talking, dominant personalities and against the gentle and quiet. The main problem of feminism in philosophy is the infantile level of human development of many of the men who are in it. This problem will not change without large-scale social changes that are still in their infancy. The most we can do is to deter the worst abuses and punish them when they occur, meanwhile trying to bring up young men who think differently, and women who assert their dignity.

But since the topic has been mentioned, let us now, indeed, consider sexual harassment. There is a tendency today for young women to think of policies against sexual harassment as both unnecessary and constraining. They feel condescended to when they are told whom they may and may not sleep with. Rational adults should be able to sort these things out their own way, and if women stand up for themselves they will not be hurt. I suppose I used to think this way too, back in the days of excessive smiling. Let me try to explain why I no longer do.

My thesis advisor, G. E. L. Owen, was a brilliant scholar of ancient Greek philosophy. He was also an alcoholic and an attempted womanizer. A Welshman who struggled to assert his stigmatized lower-middle-class Welshness against the elite British academic society that condescended to him, he viewed it as an essential part of his manly honor to attempt to sleep with every woman who came his way. This prominently included all female graduate students, one after the other. The typical pattern was as follows. (I have compared stories with others.) You had an appointment with Owen. Arriving late, he said he had left your paper, or chapter, at home. Then, if it was Cambridge, England, where the workroom was also the home, he would pour sherry, offer some to you, put on a record, and start talking about the sadness of life. If it was Harvard, where the work-room was several blocks from the home, he would try to convince you to come home to find and discuss the allegedly forgotten essay. But even if you said no, he would still produce sherry and begin to talk about the sadness of life. Much though you tried to return the topic to Aristotle, he would go further into sentimental weltschmerz. You would know that seduction was at hand when two things happened. First, he played Darius Milhaud's "Le Boeuf sur le Toit," to show how lively, funny, and virile he was. Second, he recited Auden's "Lay Your Sleeping Head, My Love," in order to show you how sad he was about age and time. At this point he would put his arm around you, grab a breast, and see what happened next. There were a couple of variants. One time when I stayed overnight in a Cambridge college guest room, he walked into my room at 8 a.m. and simply lay down on top of me, an act that in some sense I count as an attempted rape, although his physical weakness allowed me to push him away quite easily.

Now this was far from being the worst thing in sexual harassment. For Owen did not retaliate against women who said no, even repeatedly. He thought he had salvaged his honor by attempting, but such was his self-contempt that he thought all the better of those who would not have him. Only those who said yes got hurt—by being drawn into the misery of his alcoholic life, by becoming responsible for getting him out of bed and into class in the morning, by becoming the targets of gossip and criticism, and by becoming the targets for his own self-hatred, as he relentlessly belittled them in class.

Even Owen's relatively benign pattern of sexual harassment, though, created an atmosphere in which women simply had no dignity and were unable to assert it. One of my fellow graduate students, more political in those days than I, did protest to the chair of the philosophy department, who was embarrassed and had no idea what to do. At that public complaint, Owen hit the roof and refused to work with her henceforth. To this day, she suffers professionally from that early exclusion. I thought at the time that she had overreacted, since one could handle it by simply saying no. And I did, again and again. I admired Owen enormously, and I also felt sorry for him. Just as I never accused my mother of being drunk, even though she was always drunk, so I managed to keep my control with Owen, and I never said a hostile word to him. I knew I would never sleep with him, that I would go on working with him, and that he would not turn against me.

But that was really not adequate. The woman who complained was right, and I was wrong. For my dignity was always compromised by being forced to be available for the Milhaud/Auden ritual, albeit with a negative ending. And the general idea was created, in that circle, that women were there as sexual objects. Even though I was Owen's star pupil, I remained denuded of dignity. One day Bernard Williams took a walk with me along the Backs behind King's College, Cambridge, and said, "You know, there is a price you are paying for this support and encouragement. Your dignity is being held hostage. You really don't have to put up with this." I understood his point, but I didn't deeply feel it: I felt in control of the situation. So things went on as before. Although after Owen's return to England from Harvard I managed to avoid, for the most part, situations in which the ritual could enact itself, I still worked with him and even, while an assistant professor, coedited a festschrift for his sixtieth birthday. (We chose sixty because we suspected he would not live to sixty-five; he died a few months after the party.) My coeditor, a male scholar at Cambridge, kept saying to me, "Why are we editing a festschrift for this man? He has just been at my house for dinner, and he insulted my wife." And I would say, "Calm down, Malcolm. He is a great scholar with a very sad life." As in my earlier life, so here: my propensity has always been to put up with too much bad behavior, smiling. I feel I understand Anita Hill.

The first general thing I want to say about sexual harassment in the academy is that things are rarely this benign. Usually there is punishment afoot somewhere, and notice that even in this case, the woman who complained was sorely punished. I was punished, too, by the enmity of Owen's male students and former students, many of whom simply assumed that I was sleeping with him and that this was why he liked my work.

The second thing I want to say is that the availability of women for sex, or even attempted sex, creates an atmosphere in which women have no dignity. Men think that whatever advancement women get, they get through sex. Women are pitted against women in ridiculous and demeaning ways. Whether the favorites are the ones who say no or the ones who say yes, an in-group and an out-group are created in a seminar, and the academic endeavor is impeded thereby. This atmosphere hurts men, too, because they come to think that women have advantages they don't have. This hurts their relations with themselves, and with women.

The third and most important thing I want to say about sexual harassment in the academy is that the feminist analysis of sexual harassment is correct: this is not about love, it is about power. What Owen got out of the ritual was an assertion of his virility and his power over powerless women. The fact that he could do this to young and healthy me meant, to him, that he was not as decrepit and out of control as he feared he was, and was. Many men are far less sentimental, far more sadistic, in their conception of what power involves. But even the sentimental conception of power poisons the academic environment. But what of love, you ask. Can't women search for love? And can't love within an academic program sometimes be wonderful? Of course the answer to this question is yes. Love is just as wonderful as philosophy, and a love that is combined with shared goals and intellectual passions can be the most wonderful of all. And yet, I would say that if the love is between a male faculty member and a female graduate student, it is never worth the risk. The student is too vulnerable, and there are far too many things that can go wrong.

But are sexual harassment rules and policies any use? They are surely not perfect. For a complaint against a faculty member causes great upheaval, and if women are perceived as troublemakers when they say yes, they are so perceived in spades when they say no and blow the whistle. They also fail to catch the worst abuses. Notice that Owen's relatively benign conduct was of a piece with the incautious and emotional nature of his approach. A really sinister harasser is much more calculating and will usually find out whether you are likely to say yes well before he has done anything overtly incriminating. The satanic types I have mentioned will thus rarely get caught, and the one I have in mind got caught, in the end, and fired from Harvard, only because he had also engaged in financial crime, which Harvard takes far more seriously than the dignity of women.

I believe that I smiled too politely in this situation, and I now think that one should never smile when sexual harassment is afoot. One should recognize it, and name it, and publicize it, and, above all, prevent it, by education, consciousness-raising, and in general constant tiresome harping on the harms it does. It is all very well to say that women should be able to take pleasure in their sexuality and not hide it. But I fear that men are not yet ready for a world in which women's sexuality will not be held against them in some way, and held against their work. When younger men are daring and creative, doing work that challenges the traditional norms of a discipline, older men react as if a son of theirs had just won at Wimbledon. When a young woman is daring and creative in that way, not simply following the lead of her male predecessors, older men still react, far too often, as if a daughter of theirs had just taken off her dress in public. The only way to gain a respectful hearing for ourselves, and our work, and our creativity and daring, at this point in human history, is to establish that we are not primarily sexual beings. Sexual harassment rules and policies are one important step in the direction of that goal.

But in that photo I was smiling at my husband, who was holding the camera. And I was smiling at my pregnant stomach. So what of children, and their relation to a philosophical career? My daughter Rachel is now twenty-nine, a stunning dynamic individual with a mind 100 percent her own, writing a PhD thesis in German cultural history. I love being with her. From the time in utero when she pounded with determined rhythm, first the fists and then the feet, she has argued with me, and I love it, and her. She was, with respect to my work, an easy child. She learned to read early, and always loved reading; she sought out her own contemplative space, and left me mine. And she was sick and home from school only an amazing one day in her entire thirteen years from kindergarten through high school.

So if the world of the philosophical academy made it difficult for me to raise Rachel, *a fortiori* it would be difficult for women with more than one child, or children who demand a lot of attention, or children who get sick a lot, or even a normal amount. And it was exceedingly difficult. Already when I was pregnant, my thesis advisor told me story upon story of women who had babies and stopped writing philosophy. He did this out of anxiety, and with the real hope that I would both have a child and continue writing philosophy. But it imposed a stress nonetheless. Because Rachel was a small baby and I am long-waisted, I did not look very pregnant, even toward the end. I remember Owen saying repeatedly to me, "Perhaps it is a wind egg." And I think that is what he wished. I brought my Aristotle texts to the hospital, feeling that I could not stop working for even a short time without making people think I had stopped completely. I missed only one Monday night dinner at the Society of Fellows.

During the three years that I was in the Society of Fellows, however, life was very good. Leontief provided extra money for child care, and he was one of those relaxed, joyful people who could relieve stress about the whole situation. I found care that was, though expensive, good—first with an in-home sitter, later at the Radcliffe Child Care Center. It was when I started to teach that the problems began. My husband was teaching at Yale and I at Harvard, so we kept our Cambridge apartment, and he commuted to New Haven five days a week. So from the time we began teaching in 1975 until we separated in 1985, and after that, I was in effect a single parent. In some ways, I found, being a single parent was easier than trying to share responsibilities with my husband. For although there was more work to do, I could just do it, without the extra feeling of injustice, or the always vain and difficult efforts to get him to do what I took to be his fair share.

Still, the facts were these. School began at 8:30 and ended at noon, from preschool until third grade—when it ended at three. For afternoons she had to go to the child care center. This meant worrying about carpools in the morning and either at noon or in the afternoon, until she was old enough to walk to a babysitter's house for afternoon care (around the age of ten). Car pools in those days were even more hateful than they are per se, because they not only meant being dependent on others who might prove unreliable, they also meant enduring the constant critical scrutiny of non-working mothers, who were pretending that driving the carpool delighted them and was their chosen profession. Any departure from home at any time after five required a sitter, and the logistics of lining up sitters dominated a good deal of life.

Meanwhile, in the philosophy department (where my office and my heart were, although I had a joint appointment with classics), life went on as if no children existed. Colloquia were routinely scheduled at five o'clock, after the child care centers closed. The Satanic figure held his usual evening dinner/seminar for the junior faculty from six to ten, every two weeks, and attendance was morally compulsory. It was clear that participating in these discussions of Wittgenstein, which really meant listening to him and playing various scripted roles as his interlocutors, all for his tape recorder (since he wrote nothing), was the central way in which one's philosophical ability would be assessed, and that his opinion would, as it always did, greatly shape the opinions of others—not to mention the fact that, trusted by the dean, he was also in charge of the ad hoc committees for tenure in the entire university. (His career would show a good actor how the role of Iago ought to be played.) I felt that a better way to assess my work might be to read some of it and talk with me about it. I felt it was rather as if a young basketball player was told that his skill would be assessed by seeing how he could help out in the practice sessions of an aging star tennis player. I had to find and pay a sitter every time I went to one of these seminars, and I would much rather have been home with Rachel. Hilary Putnam and Robert Nozick agreed with me and brought the matter up with honest Iago. Next time we were told, "You all should understand that you don't have to come to this seminar." We interpreted this statement, correctly, as meaning that we did have to go, and we kept on going. At my tenure time, this person was not only a dogged opponent of my promotion in the philosophy department (where I got a four-to-three positive vote), but he also campaigned heavily against me with the classics department (where I got a five-to-four negative vote). Much later, after he was fired, it emerged that he and a secretary who was his mistress apparently diverted a letter from Nozick as chair that was supposed to go to the classics department, telling them why philosophy had voted in my favor, but that never arrived. I had assumed that Bob, who was out of town a lot on account of his divorce, had simply not written the letter. I should have known better.

But to return to the topic of child care, many babysitters, in short, were required, and it was impossible to mention the whole subject for fear of being perceived as uncommitted or unprofessional. Again, one had to smile cheerfully as if one's life were the same as any other professional's, while knowing that this was not so. I remember vividly the day this began to change. We had a visiting speaker; because the talk began at the usual 5 p.m., I had gotten a babysitter to pick up my daughter from day care. A few minutes into the question period, Bob Nozick stood up, and, with the carefree insouciance of which only the tenured are capable, said, "I'm sorry, I have to go now. I have to pick up my son from hockey practice." For me, this was a world-historical moment. The forbidden topic had been mentioned, as a normal part of a professional life. As always, Bob was brash, confident, and unashamed. So one need not, perhaps, be ashamed of having child care duties. Perhaps this dual responsibility could be respected in a dignified professional world. I believe that Bob, who was in surprising ways a true feminist, raised this topic deliberately, in order to pose some questions about how well the department was treating its parents. But whether or not this was true, it gave me permission to begin getting angry at the totally inadequate arrangements for the support of child care, inside the family, in the workplace, and in the larger society.

There has, I think, been a lot of improvement in our academic lives in the area of sexual harassment. In the area of child care things have changed much more slowly. I believe that men now share child care duties somewhat more than they did before. But there is less change than there should be, and in some fields, in particular law, I see a true backsliding. In large part, I believe that this backsliding results from the demands of the law firm world, which are so exorbitant that they are clearly incompatible with any family life that has home-based work in it; so young men who enter this world choose wives who say they are willing to stay at home. And women who enter it end up on a lesser "mommy" track, or remain childless. But universities are also to blame. Maternity leave is still not automatic at our university; it is given at the discretion of one's dean, and it has been refused. It is possible at many universities, including ours, for a man to apply to take paternity leave, but fewer men than women avail themselves of this possibility, because child care is still stigmatized. Work arrangements are now slightly more thoughtful about hours and their relation to duties; but only slightly. And people who complain are still stigmatized.

The problem of child care is part of a much larger problem of care labor that all modern societies are facing, especially as the population ages. To solve it, we need government programs, a new attitude toward the workplace and its demands, and more equal sharing in the home. (Nor should such programs be confined only to child care; care for elderly and sick dependents of many kinds should be included.) The academy is a relatively benign place for young women in these respects, because it offers flexible hours, and a lot of the real work can be done at home. Nonetheless, as my female graduate students get jobs and have babies, I fear for them, and I see them facing conflicts that they should not have to face. I see that some institutions are extremely supportive of young women who have children while untenured, and others are much less supportive. We have a long way to go to solve these problems in ways that make full professional equality possible for women who have children (or aged parents) to care for.

I have a very happy life now. My daughter is a great friend and traveling companion. Professionally, I survived my Harvard tenure rejection and have gone on to do work that I love and believe in. So I have moved a good way beyond the sexism that I once thought would overwhelm me. But when I was writing my 2000 presidential address for the APA Central Division, the old fears of what men would say still haunted me. I fought them, and I made a point of giving a tough feminist talk, about justice in the family and the relation between justice and care. What made me most happy was that people could hear in it an anger that I had been able to use creatively. One woman said afterward, "That was a kick-ass talk." That was among the nicest things anyone had ever said to this prisoner of politeness.

So when I say that I used to smile too much, I do not mean that women should have less joy, or that feminism should be a grim, life-negating business. I have always been a joyful person, and my work has roots in the experience of joy. For my high school yearbook I chose Shelley's ode to the spirit of delight as my epigraph, and I would choose it again. What I have discovered, however, is that there is a large difference between joy and the smile that aims to please and to be what pleases; and an even larger difference between joy and the smile that conceals an anger that is too unacceptable, too feared, to be acknowledged. When I look at that photo from 1972 and ask myself what kind of smile that is, I find it impossible to say. Today, I know (most of the time, anyway) what sort of smile I am smiling—or, as the case may be, not smiling. I like my anger, and I know it is not going to kill anyone; it might actually do good. All this seems to me to be progress.

Crashing the Top:
Women at Elite Universities

Ann Douglas

WHEN MIT POSTED ITS "STUDY ON the Status of Women Faculty in Science" on the Internet in March 1999, it made the front page of the *New York Times* under the headline "M.I.T. Acknowledges Bias Against Female Professors." Since then, Nancy Hopkins, the professor of biology who chaired the report, has received an outpouring of emails, faxes, and phone calls from female academics, confirming her contention that gender discrimination is still commonplace in top-flight universities at every level of institutional life. As a long-term veteran of elite higher education myself, I needed no persuading. I, too, have spent years, as Hopkins put it, "chronically recovering from the battle of yesterday or preparing for the one tomorrow."

Like Hopkins, I was part of the first generation of women to teach in the top-level universities. Inevitably, since I began my professional life just as affirmative action went into effect in the early 1970s, my career has been a series of firsts: I was the first woman to be offered an assistant professorship in my department at Harvard, the first woman to teach in Princeton's English department, the first to get tenure in the college division of Columbia's English department. I saw the elite universities before they had perfected their civil rights manners, before they learned how to correct, or camouflage, their gender assumptions.

I am divorced and contentedly childless. Although my work has been the most important thing in my life, I always found it difficult to think of myself as ambitious or competitive. Calculations of money and success played no conscious part in my decision to become a writer and a teacher; I was embracing a higher, even a sacred calling. I did not yet understand that by choosing career over family I had exchanged the traditional feminine domestic plot for the quest story, a search for personal and even societal salvation usually reserved for men.

When I applied to college in 1959, women were marrying younger and having more babies than at any other time in American history. Thanks to the G.I. Bill, men were going to school in record numbers, but the percentage of female college and graduate students had dropped since the 1930s. This shortage of female scholars was evident in *Who's Who*, which had fewer entries for women in the 1950s than in the 1890s. Betty Friedan was uncovering the horrors of the *The Feminine Mystique* by studying 1950s' college women as well as housewives, and my undergraduate years at Harvard could have served as a case in point.

In the early 1960s, Harvard was a Cold War university awash with federal funds, dubious corporate investments, and misogynistic assumptions. Radcliffe students took Harvard classes and received Harvard degrees, but they were prohibited from entering Lamont, one of Harvard's two main libraries, though male students could use Radcliffe's library. Nor were women eligible for Harvard's prestigious honor societies, traveling fellowships, or, presumably, most of its professorships. There were only twelve tenured women at Harvard when I entered, a number that had shrunk to eleven when I left a decade later, PhD in hand. I never had a female teacher.

President John F. Kennedy drew many of his Cabinet members from his alma mater, and James Reston jestingly predicted in the *New York Times* that soon Cambridge would have nothing left but Radcliffe. Radcliffe, apparently, couldn't supply the nation with its Cabinet nor, unaided, give distinction to Cambridge. Despite my ambitions, however, I didn't question the prevailing assumption that even the smart-est women were less viable career bets than men. Back home in the New Jersey country club set, I'd been advised that "every girl must have two social sports," for me a dreary and impossible goal. At Har-vard, devouring the major works of Jonathan Edwards, as I did during my first week of classes, was a sign of virtue. Male endorsement was reward enough—I was content to be an unrecognized heir, even the exception that proved the rule.

Some of my teachers, however, confused my enthusiasm for their subject with a passion for their person. One professor jumped me at Henry James's graveside, where he had presumably taken me to muse on the noble poignancy of literary achievement. Out of the blue, my philosophy instructor explained that he would run away with me soon but not just yet, because his wife was then eight months preg-nant. A teaching fellow told me, as a compliment, that the only thing needed to make my beauty complete was a lobotomy. Dependent as I was on male regard, I always put my money on my mind: intellect lasted, looks didn't. I regarded what today we call sexual harassment simply as another career obstacle, to be cleared without breaking my stride.

My dedication served to make me oblivious to the obstacles that faced me. It was a double bind: if I fully assessed the forces arrayed against me, how could I continue? If I didn't assess them, how would I know where I was going or how to get there? As a woman in a male world, I needed armor. Inspiration afforded the strongest kind, but armor is nonetheless an anesthetic, even a form of blindness.

In 1970, I turned down a tenure-track job at Harvard. My fascina-tion with peak male intellect remained, but thanks to the feminist movement just under way, I was now aware of the gender-restricted privileges that safeguard its preeminence and the dangers of question-ing them. The Harvard professors I loved who had praised me as a student might react differently once I was a colleague. After all, no one likes finding a critic where he expected a fan. I accepted a post at Princeton, which was then aggressively recruiting women scholars. There, I assumed it would be less risky to be my adult self, whoever that might turn out to be.

In fact, Princeton proved to be my first experience with the out-in-the-open backlash against women scholars. Long an exceptionally well-to-do bastion of gentlemanly values, the university had admitted a handful of women undergraduates in 1969. When I became one of only thirteen female professors on its faculty, and the first woman ever in its English department, many of my colleagues expressed their open displeasure. "Some of us wanted to be in an all-male school," one colleague pointedly told me, explaining why he'd rejected a Harvard offer.

To make matters worse, despite my junior status, I was quickly given a series of coveted and prestigious committee appointments. While this seemed to be a privilege, it also fueled the resentment of my male colleagues. Inevitably, token women are overexposed and overworked—even today, the Ivy League looks like a cheap Hollywood production in which a dozen female extras run repeatedly past the camera to create the illusion of a mob scene. Meanwhile I was kept constantly aware of my status as an interloper. Colleagues warned students not to take my courses in women's literature and history. My chairman called me into his office to tell me my work was faddish, "a luxury, intellectually speaking, which Princeton simply can't afford." In 1974, I resigned to take a job at Columbia, where I have been ever since.

Today the attitudes and behavior I encountered in the early stages of my career should seem part of a prehistoric past. Women outnumber men in college. Roughly 30 percent of the students at the nation's leading business schools are women; the figure is over 40 percent in medical and law schools. In many fields in the social sciences and humanities, more women than men get PhDs. The nation's female faculty has grown 114 percent since 1976, almost six times as fast as its male faculty.

Yet such figures are misleading. Despite the increase in their numbers, on several significant fronts women are losing ground in the academy, and the more prestigious the institution, the greater the discrimination. There may be more female than male undergraduates nationwide, but most of the top private colleges, including Harvard, MIT, Chicago, Yale, Johns Hopkins, and Princeton, maintain a slim male majority. Although over 50 percent of the faculty at junior colleges are women, the figure is only 36 percent at four-year institutions.

Most disturbingly, the gap between available female PhDs and women in tenure-track appointments has actually widened in the last ten years. While more women are qualified for such jobs, a smaller percentage are getting them. This imbalance is evident in promotion patterns as well. More full-time male faculty (72 percent) have tenured jobs now than did in 1975 (64 percent), but the number of tenured full-time women remains the same (46 percent). Women are disproportionately represented in the proliferating part-time, non-tenure-track jobs that now make up about 40 percent of all academic posts. The multiplication of ill-paid and often benefits-free part-time jobs, which enrich the institution at the expense of its most vulnerable members, coincided precisely with the moment when women began to earn PhDs in record numbers. The gender gap in academic salaries, after narrowing in the early 1990s, has increased in the last few years, and it is greatest at the top.

Yet gender parity within the academy is no longer seen as a pressing issue. As Jean E. Howard, an English professor at Columbia and currently the president of the Shakespeare Association of America, told me, "Feminism is no longer foregrounded in progressive politics in the academy, especially in the elite institutions. The assumption is, we've done that." Howard is quick to add, "We haven't—it's just not being talked about."

Some of the critics of the MIT report argue that what gender inequality, if any, remains in the academy merely reflects women's personal choices—perhaps they wanted to be less career-driven, to take time off to raise children. But that doesn't explain why the women who *have* pursued full-time careers still meet discrimination. There are many factors at work in today's sometimes embattled, ever more profit- and prestige-conscious elite universities, factors that shape women's (and men's) careers in a variety of ways. Yet among them is surely the old gender pattern sociologists identify as "feminization," the shift from a largely male to a largely female workforce, and its consequences. Greater numbers do not necessarily spell increased equality, especially when the group in question is female.

When "feminization" has occurred in the past, notably in elementary school teaching, the result has been a loss for the occupation in pay and status. Women move into male territory only to find that its occupants abandon it rather than share it with women, and they take their privileges with them. In such situations, female failure becomes a consequence of female success. A feminist journal of the 1970s summed up this dynamic: "Women Get a Ticket to Ride After the Gravy Train Has Left the Station."

The elite academy, however, presents a critical new variation in the feminization pattern. Gifted nineteenth-century male elementary and high school teachers, unhappy with the growing number of women in their ranks, could aspire to the all-male world of the richest private colleges and universities. But if the elite institutions are themselves overrun with women, where can the most distinguished men go? The backlash today against women in the top-level universities is intense, though unacknowledged, precisely because the stakes are so high. And if obvious discrimination is in theory prohibited, mistreatment less accessible to legal remedy can accomplish the same end.

Nancy Hopkins's awakening didn't come when she discovered how much lower her salary was than those of her male peers ("It was my fault," she remembers thinking; "I'd never asked about salaries"), but when a male colleague in effect took over a course that she had been teaching. She sought redress, only to realize that the rules were one thing, the practice something else. As Anne McClintock, a pioneer in gender studies at the University of Wisconsin, told me, "The decisions that really matter are made outside the democratic process."

The right of faculty women to be in the elite academy is no longer at issue. But their authority, their ability to lead in both the scholarly and administrative realms—particularly in areas that have traditionally been all-male preserves—is on occasion not only challenged but actively undermined. One female professor quit her tenured job at an Ivy League university after watching two female colleagues of unimpeachable intellectual and moral standing in important administrative positions be stripped of their power and accused of unethical conduct. Watching this "torture," as she put it, brought her to "a level of despondency about which I could do almost nothing." "I don't want to do bitter," she told me. "Not if I have a choice. So I ran away." She was fortunate enough to be offered a post at another top university.

Another scholar was forced out of a departmental chairmanship by an all-male administration that sided with a hostile male colleague, who had campaigned to turn her colleagues and students against her. Despite the fact that the male scholar was widely recognized as unstable, she says, the administration treated her adversary like "a sick but brilliant brother they were going to take care of at all costs."

According to another female scholar, "even when the man making the charges is less valuable than the woman he accuses, shoring up male camaraderie at the center takes precedence over the well-being of the institution." An Ivy League administrator, reminiscing about a moment when she horrified her male superiors by demanding "a penis salary, not a vagina salary" for a post she wanted to fill (the spot remained vacant), explained that women have to "stroke the fellas to get something done. Anything else, and you're a bitch. If you want to complain, you can't, because you're always going to be complaining to a man, since you wind up going to that level, and the man will side with the men." As Elaine Combs-Schilling, an anthropologist at Columbia, notes: "Power flows around the woman in a leadership position, never through her."

In my own department at Columbia, though there are significantly more women than men at the graduate-student and junior-professor levels, tenured men still outnumber women by over four to one. Behind the surface rhetoric of equality, old attitudes lie in wait, and sometimes manifest themselves in ugly and disturbing forms. A personal example:

Last winter, I was asked to poll my department as part of the process of electing our next chair. The results, which favored a brilliant and feminist candidate, were unwelcome to a small group of senior men who had the (all-male) administration's ear in a way that the departmental majority (which in this instance included most of the department's women, minority group members, and faculty under

forty) did not. One of these male colleagues accused me of falsifying
the polling; the poll was declared invalid, and, for various reasons, the
female candidate withdrew.

I was devastated. How could men who had worked with me for
a quarter-century not know that I would never tamper with the
democratic procedures on which all my hopes for progress depend?
Success, it turns out, seldom shields women from injustice, though it
sometimes protects their male colleagues from the consequences of
unjust acts.

There are, of course, women at Columbia and elsewhere who
believe that gender is not a decisive factor in their careers, and certainly not a reliable basis of identification among complex and varied human beings. This is a respect-worthy position, one that the
academy—like many workplaces—often rewards highly. Nancy Hopkins remembers avoiding one early feminist organizer lest she anger
the men in her department or be distracted from her research. Yet
ultimately, the burden of "living alone with discrimination" proved
too heavy for Hopkins. After years of silence, she began to talk to
other faculty women about how she felt. When they said, not, as she
feared, "You're crazy!" but rather, "Me, too," her life changed, and she
took the actions that led to the MIT study. The task force succeeded,
Hopkins believes, because the women involved operated like "a school
of fish, doing everything by consensus."

Today, MIT's administrators are justly proud of the steps they have
taken to end gender discrimination, which include equalizing salaries
and hiring nine new faculty women in the School of Science. In fact,
what these women asked for was good for their institution as well as
themselves. As Susanna Cole, a senior at Brown, observes, when universities recruit female students and faculty, they usually "promise
them an environment in which women will be equal. If it's not there,
they're lying," and sooner or later, lies have consequences.

When I asked the faculty women I interviewed what motivated
them today, they spoke of their work and their teaching. Research in
biology remains "the most interesting thing in the world" to Nancy
Hopkins. "The students make my heart sing," Elaine Combs-Schilling
said. But they also spoke of the challenge of still feeling like pioneers

in mostly male worlds. "These institutions are still a frontier for women," said Jean Howard. "Someone has to fight the battle in the Ivy League."

For me, it's worth fighting. I still believe with all my heart in what my great Harvard teacher Perry Miller called "the life of the mind," the gold-rush kingdom of first strikes and second chances. Its sole prerequisite is freedom; its only law, democracy.

Hiding

Lillian Faderman

I BECAME A GRADUATE STUDENT IN the UCLA English department in 1962, a time when common wisdom had it that most women who went to college were pursuing the MRS degree and that the "professional careers" for women were nursing, social work, and public school teaching. Despite common wisdom, about 40 percent of my fellow first-year PhD aspirants were female, all of us decked out appropriately in hose and low pumps and skirts that reached the shins. (Male students, too, were appropriately uniformed—button-down shirts, ties, jackets.) We women sat at our desks with legs modestly crossed as we took dutiful notes in lectures, or we tried to make intelligent contributions in seminars without appearing too aggressive. But of course, if we had serious aspirations we didn't want to appear too unaggressive either, or too feminine, because professors were almost always male, and we hoped to be accepted as their equals in the professoriate someday. On the other hand, we didn't dare appear unfeminine because . . . well, the implications of that were unspeakable. The trick was to mask femininity yet not convey masculinity. But how?

There were so few faculty women to model for us how a woman professor looked and comported herself. Of the English department's full-time faculty of fifty or sixty, only two were female. We could glean something about how a woman professor might dress just by seeing them in the halls—boxy skirt suits that conformed unobtrusively to the conventions of female dress while still hiding the femaleness that was incongruous in a serious academic setting. But since almost all our classes were taught by men, our chief model for professorial comportment, day after day and year after year, was male. It was incumbent on us to figure out, with little help, how a woman conveys "professorial." What gestures, what body language, what modulations let a woman express the role, and what must she suppress? I recall sitting in on the class of a friend, a teaching assistant, as she discussed some point of essay writing with her freshman comp students. She stood before them absentmindedly rubbing the side of her face with an open hand, feeling for the stubble of her (nonexistent) beard—just like men sometimes did when they were cogitating. I felt embarrassed for her, but once or twice I'd caught myself, too, standing before a class, stroking my own nonexistent stubble. That was what male professors did. How else to convey "cerebral" if not by emulating their masculine gesture? For women graduate students in the early 1960s, confusion about our self-presentation abounded.

But that was not the knottiest of our problems. We had only to look around us to see that the odds we'd someday be hired by a university like UCLA were worse than slim, despite what we hid or who we emulated. (My own despair was exacerbated when I remembered my undergraduate years, as a freshman at UCLA and then as a student at UC Berkeley. During all that time I'd had only one woman professor, in philosophy—and she was hired midyear, to take over classes for her husband when he became terminally ill.) Unsurprisingly, there were far fewer women in my second-year graduate class than in the first, and only a fraction of them remained by my third year. Many left after getting the MA. Perhaps some who disappeared took the MRS; others settled for a more realistic career in public school teaching. Only those few who could imagine no life other than that of an academic stuck it out and continued to struggle with the worrisome complexities of self-presentation and the despair that even if they got the PhD, they'd probably never get a good job anyway.

Despite evidence of the hopelessness of my pursuit, I was among those who could imagine no life but that of an academic. I loved books and libraries and pondering scholarly questions. I knew I would never have a husband to support me, and the occupations I'd seen up close— my mother's, my own that had permitted me to support myself when I was an undergraduate—had terrified and driven me. I felt I had no choice other than to stick it out.

Years later, when I began doing research in women's history, I discovered that had my cohort and I been around at the beginning of the twentieth century we would have had plenty of role models and encouragement for our aspirations, that there had even been women academic deans and college presidents. Perhaps had we known of those pioneers who'd succeeded in making a place for women in higher education, the knowledge would have given women of my cohort something like a "usable past"—examples of how to present ourselves and of what might be achieved, what to demand. But the names of women such as M. Carey Thomas and Mary Woolley, who had forged remarkable spaces for women generations earlier, were long forgotten; it fell to us to reinvent, however awkwardly and uncomfortably, the proverbial wheel.

The story of those women who had pioneered in higher education was not all that was hidden from us. How many scores of authors were we required to read as graduate students in English and American literature? We didn't need the fingers of two hands to count the women among them: Emily and Charlotte Brontë, George Eliot, Christina Rossetti (as an example of the writers in her more famous brother's circle), Emily Dickinson, Willa Cather, Virginia Woolf . . . There was not one woman writer on the syllabi for medieval literature, the Renaissance, the Jacobean–Caroline period, neoclassical literature, the Romantic era. Though as graduate students we were being groomed to write literary criticism, there was not one woman among the critics we were asked to read. Surely I was not the only woman student who puzzled over that daunting paradox, but none of us dared call attention to it and hence to our gender.

Did any of us have the word "feminist" in our active vocabularies? In the early 1960s, the word was never used on campus. Indeed, the only time I'd heard that word spoken aloud was in 1956, in a high school American history class. I've forgotten what it was I'd said in response to the teacher's question, but my declaration made her ask me, in front of the whole class, "Are you a feminist?" She was unmarried, in her fifties or sixties, deep-voiced, and short-haired—as butchy-looking as a public school teacher dared to be in those days. Perhaps she recognized in me a kindred spirit. Now it pleases me to think so. But then I knew the other students thought me very weird already; and though I wasn't really sure what "feminist" meant, I was sure from the sound of the word that if I admitted to being one, they'd think me even weirder. "Of course not," I answered her.

In retrospect, this is my only excuse for my fecklessness: I was already too weighed down by the burdens of stigma to reveal that I had yet another. My mother was unmarried when I was born, at a time when "illegitimacy" (the term says it all) was a shame and a disgrace in her Jewish immigrant community and everywhere else in America. I'd seen the man she told me was my father only once, when I was five years old. He denied having anything to do with my making. Nor was my "illegitimacy" all I had to hide. My mother was virtually illiterate in English, and she supported us by working in dress factories. Her job was to drape cut-out material over a stuffed half-mannequin, pin waists to skirts, and then pass the garments on to the machine operators who would sew the parts together. That's what she did from the time she arrived in this country, just before World War I, until I was fourteen and she finally got married, to a man who mopped the floors and washed the surgical instruments that the pathologists used to perform autopsies at Cedars of Lebanon Hospital in Los Angeles.

My own work experiences trapped me further into stigma. As an undergraduate, I'd supported myself first as a pinup model for girlie magazines and then as a stripper at one of the last of the burlesque houses in San Francisco, the President Follies. I'd worked for a little while before that shelving books at the university library, but the job paid minimum wage and the four-hour-a-day shift cut seriously into my study time. As a model or a stripper I could earn decent money and spend much more time on my homework assignments.

Was there anyone among my fellow graduate students at UCLA who had had so checkered a life story? If there was, she hid her background as painstakingly as I did. Class stigma, poverty, the concomitant sordidness of desperation and anger—those were things you learned about through the novels of Theodore Dreiser and Upton Sinclair. The professoriate at mid-century was a profession of gentility, and the assumption was—it seemed to me, anyway—that only the genteel would aspire to it. How could I survive in such a milieu, I thought, if I didn't hide?

But my roots and occupations weren't even the most dangerous of my secrets. My sexual orientation was. When I entered UCLA as an undergraduate student in 1958, I and all the other freshmen had to take a battery of written psychological tests. Scattered among questions on mental and moral habits, character traits, phobias, and compulsions were various queries about homosexual desire. I remember them as something like, "Are you attracted to persons of your sex?" "Have you ever dreamed of kissing a person of your sex?" "Have you ever had sexual relations with a person of your sex?" As a lesbian used to hiding my orientation from the straight world since I was sixteen years old, I knew enough to answer "no" to all such questions. I imagine that all homosexuals who were smart enough to get into UCLA in the 1950s were, like me, smart enough to answer no. We couldn't have gotten as far as we had, we couldn't have made it through high school with good grades and good recommendations supporting our college applications, if we hadn't known when and what to hide. Thirty years later, I discovered how crucial those survival instincts had been. I was doing research for my book on lesbian history in twentieth-century America, *Odd Girls and Twilight Lovers*, when I stumbled on a 1955 article titled "The Sexually Deviant Student," by Milton Hahn and Byron Atkinson, the Dean and the Assistant Dean of Students at UCLA, published in the journal *School and Society*. The article lamented "the attraction of colleges, both public and private, for overt, hardened homosexuals," and the writers recommended that "sexually deviant" students be forced to undergo psychiatric treatment to change their sexual orientation. If they refused, the writers said, they must be routed out of college.

The awful fear that I would be found out by people such as the authors of "The Sexually Deviant Student" followed me throughout my student years. Never once as a student did I utter a word about homosexuality on campus. Nor did anyone else—though in my courses we read, discussed, and listened to lectures on Henry James, Somerset Maugham, E. M. Forster, T. S. Eliot, W. H. Auden, Stephen Spender, Virginia Woolf, Walt Whitman, Willa Cather . . . We studied the plays of Oscar Wilde for several weeks in a drama seminar, and not one mention was made of Wilde's relationship with men, his trial, or even the cultural roots of his campy humor. Homosexuality was such anathema in the academy that a student could hear of it only in abnormal psychology class.

About twenty-five years later, in 1989, I returned to UCLA as a visiting professor and was befriended by a senior member of the English department from whom I'd taken a course when he was a young (and, of course, very closeted) assistant professor. He told me in 1989 that a number of the faculty who'd taught in the English department in the 1960s—including both the women—had been homosexual. How sad, I thought, that I hadn't known it when I was a student; knowing would have been such a comfort and relief to me, and probably to other lesbian and gay students, too. But like us students, lesbian and gay faculty members hid in order to survive. In 1954, a woman physical education professor at UCLA had actually been dismissed because it became known that she was a homosexual. Lesbian and gay professors smart enough to teach in the UCLA English department were smart enough to keep mum.

Though I carefully hid my sexual orientation from everyone but a few other lesbian students when I was in graduate school, I did stop short of "front dating"—a practice very common in mid-century, in which a lesbian and a gay man would appear together at straight gatherings as "beards" for one another. But the various other hiding machinations which I felt compelled to perform—and which made great sense then—seem quite incredible now. One of my drollest experiences with hiding concerned a book. During my first year, I'd gone to the UCLA English Reading Room (the quaint name characterized the atmosphere of this space that was reserved for faculty and graduate students) in order to find a collection of essays by E. M. Forster. On a shelf of the Reading Room's library next to books by Forster was one by Jeannette Foster. It bore the intriguing title *Sex Variant Women in Literature.* I looked around to be sure no one was watching before I picked it up. It was a book-length bibliography describing all the fiction and poetry, from antiquity to 1954, which dealt in any way with the subject of lesbianism that the author, who'd worked for the Kinsey Institute, could find. The book had been published in 1956, by a vanity press. What legitimate publisher would have dared to publish such a book at that time? In the foreword, Foster (a lesbian all her life, as I subsequently discovered) disclaimed any intimately personal knowledge of the subject. But she declared that her objective knowledge about what she called "sex variance" (a sort of euphemism for lesbianism) had "enabled" her, during the years she taught in college, "to help [her students] in averting more than one minor tragedy."

I was as cautious as the author. Through the rest of semester I read the book cover to cover, but only standing up, thirty minutes or so at a time, in the dark stacks of the English Reading Room, with another book in hand to use as a beard lest anyone pass me and look over my shoulder. It's a point of irony and amusement to me that ten years later, in the early 1970s, when a new social climate had finally brought astonishing changes even to academia, it was Foster's invaluable bibliographic study that enabled me to kick-start my own work on lesbian history.

If you weren't around in the 1960s but know a little about American social history, it may seem surprising to hear how long into the second half of the twentieth century universities continued to be conventionally rigid with regard to gender, class, and sexuality. The 1960s was the decade of the hippie phenomenon, in which middle-class kids were proudly rejecting their parents' values and declassing themselves. It was the decade of various radical ethnic movements (Black Power, La

Raza, Red Power, Yellow Power), which abhorred white gentility and all the outrageously unbalanced privilege connected to it. It was the decade that gave birth to the second wave of feminism. And at the end of the sixties, with the "hairpin drop heard round the wall," as the Stonewall Riots have been called, the gay revolution began. But until the 1970s, almost all institutions of higher learning remained quite impervious to the social upheavals that had been taking place in America throughout the sixties.

During the winter 1966 meeting of the Modern Language Association, I interviewed and was hired for a job at Fresno State College (as California State University, Fresno was then called). The English department had thirty full-time faculty members, but when I arrived on campus in fall 1967, I discovered I would be its only woman. Of a university faculty of about seven hundred, there was one woman in chemistry (also hired that year), one in anthropology, one in history, another in biology, and a smattering in the fine arts and foreign languages. The preponderance of women was in the departments of nursing, social work, education, women's P.E., and home economics. (Where did the women who managed to stick it out through the PhD go in those days? I'd already known there were no significant numbers of them in permanent positions at research universities; now I found there were hardly any at the state colleges.)

During my first week on the job, I ran into one of my senior colleagues in the English department mail room. "How are you liking it here so far?" he asked amiably.

"Fine, but . . ."—the words slipped out of my mouth before my brain could censor them—"I'm surprised there aren't more women on the faculty."

"Oh, there were a lot when I came here," he said, "left over from the war years, when there were no men around to teach. But we got rid of them all by the fifties."

I must have turned the color of the wall behind me, because he was quick to add, as though to assure me, "Only because we wanted to upgrade, and they didn't have PhDs." What I kept hearing in my mind for the longest time was "we got rid of them all."

And yet one had only to tune into the world outside of academia to understand that huge social transformations were beginning. Knowing of them was a heady experience for me. I know I resonated deeply with the demands for visibility from those who'd had no voice and no social presence because I'd long had to hide so much of myself. Once I obtained a position in the academy, it became my goal and chief mission to bring those voices into the academic world. It figures that the first book for which I sought a contract was a textbook titled *Speaking for Ourselves*. It was published in 1969 and was the first college anthology of multiethnic literature.

Looking back over more than forty years now, it's clear to me that my major interests and the thrust of all my work—as a member of a faculty, an academic administrator, and a scholar—were largely determined by my earlier life on the margins and by what I'd once felt deeply constrained to hide. With the perceptions gleaned from that vantage point, it felt crucial to me to change the academy in my little corner and as far beyond as I could. In 1971, a music professor, Phyllis Irwin (who became and is still my life partner), and I designed for our campus one of the first women's studies programs in the country. In 1973, as an administrator at Fresno State, I drew up the campus's affirmative action guidelines and, as the director of the Experimental College that same year, I encouraged the offering of some of the first lesbian and gay studies courses. In 1974, while I was still an administrator, I became pregnant by donor insemination, and our son was born in January 1975. It was while I was pregnant that I began to write on lesbian literature and history.

Once I dared begin that work, I wrote in white heat, with passion and focus and diligence. Between 1977 and 1979, I published eight articles on lesbian literature or history, and my book *Surpassing the Love of Men: Romantic Friendship and Love between Women from the Renaissance to the Present* came out in 1981. In that early work and in all my subsequent books and articles, what's been most important and gratifying to me has been to challenge and to help destroy the received prejudices and internalized fears that make hiding necessary. I'd venture to say that the work that is always dearest to us is that which heals the old deep wounds.

Feminist Accused of
Sexual Harassment

Jane Gallop

I AM A FEMINIST PROFESSOR WHO WAS accused by two students of sexual harassment. What kind of a feminist would be accused of sexual harassment?

"Feminist sexual harasser" seems like a contradiction in terms. I find myself positioned at the center of this contradiction. Although the position has been personally quite uncomfortable, professionally I can see it as a rare vantage point, an opportunity to produce knowledge. I have long suspected that a contradiction in terms might present an occasion to confront and rethink the terms themselves.

As a feminist theorist of sexuality, I consider it my business to understand sexual harassment. And so I'd like to take advantage of my peculiar position as an accused harasser to provide a fresh feminist view of the issue. Theorizations of harassment generally focus on what is clearly the classic scenario: the male boss uses his professional clout to force himself upon a female subordinate—sleep with me or you'll lose your job, sleep with me and you'll get a raise, a promotion. Rather than refer to this classic case, I want to produce an understanding of sexual harassment based instead upon the limit case of a feminist so accused.

The classic scenario is explicit and quid pro quo (demand for sex in exchange for professional support). The concept of harassment also includes more implicit forms, where the sexual demand or the professional threat is not stated but understood. Implicit sexual demands might ultimately include any charged talk or behavior; implicit professional threats could possibly cover the entire range of professional interaction. While these possibilities are potentially already limitless, the range of harassment is also expanding in other directions. Harassment need not be perpetrated by bosses; peers can harass, even subordinates. And gender can be a variable: increasing numbers of cases involve a man claiming to have been harassed or a woman accused of harassment.

The classic scenario—easy to recognize and deplore as sexual harassment—expands its application in every direction. I want to ground my theorizing in a limit case precisely because I believe that there should be limits to this bloated general application. I hope that my example can expose the limitations of loose analogies and impede this rampant expansion of the concept of sexual harassment.

Feminism has a special relation to sexual harassment. One could in fact say that feminism invented sexual harassment. Not, of course, the behavior itself, which presumably has gone on as long as men have held power over women. But, until feminism named it, the behavior had no official existence. In the mid-seventies, feminism got women to compare notes on their difficulties in the workplace; it came out that women employees all too frequently had to cope with this sort of thing. Feminism named this behavior "sexual harassment" and proceeded to make it illegal.

Today the general public knows that sexual harassment consists of some form of unwanted sexual advance and that it is some sort of crime. Inevitably people assume that it is sex that makes harassment criminal. Feminism's interest in prosecuting harassment is then chalked up to feminism's supposed hostility to sex.

But, whatever the feelings of individual feminists, feminism is not in principle a movement against sexuality. It is, in principle and in fact, against the disadvantaging of women. Sexual harassment is a feminist issue not because it is sexual but because it disadvantages women. Because harassment makes it harder for women to earn a living, feminists declared it a form of discrimination against women. This framing was so persuasive that, within a few years, harassment was added to the legal definition of sex discrimination. Since discrimination on the basis of sex was already illegal, once harassment was included within the category of discrimination, it immediately became a crime. Sexual harassment is criminal not because it is sex but because it is discrimination.

When I was charged with sexual harassment, the accusations were made on official university forms that bore the heading "Complaint of Discrimination." Under that heading, the students filed formal complaints against me, checking the box marked "Sexual Harassment." The form includes twelve such boxes, each pertaining to a type of discrimination (race or color, sex, national origin, etc.). The form itself makes it clear that harassment is treated as a subspecies of the general wrong, discrimination.

After reviewing the evidence and interviewing the witnesses, the university officer who investigated the charges against me was convinced that I had not in fact discriminated—not against women, not against men, not on the basis of sexual orientation, not on any basis whatsoever. She believed that my pedagogical practices had been, as she put it, applied in a consistent manner. Yet she nonetheless thought I probably was guilty of sexual harassment.

When it is possible to conceive of sexual harassment without discrimination, then sexual harassment becomes a crime of sexuality rather than of discrimination. There is, in fact, a recent national trend toward findings of sexual harassment where there is no discrimination. This represents a significant departure from the feminist formulation of harassment.

Although the shock value of my case resides in the supposition that it is impossible to be both a feminist and a harasser, the spectacle fascinates because it suggests the possibility that a feminist *could* be a sexual harasser—which would mean that either feminism or sexual harassment (maybe even both) are not what we assumed they were. A feminist sexual harasser is no longer a contradiction in terms; rather, it is the sign of an issue drifting from its feminist frame.

I was construed a sexual harasser because I sexualize the atmosphere in which I work. When sexual harassment is defined as the introduction of sex into professional relations, it becomes quite possible to be both a feminist and a sexual harasser.

The classic harassment scenario clearly involves both discrimination against women and sexualization of professional relations. Because people always refer to that classic case, it has been assumed that sexualizing the workplace is automatically disadvantageous to women. But if we base our thinking in the more exotic possibility of a feminist sexualizer, these two aspects of harassment no longer fit so neatly together. And sexualizing is not necessarily to women's disadvantage.

It is no coincidence that I happen to be both a feminist and someone whose professional relations are sexualized. It is because of the sort of feminist I am that I do not respect the line between the intellectual and the sexual. Central to my commitment as a feminist teacher is the wish to transmit the experience that brought me as a young woman out of romantic paralysis and into the power of desire and knowledge, to bring the women I teach to their own power, to ignite them as feminism ignited me when I was a student.

The chill winds of the current climate threaten to extinguish what feminism lit for me. What felt liberating to me as a student is today considered dangerous to my students. Today's anti-harassment activism is, of course, a legacy of seventies' feminism. But the anti-sexual direction of the current trend makes us forget how women's liberation turned us on. The present climate makes it easy to forget and thus crucial to remember. And so, at the risk of sounding as old as I am, I want to tell you what feminism on campus felt like back when I was a student.

———

In 1971, there was a weekend-long feminist event on campus, lots of workshops and seminars, which combined teaching the issues and organizing us for activism. As part of this event, Saturday night there was a dance—women only, featuring a women's rock band (the first I'd ever seen).

Outraged at the idea of a women-only dance, male students came to crash the party. A large group of us women threw ourselves against the door. It was a thrill keeping the men out, feeling the power of our combined weight, heaping our bodies together in this symbolic enactment of feminist solidarity. And then, after the men gave up, we decided to celebrate our triumph, our women-only space, by taking off our shirts and dancing bare-breasted.

Our breasts were political. In those days feminists were said to burn bras. Restricting and constraining movement, bras provided a metaphor for women's bonds. We didn't wear bras. We stripped off our shirts in triumphant defiance of the men we had kept out. With no men around to ogle our breasts, we were as free as men to take off our shirts in public; so we were asserting equal rights. But our breasts were not just political.

I remember Becca that night, a gorgeous young woman a year or so older than me. She had been one of the first to the door, expertly throwing her long, rangy body against the would-be intruders. And she was the first to take off her shirt and start dancing, revealing the most beautiful breasts I had ever seen. We all danced together in a heap, intoxicated with the joy and energy of our young feminism. The bacchanalian frenzy did not in the least cloud my focus on Becca's breasts. I was dancing with those beautiful breasts, dancing all the harder because I so wanted to touch those breasts.

While I'll never forget Becca's breasts, they were not the most memorable sight at the dance. Earlier that evening, two women had made a spectacular entrance. One of them taught my first women's studies course, which I was taking that semester. One of the campus's best-known feminists, an early leader in the national movement for women's studies, a published writer over six feet tall, this teacher was a woman whom I looked up to in every way. She walked into the dance accompanied by a beautiful girl I had seen around and knew to be a senior. The teacher was wearing a dress, the student a man's suit; their carefully staged entrance publicly declared their affair.

I thought the two of them were just the hottest thing I'd ever seen. I profoundly admired the professor; I found the senior girl beautiful and sophisticated. I wanted both of them. Although I would have loved to have an affair like theirs, I didn't feel left out and envious. I felt privileged to be let in on the secret. I felt it as our secret, the secret of our women's party. This couple could no more safely appear around campus together like that than we could safely walk around with our shirts off. But the relationship could be revealed within our women-only space for the same reasons Becca could expose her breasts. Not because they weren't sexual, but because we as a community could recognize them as our sexuality, could affirm them as part of the new possibilities opened to us as women by feminism. The couple were performing *for us*: we were not only their special, exclusive audience, but they presented us with the spectacle of our daring communal possibility.

The long-haired senior was usually seen on campus in rather feminine clothes. Her getup that night was quite clearly meant for their joint appearance. Although their butch-femme attire functioned as a revelation, what it revealed was not some hidden sexual truth about them, but rather sexuality as the very possibility of taking on roles. In those days feminists saw social roles as traps, in particular masculine and feminine roles. We just recently liberated women were so afraid of being trapped by roles that we tended to embrace a broadly flattening egalitarianism. This couple walked in and implied that we didn't have to fear being obliterated by roles, that we were strong enough to take them on. And sexy enough to get off on them.

Although their costuming referred to male/female roles, their performance made us think of the roles they played outside that room: teacher and student. Perhaps, they seemed to be saying, teacher and student, like butch and femme, could be roles we explored for our pleasure and empowerment. It was crucial to this feminist spectacle that the student was the one wearing men's clothing. This seemed a role reversal. Her suit hinted that their connection made it possible for this student to take on power with the teacher. Our institutional roles did not have to limit our relationships, and they also did not have to be ignored in some colorless egalitarian utopia where all women were the same.

This was a performance custom-made for our community, using gender as a sexual metaphor to make explicit a possibility the community as a whole was exploring. Campus feminists came together in the context of feminism but also in the context of the university. In those days, feminism offered students the rare opportunity to mingle with faculty in a manner not circumscribed by our institutional roles.

Feminism was as new for our teachers as it was for us. We were all reading and being changed by the same books; we were going to the same political events and social gatherings. In the context of feminism, students and teachers worked and played together in some assumed commonality as women, a commonality that seemed to override the various social and institutional roles that separated us.

Not that our roles totally disappeared. What happened was more exciting and more empowering. We belonged to the same women's community as our teachers *and* we never stopped seeing them as teachers. It was heady indeed to attend meetings with faculty women, to feel part of a community with them. It made us feel like adults, like intellectuals, like we could in some way share in the aura of these knowledgeable, accomplished women. It was in this context, where faculty treated us as sister feminists rather than just as students, that I became a better student, a student who believed in my work, the sort of student who would ultimately become a professor.

This campus women's community was not just extracurricular. We didn't just happen to be teachers and students; we were actually interacting regularly in classroom situations. The feminist students were taking the new women's studies courses; the feminist faculty were teaching those courses. And for both students and faculty, these experimental new courses were the ones that really mattered.

We considered women's studies an academic wing of feminism where the learning that was liberating us could become part of the university curriculum. At the time, women's studies was not yet a formal program; a steering committee was set up to conceive its shape before we applied for official university status. The decision was made,

on principle, to include students on what would more traditionally
have been a faculty committee. As an undergraduate, I got to serve
on the committee, and I felt privileged to join the faculty in building
women's studies. The inclusive composition of this committee beto-
kened our vision of women's studies as different from the rest of the
university: knowledge would be more egalitarian and more alive.

This commitment to a freer, less rigid knowledge meant exploring new kinds of pedagogical relations. We didn't want teacher and
student to be identities determining what we did and said; we hoped
they could be roles we might take on for our benefit, roles that were
sometimes useful, sometimes irrelevant. In our vision of a feminist
university, we imagined teachers and students not separated by some
uncrossable chasm, but joined in a shared pursuit of knowledge and
women's liberation. And it was this brave if naïve vision of faculty and
students pursuing a new feminist relation to knowledge that I saw
bodied forth in the spectacle of a feminist teacher–student affair.

I looked at this bold proclamation of sexuality and I saw my
teacher, the one teaching my first women's studies course, which I was
so excited about, which was changing my life for good. I saw one of the
leaders of the movement for women's studies, not just on my campus
but nationwide. And I didn't separate what I learned here about my
teacher from the other ways I knew her. Her appearance at the dance
became part of my image of my women's studies teacher and part of
my image of women's studies.

That was the first time I ever thought of teacher–student sex in
relation to feminism. And feminism shed a rosy glow over the prospect. Feminism provided the occasion to fantasize teacher–student
sex alongside other brave new possibilities: from a women's rock band
and dancing bare-breasted, to having the physical force to resist men's
intrusion, to the dream of campus women of all ages and institutional
ranks joining together to reshape the university and knowledge itself
in the image of our feminist excitement.

Twenty-five years ago, I thought women's studies was hot. And since
that time I've devoted myself to the feminist pursuit of knowledge.

After college, I went on to graduate school and wrote a feminist dissertation. In the late seventies, I got a job teaching at a university, and I've been teaching women's studies courses ever since. In the eighties, I set up and ran a women's studies program at a college that did not yet have one. For more than two decades, I've been pursuing the dream of women's studies, led by my desire for the community that turned me on as a student.

Nowadays, women's studies is a lot older and more established; it doesn't feel so much like a bold experiment. While it still is said in women's studies circles that feminist teachers and students ought to have a non-hierarchical relation, ought to work together as sister seekers of knowledge, in fact the relation between feminist teachers and students is not what it was when women's studies was young. Students and faculty are no longer discovering feminism together; today, faculty who have been feminists for decades generally teach it to students for whom it is new. We are no longer discovering books together; instead, feminist faculty teach feminist classics we've read half a dozen times to students who are reading them for the first time. Whatever lip service we might still give to an egalitarian classroom, we function as feminist authorities, trying to get our students to understand a feminism we have long known. In this context, relations between us are defined much more by our roles as teacher and student than by any commonality as feminists. These days, rather than playing with our pedagogical roles, we seem to be trapped in them, our ability to connect as women very much limited by them.

Yet my students still want a feminist education that feels like women's studies did to me in 1971. And so do I, deeply. I want it for them and I want it still, again, for myself.

Sometimes it works. Sometimes a class or some more informal gathering suddenly comes together, and I feel the electricity, the buzz of live knowledge, the excitement of women thinking freely together. I always try to get us to that place where learning begins to dance. When we get there, my students love me and I'm crazy for them.

But when, as is more often the case, we don't get there, we are all disappointed. And then the students are likely to blame me.

For about a decade now, students in my feminist seminars have been complaining, in their anonymous evaluations, that I am "authoritarian." They expect a feminist teacher to be different, but my authority *as a feminist* feels too much like the male professor's authority in other classrooms. This experience of the feminist teacher as authority seems to betray the very principles of feminist teaching. In the context of feminism, these complaints of authoritarianism and the complaints of sexual harassment are saying the same thing: that I abuse my power, get off on my power at the students' expense, that I am just as bad as the men.

During the time I was under investigation by the university, the two graduate students who had filed harassment complaints against me called a meeting of all the grad students in the department, a predominantly feminist group. The purpose of the meeting was to get the grad students to band together so they would be strong enough to curtail my power. At this student-only meeting, in the tradition of the feminist "speakout," students shared with each other the abuses they had suffered at the hands of faculty.

And in that context, charges of sexual harassment mingled freely with complaints about other manifestations of power. Little distinction was made between sexual harassment (the criminal charge) and authoritarianism (a complaint about teaching style). In the eyes of the students gathered together to resist me and faculty oppression, they were virtually the same crime, the crime of having power over them.

Well-versed in anti-harassment rhetoric, one of the students states in her complaint against me: "it is at the level of the institutionally enforced power differential that I wish to locate my harassment charge." She found it humiliating that I had power over her and considered it a betrayal of feminism. Harassment for her in fact meant precisely experiencing what she calls "the power differential." Now that there are feminist faculty securely installed in the academy, students can experience feminist teachers as having power over them. And that makes it possible to imagine a feminist teacher as a sexual harasser.

Back when I was a student, our feminist teachers tended to be in rather tenuous institutional positions; they didn't have much institutional power. We didn't experience what power they did have as power over us, but rather as power for us—power for women, power for feminism. Bad power was men's power, the power society granted men to exploit women, impose upon women, abuse women. Twenty years later, thanks to feminism's academic success, students could look at me and see me as just like the men, just as bad as the men. And therefore worse.

A campus activist against sexual harassment, a student from another department who had never even met me, was quite willing to comment on my case to a reporter: "Jane Gallop is as bad as—*no, worse than*—the men who do this kind of thing." A woman "as bad as the men" is inevitably, because she is a woman, considered to be worse than the men. Although several men in my department have been accused of sexual harassment, none of those cases prompted students to rally against the accused.

Feminists often condemn the woman who is like a man as a traitor to feminism, a traitor to her sex. But the condemnation of what feminists call "the male-identified woman" bears an uncanny resemblance to a larger social prejudice, the vilification of women who are like men. Feminism has taught us a lot about that sexist image, how it works to limit and constrain women, to keep us in line, but feminists are not themselves always immune to it.

And what it means for a woman to be "just like a man" always comes down to two things: sex and power.

In 1993, at the very moment I am under investigation, Michael Crichton writes *Disclosure,* the first popular novel about sexual harassment. This novel by a best-selling author, a book that became almost immediately a Hollywood movie, marks a turning point: harassment has taken root in the culture's imagination. Sexual harassment moves from the news to the novel. And mainstream culture's first attempt to imagine harassment conjures up not the classic scenario, but a male victim and a female predator.

Disclosure sports the epigraph, "Power is neither male nor female," and this view of power seems to be behind the choice to portray a role-reversal harassment. The epigraph is actually spoken within the novel. The woman lawyer who functions as the book's authority on harassment explains to the male victim: "the figures suggest that women executives harass men in the same proportion as men harass women. Because the fact is, harassment is a power issue. And power is neither male nor female. Whoever is behind the desk has the opportunity to abuse power. And women will take advantage as often as men." This sounds like the moral of a story about a female sexual harasser.

Crichton is a writer known for the extensive research behind his books, and this one is no exception: *Disclosure*'s understanding of harassment is very up-to-date. Explanations of sexual harassment are beginning to move away from the idea that gender is the key factor and toward a gender-neutral notion of power. While a number of feminists have embraced this move, I consider it to be a serious departure from feminism.

Sexual harassment was originally understood within a more general feminist analysis of sexism. Feminists saw that the specific power men exercise over individual women—as a boss or a teacher, say—is enormously magnified by widespread societal assumptions that men should dominate women. In a society that expects male sexuality to be aggressive and female sexuality submissive, a boss can sexually harass his female employee with a devastating combination of economic, psychological, and social coercion. The boss's pressure on his employee is backed not only by literal economic power and general psychological intimidation, but also by social expectations that relations between the sexes are supposed to be like this.

When we move beyond the gender configuration of the classic harassment scenario, some important things change. The link between sex and power is not always the same. Whereas male heterosexuality in our culture connotes power, both homosexuality and female sexuality tend to signify weakness and vulnerability. If we imagine a sexual harassment scenario where the victim is male or the culprit female, the abuse of power would not be reinforced by society's sexual expectations. Outside novelistic turnabouts (and Hollywood fantasies featuring Demi Moore), a woman is much more likely to undermine than to enhance her authority by bringing her sexuality into the professional domain.

Not unlike *Disclosure*, my accuser locates harassment "at the level of the institutionally enforced power differential." Both reflect a current trend in thinking about harassment that reduces power to mere institutional position. And thus forgets the feminist insight that the most destructive abuses of power occur because of widespread, deeply rooted social and psychological reinforcement.

Troubled by this move to a gender-neutral understanding of sexual harassment, I take *Disclosure* as a dramatic portrayal of its real danger. Rather than worrying about male exploitation and women's disadvantage, the novel's reader is confronted with the image of an evil woman; the reader identifies with and fears for the poor man she preys upon. Under the guise of despising sexual harassment, we find ourselves once again vilifying women who presume to be sexual and powerful like men are.

Embracing a gender-neutral formulation of harassment, we leave behind the concern with sexism only to find ourselves faced with something quite traditionally sexist: an image of a woman who is evil precisely because she is both sexual and powerful. Meredith Johnson, *Disclosure*'s villainess, is a single career woman who is sexy and sexually aggressive, professionally adept and successful. She corresponds to the pop-cultural image of a liberated woman. Although feminists have condemned women who are just like men, society at large tends to think of women who are like men as "feminists." We might see Meredith Johnson as the fantasy of a feminist sexual harasser.

Disclosure marks a real turning point in the response to sexual harassment. Or maybe a turn of the screw. As outrage at sexual harassment becomes popular, a role-reversal fantasy allows a wide audience to embrace the feminist issue of sexual harassment and at the same time turn it against liberated women.

As the century draws to a close, it appears that the campaign against sexual harassment may, in fact, be *the* success story of twentieth-century feminism. At a moment when abortion rights are endangered, when affirmative action is becoming unfashionable, when everyone is jumping on the family values bandwagon, when few women want to be thought of as feminists, there is a broad-based consensus that sexual harassment is despicable, and measures against it have become very popular.

Although feminists targeted sexual harassment in the 1970s, outrage against it did not become popular until the nineties. The Hill-Thomas hearings in late 1991 are generally credited with producing this effect. Although I have my own suspicions about the way that a black man makes it easier for the majority to see male heterosexuality as a threat to the social order, my concern here is rather with the more general question of how sexual harassment is understood at the moment when the nation finally rallies against it.

While the battle against sexual harassment has been feminism's great victory, I'm afraid that's because it has been too easy to separate the issue from feminism. Feminists took up the issue because we saw it as a form of sex discrimination, but sexual harassment is increasingly understood as having no necessary link to either discrimination or gender.

In 1990, Billie Wright Dziech, a national authority on sexual harassment, predicted that "genuine change can occur only when sexual harassment is approached as a professional rather than a gender issue." Three years later, the change Dziech was calling for seems to have occurred. Crichton's *Disclosure* approaches harassment in just that way: gender doesn't matter, what matters is who is "behind the desk." That same year, a university official finds it possible that I could be guilty of sexual harassment without having discriminated against anyone. The university's lawyer comments that they must take care to punish me as harshly as the men so that the university won't be accused of sex discrimination.

By the end of 1993, Dziech announces that the discussion of sexual harassment has entered a "new phase": the issue has moved beyond its feminist framework and taken on a life of its own. Although feminism brought the problem to public awareness, the larger public does not necessarily share the feminist assessment of the problem. Once separated from the issue of sex discrimination, harassment can be linked to other versions of socially undesirable sexuality.

As sexual harassment breaks loose from its feminist formulation, the crusade against it might even become not just independent of feminism, but actually hostile to feminism. Dziech imagines one particularly chilling possibility: "eventually the political right will embrace protections against sexual harassment as part of its agenda for a return to traditional values." A return to traditional values always implies women returning to our proper place. And then we might see not just the odd spectacle of a feminist accused of sexual harassment but the more general prospect of feminists being so accused precisely *because* we are feminists. Once sexual harassment is detached from its feminist meaning, it becomes possible to imagine feminism itself accused as a form of sexual harassment.

I Dreamed Again That I Was Drowning, with a Postscript

Annette Kolodny

4 a.m., May 9, 1978

THE WATER IS COLD. MY CLOTHES cling to me in layers, weighing me down. Every part of my body is chilled, and none of my exertions warm me. Around me the water is dark and choppy, but there is still light—it seems to be early evening—and I can see for some distance. What I see are shores on two sides. On one there is a road where cars pass too quickly for the drivers to catch any glimpse of me. On the other there is a paved walkway, parallel to the water, but no one comes just now. I am trying desperately to swim toward the walkway shore, but a current keeps me in place. Exhausted, I tread water, trying at least to stay afloat. I am not a good swimmer, I remember I have always been afraid of the water, and I am not very strong. I cannot keep this up much longer.

Then I see a woman coming along the footpath. There is something odd about the perspective because, although the shore is some distance away, I can see her distinctly. She wears sensible low-heeled shoes and a tailored paisley print dress in shades of brown. Her improbable red hair is shoulder length with a prominent gray streak on one side. She wears no makeup, and her face is slightly pockmarked, the scars of adolescent acne. At some point, I realize that I know this woman.

For a time, she doesn't see me even though I am shouting and waving my arms, thrusting my body out of the water to catch her attention. Then she does see me; and her face momentarily registers concern. Her mouth opens and her eyes narrow to a squint as she strains against the glare from the water to focus on me. I am trying to shout that there is a life preserver further along the walkway—a white inner tube with a long rope attached. I hadn't noticed it before, but it is there now. If she comes down to the water's edge, she can throw it close to me. She seems to understand, she looks around, she sees the thing lying on the grass up ahead.

But she hesitates and does not go toward it. Instead, she shouts back to me, explaining that if she comes any closer to the water, the waves will spray her dress. Apparently, my movements have so agitated the water that it splashes hard against the bank. I am crying and pleading, screaming with all my force; I hear my voice crack with the effort. My movements have become frantic. The woman on the shore watches, her body stiffening. She is indignant that I am demanding so much of her. She has a right to refuse, she feels: I should understand that she cannot get her hem wet. Finally, she turns and continues along the walkway, her back to me.

I am weeping, swallowing large mouthfuls of dark brackish water. I am gulping for air, I am having trouble breathing, I am sinking. . . .

I wake up bathed in sweat, and I am crying.

Thank God, thank God Dan is here beside me. I nudge him and tell him I have had a nightmare. He grunts from somewhere deep in sleep and rolls toward me, putting his arms around me. He says something, but I can't make out the words, they are incoherent. He isn't really awake. But he *is* holding me, slowly running his hand up and down my arm, comforting. In a few minutes he will sink back into deep sleep and roll away again. In the morning he probably won't remember any of this. I could wake him if I wanted, force him to full consciousness and make him listen while I retell the dream. But I won't—he's heard it too many times before. He held me when I was crying, he heard me even from sleep. It is enough.

1 p.m., May 9, 1978

I slept till noon again today, and still I feel exhausted. Last night I dreamed again that I was drowning.

It is now almost three years since I filed a discrimination complaint against the University of New Hampshire in 1975. I charged the school with sex discrimination and anti-Semitism. The Department of English had twice denied me promotion to associate rank, eventually promoted me, and subsequently voted not to tenure me. When the New Hampshire Commission for Human Rights found probable cause in my favor, the university refused to attend settlement hearings or to redress any of my grievances. The school again refused to come to the bargaining table when, thirteen months later, the Equal Employment Opportunity Commission made similar findings. This last year I have employed legal counsel, filed suit in federal court, and am in the throes of preparing for trial. My lawyers say it will be a landmark case.

Something else has happened this last year: both the women junior to me in the tenure track have been tenured, and one woman brought in as a full professor—subsequent to my initial discrimination complaint—has also been tenured. One by one, they are turning into people I no longer recognize, except in my dreams. Sheila, my closest friend and confidante when she was still an assistant professor, now says she can't be seen talking to me, on campus or anywhere. "It hurts my credibility," she explains. Amanda arrived last year from a small college in the Midwest where she already held the full professor rank. We had mutual friends from graduate school. From the first week, Amanda told everyone—department colleagues and others— that the denial of my tenure was "a clear case of discrimination." She was sure I'd win. But this year Amanda was given tenure at New Hampshire, and she's now begun blaming it all on my style. "It's your style, Annette," she keeps saying to me, although she never explains what she means. Amanda has shoulder-length red hair with a gray streak on the right and skin scarred by acne. Amanda was the woman in last night's dream.

Like Sheila, Jennifer is the other junior woman who has just been tenured. A week after she learned the good news, she told me she believes people get what they deserve. More recently, she has begun to ask why I don't leave. "You've done all you can here, there's nothing more to be done on this campus. So why don't you just go someplace else?" She seems to think it would be easy, as if the lawsuit and the denial of tenure have not marked me, as though the department has not told prospective employers that I'm "abrasive," the new code word for feminist. Jennifer also has been in my drowning dreams. She didn't throw me the life preserver, either. She was late for an appointment, she said, and hurried along the concrete path.

Now that these women are tenured, I have asked them to speak up for me and for women's issues at department meetings; I have asked them to tell my lawyers if there are breaches of professional procedure in the votes on my various appeals; I have asked them to support me in every way they can. But it's been three years now, and I am becoming a burden to them. "You expect too much," Jennifer tells me. "Don't ask people for anything," advises Amanda, "let them do what they can do on their own—and understand if they feel they can't do anything." "I've got to back off where you're concerned," Sheila tells me again and again. "It jeopardizes my standing in the department." The drowning dreams began this year. Always, it is Sheila or Jennifer or Amanda who will not get her hem wet, who cannot be late for an appointment.

I am, of course, the truth too awful to allow. Each woman wants to believe that her tenure and promotion were earned, deserved— not the result of my lawsuit and the department's attempt to prepare itself for trial. And, to be sure, each woman *did* merit her tenure and promotion, as did many women before them whom this department let go. I was the first woman and the first Jew ever reviewed for promotion to associate rank in the department's entire history. Before me, no woman and no member of any ethnic minority group had gotten even that far. But if my women colleagues acknowledge that the department made a mistake in my case, how can they rest comfortably with the department's decision in their own? Adamant, Sheila and Jennifer keep insisting, "They hired Amanda McKinney. She does feminist criticism. And they tenured us. So how can you say the department discriminates? They hired Amanda McKinney!" The refrain bludgeons. They have ganged up on me.

The terrible irony is that my women colleagues have invested their self-esteem in the judgments of men whom previously they would ridicule and sneer at in private. At dinner parties, Sheila and Jennifer used to parody one or another of the senior men or make fun of the pretensions of a department chair. But now those men have presumably found each woman worthy, and the approval of others is difficult to dismiss. It is easier to dismiss *me*, to see *me* as the problem.

Sometimes I think maybe I am crazy, maybe I have some other personality I don't know about. I've read the testimony of some of the senior members and don't recognize the person they describe as me. I don't remember saying some of the things they say I said, and I don't believe I've ever held some of the opinions or attitudes they attribute to me. Their versions of certain meetings and encounters bear no resemblance to my memories of those occasions. What's so scary is that their testimony is consistent; they all agree with one another. I seem to be the only one with a different version. My lawyers say not to worry. The university lawyer is simply coaching his witnesses into producing a coherent story to offer the judge. They don't have any professional grounds for the denial of tenure—I've outpublished them all, the department chair concedes that my teaching is "outstanding," and my committee work has always been diligent—so they're building a case based on personality. They're going to characterize me as "uncollegial," whatever that means. The second time I was denied promotion, the reason given was "collegiality." I went to the department chair to ask what it meant. He said he didn't know, wished they wouldn't use the term, called it a "will o' the wisp." But he, too, had voted against me—always has.

My lawyers' assurances do not comfort. These people are inventing a personality for me, forcing me to live inside it or defend against it. How can three men say the same thing about an incident that I remember differently? Am I crazy? I appeal to Dan: "Am I really this person they say I am? Do I ever do or say these things?" I sometimes fear I am losing my grip on my own reality. In department or committee meetings, I take notes frantically, fearful of forgetting, of being convinced by others that something different transpired. "I'm not this person, am I?" I keep asking Dan. I need to hear it from someone who sees me daily. I need to know I am not the monster they say I am.

I am trying to write an essay about the accomplishments of feminist criticism over the last ten years. What I really want to write about is what it feels like to be an outsider, a pariah. I want to write about being angry and scared and how it feels to be abandoned. If it weren't for Dan, I would be crazy now.

I find the essay difficult to work on because I am afraid it may be the last one I'll ever write. Unless this lawsuit is settled quickly, or I can find another job, I'm afraid I won't have any career. I have already been blackballed at several schools—friends have told me about department meetings at which someone fears I'm "too political," "too feminist," "too strident," too something. And my lawyers say a trial will take at least a year, with another three to five years of appeals when the university loses. The essay has become a sort of life preserver: it reminds me of what I'm fighting for. I was going to put "drowning" in the title and use my dream as a metaphor to hold together its disparate sections. But every time I try to use drowning as a symbol, I start crying. Not for fear of drowning so much as for the pain I feel when I remember the woman continuing along the walkway. I cannot bear the desertion. I will title the essay after another dream, one not so awful because I survive it each time. In that dream, I am dancing through a minefield. . . .

May 1987

The preceding section is a partial transcription of a 1978 entry from a handwritten journal that I kept erratically from December 1975 through November 1980. It was at the end of December 1975 that I first learned that the Senior Members Committee of the Department of English at the University of New Hampshire had voted 10 to 0 against my promotion to associate professor. Almost five years later, in October 1980, two weeks before trial was to begin, the university opened negotiations for an out-of-court settlement. By late November, the settlement was final. In both its stipulations and its financial terms, the settlement was what my lawyers had all along predicted: a landmark. During the three years of pretrial litigation, we had set important legal precedents from which Title VII complainants after me would benefit.

Unpacking the journal after all these years, I am forced to remember the anguish of that period: the repeated deep depressions, the paralysis of mind that slowed my writing, the endless nights when I could not sleep or when sleep brought only nightmares and the unremitting sense of anger and isolation. Rereading the journal today, I am struck by the rancor and bitterness expressed toward my three women colleagues. In the first two years of journal entries, my anger is directed at the senior men who resolutely tried to keep the tenured ranks a private Christian men's club. As I had recorded in an early entry, one of those men told me, "It *is* a club, Annette; we can keep out anyone we want to." But as the women on whom I depended for emotional support gradually pulled away, they became the focus of my desperation, and, finally, my anger. By the third year of journal entries, I was hardly writing about the men at all. A small clique of tenured men had discriminated against me as a woman and as a Jew. I could understand that, and I could fight it. But the women, I felt, had betrayed me, abandoned me, even used me. That I had not expected, and I knew no way of fighting what I did not even want to admit.

Under these circumstances, I am amazed that I didn't crack—though the journal entries suggest I came close more than once. I did not crack because, although I didn't always recognize it at the time, I had been embraced by extraordinary caring. My lawyers and one paralegal—all women, all committed feminists—negotiated the legal system as my advocates and, in that process, became my friends. A nationwide network of colleagues from both the American literature and women's studies communities responded to my letters of appeal with contributions to my legal fund, letters and phone calls of warmth and encouragement, offers of expert testimony. My students—women and men, graduates and undergraduates—dutifully kept the lawsuit out of the classroom and then organized on my behalf all over campus; they threw parties and fundraisers to let me know they would share the burden. My colleague Gary Lindberg steadfastly remained independent within the English department and supported me, without reserve, never letting me know the prices he paid. Judy and Peter Lindberg, his wife and son—together with Gary—were more than friends: talking and listening to music together, often until dawn, they became extended family. And, finally, my husband, Daniel Peters, was always the target of my anger and frustration, the recipient of my grief and depression. In our society, men are rarely trained to nurture or give care, and Dan was certainly no exception. But if he did not always anticipate my needs or divine the depth of my depression, he nonetheless provided the crucial assurance that would see me through. In endless patient responses to my appeal, "I'm not this person, am I?" he helped me hold onto reality. In words, in little gifts, in loving gestures, he let me know that even when I did become irrational, even when my fears overcame me, he would keep loving me and believing in me. All else might fail, but Dan, I knew, would never betray me.

I read the journal now almost as if it were someone else's. I don't quite recognize the person writing those pages, but I want to put my arms around her and tell her it will be all right. Part of the anguish, you see, was that I could never be sure of that.

Happily, in the end it *has* been "all right." After several uncertain years, my career stabilized, and schools competed with one another to hire me. Nowadays, I am quite secure; I teach, write, and publish about all the things that are important to me. I no longer have nightmares, I never have dreams of drowning, and I take great pleasure from swimming regularly. Not incidentally, as I write, this coda to the journal entry, I approach my forty-sixth birthday. When I look in the mirror, I find I like the person I see there. I know that the woman in the mirror will never abandon another woman because, ten years ago, something irrevocable happened in New Hampshire. Lines were drawn. Sheila, Jennifer, and Amanda believed they could avoid taking sides; they thought they could avoid getting their hems wet. In their view, they were not actively doing anything to harm me; they were simply "not getting involved." What they never understood—

but I always will—is that their supposed neutrality gave the men in the department tacit permission to continue refusing me promotion and tenure. The women's silence encouraged the men's recalcitrance. The neutrality of Sheila, Jennifer, Amanda, in other words, was itself a position. It is a position that leaves *all* women isolated from one another, vulnerable to drowning.

I have never forgiven those women their lack of courage. Even today I avoid seeing or speaking to them at professional conferences. I have never forgiven the University of New Hampshire for trying to exile me from its private "club." For all the loveliness of the New Hampshire countryside which I adored, and for all the friends we left behind there, for me the town of Durham is forever a tainted place. Above all else, however, I can never forgive the mask of institutional decorum that made it impossible for Dan and me to return for the memorial service—held on campus—after Gary Lindberg died in 1986 of Hodgkin's disease. I needed that ritual of mourning for a loving friend who had made my own survival possible. And, finally, I will never be reconciled to the fact that the University of New Hampshire mired me in debt and emotional anguish during the last years in which I might reasonably have planned on pregnancy. Forced to concentrate all my energies on professional survival, I watched the biological time clock run out.

I realize as I write these words that the rage I felt ten years ago is still with me. Anger recollected in tranquility does not transmute; it is still anger. Perhaps it is not as sharp, certainly not the constant companion it was then. But it is there, a familiar vibration, and one I think I've earned a right to. The common wisdom, of course, is that we must let go of our anger, forget our pain, lest they eat away inside and turn us bitter. My trusted friends do not give such advice. They know what is really being asked of us by such so-called "wisdom": that we forget our history. When we can no longer call up the feelings, after all, the events of our past are dead to us, without meaning or motivation. I want my past to remain vital to me because I need to keep learning its lessons.

They are not easy lessons, to be sure, nor have I yet fully comprehended them. But they are lessons that no individual or political movement can safely evade. As a result of what happened to me in New Hampshire, the contradictions in my life opened out like a hall of mirrors. I fought, I believed, for principles and for people. Even so, the people who stood to gain the most from what I was doing proved the least helpful. The rabbi assigned to the university said he'd never heard any complaints of anti-Semitism on campus; the more senior faculty women in my department would take no risks on my behalf, instead condemning me for risking all. The two people who stayed with me, ironically, were two WASP males: my husband, Dan, and my friend and colleague, Gary. If the personal is political, then what sort of politics emerges from such truths?

I don't have the answer to that question, but I know it is one I—we—must pursue beyond the cliché of cognitive dissonance. The question leads, ineluctably, to an examination of the corrosive *professionalization* of identity within patriarchal institutions that constrains women from bonding with one another. So long as I remain within academe, this is something I must strive to understand and overcome. To do that, I must hold firm to my memories—the pain and the anger both—and cherish the challenge they engender. Bitterness, I suspect, comes from trying to bury what will not die. Bitterness is the attempt at repressing anger, refusing contradiction. The woman I see in the mirror is not bitter. She knows that to embrace one's anger is to return from exile from one's self.

Thanksgiving 2007

"I Dreamed Again That I Was Drowning" was written for a collection of essays entitled *Women's Writing in Exile*, published in 1989. The general themes of the book were the many ways in which women experienced ourselves as excluded or even exiled from literary history, the craft of writing, or the academic institutions to which we hoped to contribute as teachers and scholars. It was a decidedly feminist statement. Until Susan Gubar called to ask if she could reprint the essay in this current collection, I had not looked at it since it went to press in 1989. Coming upon the essay afresh, five months after my June 30, 2007, retirement from the University of Arizona, I found that I recognized the anger and anguish in both the journal entries and in the follow-up comment. But I no longer *felt* either the anger or the anguish. Rather than rage, I simply felt a deep sorrow for my younger self who had had to go through all this. When, on occasion, my graduate students come across this essay, they invariably ask the same two questions: "Knowing what I know today, would I do it all again?" and "Have I ever seen or spoken with the three women colleagues described in the essay?" For the record, I will now try briefly to answer both questions.

Much though I have loved both teaching and scholarship, if I were twenty-one again I am no longer certain that I would seek a career as a college professor in the humanities. Under the pressure of the ultra-conservative right and the related pressure of chronic underfunding—especially in the public universities—the humanities no longer seem to me an inviting haven for audacious intellectual inquiry or a place to build a reasonable career. I am seeing too many budding young scholars frustrated by the lack of tenure-track positions, forced to carry heavy course loads as adjuncts, or pushed into a quasi-nomadic existence as they repeatedly move from job to job. There is little that is satisfying in this kind of teaching, there is never time for one's own research and writing, and there are certainly no meaningful financial rewards, let alone job security. Under such conditions, the love of one's field or discipline is hard to sustain. That said, knowing what I know today, if I were again unfairly denied promotion and tenure, yes, I would fight the injustice all over again. I believe that silence in such situations only deadens the soul.

While I deeply regret having had to spend five years of my life in pursuit of a Title VII discrimination lawsuit, I am also aware that that experience educated me about how higher education institutions function and prepared me for the role I would later play as dean of the College of Humanities at the University of Arizona, 1988–93. I take pride in the fact that under my administrative leadership, the College of Humanities reviewed and revised tenure and promotion procedures in all departments, and, in our new documents, clearly stipulated that promotion and tenure committees would include "only faculty members who have met the current criteria by which the candidates under consideration are being judged" (*Failing the Future* 258). Among other things, this phrasing minimized the possibility that new and innovative scholarship would be rejected by those who were not still active in and knowledgeable about their fields. It was a move that truly helped level the playing field for the outstanding women and minority faculty members hired during my tenure as dean (all of whom, I am pleased to say, successfully negotiated the tenure and promotion process). I don't know that I would have understood how crucial is the language in a promotion and tenure document unless I had experienced what I did at the University of New Hampshire where faculty members unfamiliar with the new feminist criticism (or with interdisciplinary American studies) simply dismissed everything I did as "faddish."

I'm equally proud that I instituted a host of family-friendly policies which also helped to level the playing field, especially for women. We developed clear procedures for family-care-related adjusted workloads and delayed tenure clocks. And by the time I left the dean's office, almost half the department heads were women. Would I have thought to do any of this or would I have been so determined to initiate institutional change had I not myself earlier been a victim of institutional discrimination and procedural misconduct?

As for the women cited in the essay, yes, I did see them in later years and yes, I do believe they read the essay. On two occasions, I spotted the woman named Sheila in the essay (not her real name) at large Modern Language Association convention cocktail parties. Sheila was standing alone at both these parties, while I was in the company of friends, colleagues, and my graduate students. Neither of us greeted the other, although we did make eye contact. On both occasions, she left the party within minutes of my arrival. I have never seen or spoken to her since.

The woman I name as Jennifer in the essay was in front of the Folger Shakespeare Library in Washington DC one spring afternoon when my husband, Dan, and I happened to be strolling by. She greeted me and chatted away about her research, very friendly, as though nothing had ever happened all those years ago at UNH. I was so taken aback by her seeming imperviousness to the pain she had once caused me that I didn't know how to respond. So I just smiled, wished her well with her research, and got away as fast as I could without being obviously rude. Later, I wished that I *had* said something to her, but I somehow felt she must have read the essay and that this was her way of coping.

I never told Jennifer that the department chairman who hired me at UNH told me in confidence—some weeks before the senior members committee denied my promotion and tenure—that he intended to fire her at her next two-year review. He complained that she hadn't published anything and that her student teaching evaluations were consistently poor. He said students complained about her all the time, and he wanted to let her go. At this point, the department chair had no inkling that the senior members would subsequently turn down my promotion and tenure bid, and he and I were on a friendly footing. I urged him not to let her go but, rather, to work with her to improve her teaching and help her become eligible for promotion and tenure. I don't know if he ever did. But I do know that once I filed my discrimination suit, Jennifer was tenured and promoted almost immediately. Her student teaching evaluations had not improved, nor had she published much.

About fifteen years ago I arrived late for a large, well-attended Modern Language Association convention session on feminist criticism. I made a beeline for one of the only empty seats near the back of the room and, after a few minutes, realized that the slouching woman seated next to me was the woman I called Amanda McKinney in my essay. Almost without thinking I turned, nodded, and smiled. Amanda didn't respond. When the speaker on the platform finished her paper, and just as the audience began to applaud, Amanda got up and rushed out of the room. I have never since seen or spoken with her either.

In retrospect, I still harbor a deep regret that these three women were never able to believe that the four of us, standing firm together— with the support of sympathetic male colleagues in our own department and the help of women colleagues in other departments—could have forced change in the English department and secured my promotion and tenure (as well as their own). Although all three identified as feminists, they seemed to have no confidence in the popular adage of the day, "Sisterhood is powerful." So, instead of taking advantage of a moment that was ripe for coalition-building across campus, in effect they forced the campus to become polarized. In consequence, it was my lawsuit that forced change—at the expense of my health and, for a time, my career.

By the time the lawsuit was settled, the entire senior administration—dean, provost, and president—were gone, and UNH was preparing to inaugurate its first woman and its first Jewish president, Evelyn Handler. The fledgling women's studies program, which I had helped to establish, now had a permanent budget. And the institution as a whole began making serious efforts to diversify its faculty. In later years, friends in other departments told me that Sheila, Jennifer, and Amanda had become increasingly isolated in an English department that had changed radically. I also know that, in more recent times, the UNH English department has repeatedly tried to hire my graduate students for its faculty. So far, none of my graduate students has been enticed.

Note

With the exception of the Lindberg family and my husband, Daniel Peters, all names are fictitious. Those characterized as departmental colleagues are composites drawn from several persons. Chronology and other details have been altered to protect the privacy of individuals.

In helping me to examine the implications of my journal entries, Susan Koppelman has been a generous friend and loving resource. I am also grateful to Judy Lindberg, Nancy Gertner, Ann Lambert Greenblatt, and Sandy Eisdorfer for their careful readings and valuable suggestions.

WORKS CITED

Kolodny, Annette. *Failing the Future: A Dean Looks at Higher Education in the Twenty-first Century.* Durham, NC: Duke University Press, 1998.

————. "I Dreamed Again That I Was Drowning." In *Women's Writing in Exile,* edited by Mary Lynn Broe and Angela Ingram. Chapel Hill: University of North Carolina Press, 1989. 170–78.

"Anyway, *We* Certainly Don't Want to Be Lumped In with Black Studies!"

Frances Smith Foster

Once Upon a Time . . .

WE HAD BEEN MEETING FOR AT LEAST an hour, venting, lamenting, scheming, analyzing, and strategizing about an effective response to the most recent threat to the women's studies department. After many years of struggle, *we* had managed to create what is believed to be the first department of women's studies in the United States. The latest budget crisis had provided another opportunity for assault by those who chronically feared and resented the emergence of what they called "bullying punitive disciplines" whose "narrow political interests" threatened "traditional academic values." Their proposed "rational and objective" cost-cutting solution was to combine Chicano studies, Afro-American studies, Native American studies, and women's studies into a single unit.

I, like my colleagues, was vehemently opposed to this scheme. The civil rights struggle had given birth to both ethnic studies and women's studies movements, and thus we were siblings of a sort. When threatened from the outside, we had usually displayed a unified opposition. But like brothers and sisters, we also had our individual identities and fundamental differences. For one example, women's studies centered on women and assumed feminist primacy, or at least gender equality. Native American, Chicano, and Afro-American studies, on the other hand, found much of this extremely problematic. Feminist pedagogy was quite similar to that of ethnic studies, but our ideas about sexuality and the primacy of what many labeled "women's issues" were not. From a women's studies perspective, the ethnic studies departments were, in fact, being constructed around the accomplishments and needs of men. Especially within a context of merged faculty and decreased funding, we knew full well that if we were pushed into one unit, it would quickly come to shove. I could not imagine any way that such confrontation would not further complicate my life because, unlike the others at this meeting, I also taught in Afro-American studies. I believed, however, this meeting was the necessary prelude to collaboration with the other Others. The obvious first step was for women's studies to agree upon a plan that worked in its own best interest, but I assumed that we would afterward, as in other times, confer with the other groups and try to create a joint strategy. So when my ears heard the sounds, "Anyway, *we* certainly don't want to be lumped in with black studies," my brain was slow to interpret. I was nonplussed, shocked, and then furious.

"Oh, no, she didn't!" I thought. Questions and suspicions attacked my brain like the motorcycle monkeys in *The Wiz*. At San Diego State University, where this was happening, the department was named "Afro-American Studies," so why did my women's studies colleague say "black studies?" Did "lumped" imply rejection of conflation, or did it reveal unconscious (?) identification of "black" and "coal"? I realized my colleague was trying to lay a cornerstone for consensus, but that was the reason for my distress. "Anyway" and "certainly" seemed to assume that regardless of whatever else *we* might do or say, *we* had to avoid being blackened—or at least smudged—by too close an association with the Others of color. But was I an invisible woman here?

Did she really believe I "certainly" agreed? Why were some nodding in agreement? Why did no one else around the table seem to have a problem with her comment? Didn't someone else recognize that my academic home, my research specialty, my naturally curly hair, brown skin, and cultural identification already connected *us* in women's studies with *them* in Afro-American studies, at least? Who was this *we* of whom she spoke?

This meeting, like most, included women's studies faculty and faculty women of the advisory committee. I was a "sister/outsider." Officially I was not women's studies faculty. Although it had department status, in the early 1980s women's studies did not yet have enough tenured faculty to represent the department in business requiring senior faculty. I was one of only a handful of tenured women, and the only woman of color, at SDSU who could, or would, agree to serve on its advisory committee. Like the other members of the committee, I had worked long and hard with the women's studies faculty. I taught women's literature and African American women's literature classes under the department's rubric. I participated in departmental projects, protests, and celebrations. While I was the only woman who did not appear to be of European ancestry, what had begun as collegiality had moved to what I thought was friendship between me and several women around that table.

And yet, if truth be told, my sense of not quite belonging, not quite being trusted, did not begin with this incident. Often enough, at other women's studies meetings, my colleagues had alternately displayed indifference to, or ignorance of, my perspective on some questions and excessive attention to "my" perspective on others. Other times, I had overheard remarks that suggested less tolerance for political, sexual, and cultural difference, but this was the first time someone had actually said something like this in my hearing. My faith in women's studies' stated and often demonstrated desire and intention of becoming more inclusive made me believe we would overcome our residual prejudices or bigotries. Now, my grandmother's words rose up over the questioning noise of the motorcycle monkey in my head: "Remember, honey, every shut eye ain't sleep, and not everyone who grins in your face is your friend." I had dropped my guard, and I got sucker-punched with words that hit so hard that I could neither breathe nor speak.

These words and their effect are vividly seared into my memory, but what happened next is not. I recall that I didn't know what words to say or how to say them so that she and the others would recognize my situation and why I didn't—couldn't—continue to focus upon the original agenda. I imagine that I sat silently through the rest of the meeting. If anyone noticed, she didn't mention it then—or later. I don't think that I lost any sleep over the incident. I suspect that by the end of that day, other meetings, other moments had diverted my attention. When I was asked for a tentative title for this essay, however, the words leaped into my consciousness, and I discovered that after all these years, the salient aspects are still alive—and still painful. But, or maybe because of this, I decided to explore this incident to try to understand how and why this memory persists after forty years. I want to know better why, after many, many happy days and close friendships that developed from my women's studies experiences, I still sometimes feel the odd woman out.

The personal is (still) political

Were I convinced that mine was a unique or rare experience, I would not have decided to share it. But my experience is more archetypal than isolated. In the seventies, most women of color in the academy were confronted regularly with such situations. The words may have varied, but their meanings were the same. In 1989, Barbara Christian reported the question as, "But who do you really belong to—Black Studies or Women's Studies?" "In the last decade," Barbara wrote,

I, and many of my sisters, have been asked that question, not so often in words as in the social gestures and roles demanded of us in Black Studies and Women's Studies, both marginal institutions in the universities. When we black women scholars who came out of the sixties see each other, we inevitably discuss that question and even though we know the correct answer is "Both Black Studies and Women's Studies," the realities of a university process belie such a pat response. (86)

The realities of university bureaucracies belie a pat response, but as I have pondered the problem, I have come to understand that the question itself is faulty, and the answer of "both" would be insufficient. Women of color have been eloquently helpful, but so too have white women such as Elizabeth Spelman, who in *Inessential Woman* uses an old philosophical saw to cut new wood. Spelman articulates the illogic and ignorance of asking someone whether she "belonged" to women's studies "or" some other group by posing this dilemma: An African American woman stands before two doors. One was marked Black, the other marked Women. Which one should she choose? My answer is "Both, and neither." If the doors were to a restroom and my need was urgent, I'd choose the first available one. But either choice would be a dangerous expediency. I am an American woman of African descent. I am also a mother, grandmother, sister, aunt, niece, who does not live near any of her family. I am a former PTA member, a former soccer mom, a former wife, a member of National Public Radio, and a Christian who does not attend church on Easter but does believe in ghosts. In other words, I am a human being like other humans and no one category can define me. "Either/or" can work quite well at any given moment when making a necessary decision, but each decision is made in its own context, and while precedent or pattern can be expedient, foolish consistency belies growth, change, and creativity.

There was a second reason why Barbara Christian published her essay, and there is a more compelling reason why I am writing this one. In 1989, Barbara says, her students were still "being characterized as marginal to these already marginalized university programs." So, too, were my students and the students of other women of color identified with women's studies. Our students of color were feeling fragmented, diluted, and defensive. They were doubting the wisdom of being identified as feminist scholars of color. Some defined themselves as "womanist," "Africana," or "third world." Our students of European heritages were also wrestling with their places and options.

In that same essay, Barbara identifies as central issues "the inappropriateness of studying gender, race, and class as pure categories" and the need for strong, well-wrought critiques and a critical mass of well-qualified "young women scholars of color who will be inclined to pursue this perspective and who will be hired" in women's studies departments as well as other disciplines. This is not to claim that women of color were solely responsible for elevating race, gender, and class to an iconic status. Mathematicians have long embraced the knowledge that geometric figures can have points common to others while remaining distinct. Regardless of what we think of his practical applications, Booker T. Washington's metaphor of fingers being separate but part of the same hand is apt. The idea of intersectionality, like most truths, came to many people. Nor was our insistence upon the efficacy of borrowing, appropriating, collaborating, and giving honor to whom honor is due ours alone. But we were pretty insistent upon these things, and it is only fair to acknowledge that. Today I believe that the more things change, the more they stay the same. My women's studies students are predominately white, middle-class, curious, but smugly convinced that racism and sexism are almost extinct. My current women's studies department has had as many as four African American faculty offering courses in one semester. However, we African American faculty are expected, indeed hired explicitly, to teach courses that focus upon women of color, while our Euro-American colleagues tend to "add one" or "add to" or "mix in" a bit of color to their syllabi. Each year's new PhD class seems to include at least one woman whose ancestry is not European, but rarely do these women complete their degrees without some trauma they believe racism caused. This is unacceptable! Rather than abdicate or segregate ourselves, I, like many others, think it best to enter into what Johnnella Butler called "Difficult Dialogues."

Flashback: "To Be Young, Gifted and Black"

So, how is it that I came to be an African Americanist with women's studies affiliations, anyway? Well, I guess you have to understand something about my life and the community within which I was reared. I was born and raised in the northern city of Dayton, Ohio. It was— and still is—neatly divided by the Miami River into the Westside and the rest of Dayton; that is, into black neighborhoods and white ones. I grew up in a segregated community, and that community gave me spiritual, emotional, social, and intellectual nourishment. It allowed me to define myself and my goals with freedom fettered only by the understanding of *noblesse oblige*. What I achieved was always to be shared with those less blessed. I went to an all-black school with black teachers. Our family doctor, our pharmacist, our dentist, our minister—all the professionals and all the folks with whom I had personal, regular interactions were black—or as they called themselves then, "colored" or "Negro." They encouraged me without direct or obvious references to institutionalized racism or sexism or any other seemingly intractable obstacles to their dreams or to mine. The only white people I knew as individuals were our next-door neighbors, Mr. and Mrs. Donahue, and the white friends I made every year at Camp Shawano, during the annual excursion for some of us from our Negro Camp Fire Girls group. Sometimes I actually saw one or two of them once or twice afterward. But overall, my sojourns out of the Westside were infrequent, focused, and almost never alone. "Racism" was not even a vocabulary word.

Later, I realized this was a deliberate strategy developed by my parents and guardians. But by then I was singing it loud: "I'm black and I'm proud" and "To be young, gifted and black . . . that's where it's at." Even then, racial discrimination was something I read about, but it did not apply to my life. I recall being aware that all the clerks at McCroy's five- and ten-cent store, Shift's shoe store, and Elder's department store were white. I didn't expect them to give friendly, efficient service, and they didn't. But I didn't expect to be insulted or refused service, and I was not. Occasionally a bunch of boys with duck-tail haircuts and leather jackets might jeer or jostle me, but bunches of boys were often troublesome to girls. White people sometimes moved away when I took a seat beside them, but I chalked that up to their being hainty, not to my being black. Somehow, I knew that such behaviors were why my mother advised me to do what I had to do and come straight back home. When I wasn't in an all-black environment, I was sometimes uncomfortable, but I was not afraid.

In that environment, segregation was a vocabulary word. What I knew about racial discrimination, I read in books—until I attended Miami University. Here in the farmland of southwestern Ohio, I entered a public university of 5,000 undergraduates in which fewer than 100 were black—and that included the Africans.

The chorus to Miami's alma mater is

> *Old Miami, New Miami,*
> *Days of old and days to be;*
> *Weave the story of our glory,*
> *Our Miami, here's to Thee!*

It didn't take long to learn that the weave of "Old Miami" and "New Miami" was uneven and had big holes. I arrived at Miami in 1961, the first year of a new university dormitory integration initiative. Instead of assigning all the African American students to one residence hall, it had opted for a Noah's ark strategy. We were paired as roommates in dorms all across the campus. And despite a room shortage that required several students to live in the recreation room, no African Americans were bunked in that temporary site. In fact, my roommate and I had been assigned a three-person room, but when a white friend asked to live with us, the housemother refused. Our friend had to wait until a room or a space became available with white women.

When I registered for classes, older black students warned me, "Don't take American history from Professor X. He says that no Negro will ever achieve more than a C in his class." "Take Professor Cottrell's sociology class. He's fair to us." "Math? Forget it! No black folks major in math." I avoided the classes and subjects known to be hazardous to my academic health. When I realized my projects in home economics were not being graded fairly and that my idea about becoming a Betty Crocker chemist was far-fetched, I switched majors.

One year, some of my new white friends suggested that I try out for cheerleading. This was a political move of a sort. Almost all the black males at Miami were on an athletic team, and it seemed appropriate to integrate cheerleading as well. But cheerleading was also a big part of my personal history. In my hometown, sports were the center of social life. For girls, cheerleading was the most prestigious sport, and I loved it. I had won a varsity spot in seventh grade and every year since then. I had been cheerleader captain for two years, and I knew I was good. My new white friends helped me learn the cheers, and I was undaunted by the large number at tryouts. I watched my competitors, and I knew I was better than most and as good as any. I fully expected to be chosen. When I was eliminated on the first day, I was nonplussed, shocked, and then furious. Later, one of the cheerleaders tearfully told me that my hair wasn't long and my tan did not come from hours in the sun with baby oil and iodine. When she and others had urged me to compete, they had thought the time was ripe. It wasn't.

Sexism entered my vocabulary much later. I enjoyed being a girl. I loved to sew, and I was an excellent cook. I expected to get married and have babies. I originally chose to major in home economics because it seemed the most practical combination of my personal and professional ambitions. If I didn't work for Procter & Gamble in nearby Cincinnati, inventing food mixes and recipes, then I would go along with my former high school principal's plans that I earn my education certificate, return, and join her faculty. There I could help students learn, as I had, how to make beds with crisp, tight folded corners, sew clothes that were chic and less expensive, and conjure palatable meals from the powdered eggs, heavy flour, and tins of peanut butter distributed during the pre-food stamp welfare days. When I changed my major, I changed my goals. As an English major, I expected to teach in a public school system or work in a government office. In my mind, none of my options were determined by sexism. I didn't know the term "patriarchy," and the special conditions imposed upon women students at Miami University (as in most other institutions) did not strike me as onerous. So what if we couldn't ride in cars without written parental permission on file? Cars were forbidden to undergraduates, and Oxford was small enough to walk anywhere we needed to go. Why lament curfews for female students but not for male ones? Once we went in the dorms, they had nothing else to do but go back to the dorms themselves. And we all needed study time, anyway.

So how is it that I became and remain a professor of African American studies and American studies and English and women's studies? The story is longer than this essay allows and requires fast-forwarding. I made dean's list, was inducted into Phi Beta Kappa, and graduated cum laude with a BS in Education and a certificate to teach English on the secondary level. When I signed a contract to teach in the Cincinnati public school system, I asked to be placed in an inner-city junior high school where I would be teaching kids like I had been. Instead, I was one of two African American women assigned to Western Hills High School, which was not only 99.9 percent white but situated in an enclave of German Catholics who did not take kindly to any folks foreign to that experience. I decided to move to Detroit as part of the Black and Proud migration. It was the sixties, and I became involved in protesting racial discrimination in the north, unionizing public school teachers, and liberating theology. I taught high school English at Cass Technical High School, counseled science and biology students, and coached the women's tennis team (undefeated that year) and the cheerleaders. My housemates and friends were teachers, social workers, and "firsts" in several professions. My best friend worked for Motown Records, and my boyfriend played for the Detroit Lions. We all lived, mostly by choice, in "the ghetto." My awareness of ways that class, gender, and race wove structures of oppression that individual effort alone could not undo became immediate and personal realities—especially after surviving the fires, lootings, gunshots, and curfews of the so-called "race riots" during the late 1960s.

Although I marched against the Vietnam War, I married a black naval officer who went to Vietnam three times. (His antiwar sentiments were strong, but given a choice of being drafted as an enlisted man or taking advantage of the Navy's new emphasis upon increasing its minority officer cadre, he had volunteered for officer's training school.) Both of us read all the African American history and literature we could find. When I earned an MA in British and American literature at the University of Southern California, the closest that my comprehensive exam came to African American literature was a question on a novel by William Faulkner. But I had also published two articles on African American literature, taught one of San Fernando State University's first courses in African American literature, and birthed a baby girl. We moved to San Diego, and I became a freeway flyer, teaching courses at University of California's Third College and at San Diego State University. At SDSU, I worked with three men to create a relatively gender-sensitive proposal for an Afro-American studies department, and after the birth of my second child and the completion of my PhD, I was hired on tenure track. Although several women taught in Afro-American studies, my attitudes towards gender roles and sexuality were not dominant. But my dissertation on slave narratives had led me to wonder about the paucity of writings by enslaved women and about African American women generally, and my scholarly focus was not considered as revolutionary or relevant to the black studies movement as others. Women's studies needed me, and I needed them. And that essentially brings us back to the beginning of this narrative and to the story of my research career.

Still Brave . . .

Since then, my research has included the rediscovery of nineteenth-century African American women writers. I found Mary Shadd Cary, Frances E. W. Harper, Harriet Jacobs, Elizabeth Keckley, Jarena Lee, Maria W. Stewart, and many, many others, and I discovered that to a woman, they were not merely writers but doers of the word. For them, as for me, education was power and writing was fighting. I discovered also that these accomplished and influential women had faced racial and gender divides but refused to choose their interests or issues based upon external categories and definitions.

Like them, I have had white women argue with me that I did not experience what I said I did, that I have foolish notions, that I am overreacting, exaggerating, or that maybe I'm right but first I should focus upon achieving gender equality and that will open the space for equality of race, class, religion, age, etc. I have maintained and even cultivated friendships with people of varying political, religious, and social opinions despite, or maybe because of, having those relation-ships questioned, discussed, and criticized, and despite being advised to exercise greater discretion about whom I hang out with lest some-one mistake me for a lesbian, a conservative, or an effete intellectual. The lives and letters of the women and men I have researched have helped me know the larger contexts for my own texts. Some of the strategies they used to negotiate racial and gender divides have proved useful to me also.

Learning from the past gives strategies and strengthens resolve, but life is lived in the present. As I was beginning my academic career and feeling I had a foot in two camps but was on the margins of both, I began to meet women like myself. Let me tell another story.

I was in a room at the University Inn in Madison, Wisconsin, fret-ting over the presentation I had come to make at a symposium on black women's studies, wondering how my work intersected with the other two invited guests, and generally working myself into insom-nia, when a man tried to force his way into my room. He was loud, he was angry, and he was probably very drunk—otherwise, he would have realized that the party to which he was demanding admission was next door. Finally, his hearing connected with his mind, and he left. So later, when someone else knocked insistently, I remained silent and watchful until she said, "Frances Smith Foster, are you in there?" With my hair in rollers, cream on my face, but curiosity win-ning over vanity, I peeped out to see a small Afro-wearing woman—a stranger to me, but clearly someone who knew my name. I opened the door, and Barbara Christian walked into my life. Talking a mile a minute in a just slightly Caribbean accent, she flopped on the extra bed and asked if I had seen Barbara Smith yet. I discovered that both of us were in African American studies and women's studies and felt ourselves marginalized within marginalized communities. We both resented and resisted choosing to identify primarily with one side or the other, but we also thought that black women's studies was an idea whose time had not come.

The three of us, Barbara Christian, Barbara Smith, and I, were liv-ing in different circumstances. Barbara Christian's highly publicized battle to gain tenure at UC Berkeley was better known in some circles than her pioneering scholarship. Smith sometimes held adjunct status at universities in and around Boston, but she was becoming famous (or notorious) as a black lesbian community activist and founder of the Kitchen Table Press. And I was teaching eight classes a year at what I learned was considered a second-tier university while taking on more and more administrative assignments. But we all had come to Madison at the behest of Nellie Y. McKay, an African American transplant from New York City, a Harvard PhD, and a pioneering figure in African American, women's, and literary studies. Nellie and her good friend Susan Stanford Friedman were the driving forces behind this three-day symposium at a very, very white university in a very white town in a virtually white state.

The symposium helped me clarify many things in my own mind, and it was the people who were seemingly living in an advanced stage of diverse sisterhood that began my love affair with UW–Madison and many of its people that has lasted to this day, but that's another story. Suffice it to say that Madison showed me ways of living the best thoughts of ethnic studies, women's studies, and literary and other more traditional studies. The women and men with whom I interacted were scholars in the humanities, the social sciences, and the physical sciences. Some, such as Gerda Lerner, Elaine Marks, and Ruth Bleier were internationally known scholars who worked surprisingly closely with undergraduate and graduate students. They were also community leaders, elected officials, and just plain Midwesterners who appeared to be comfortable and valued on the campus. UW–Madison was no utopia, but it had a critical mass who clearly cherished similarities, respected differences, and struggled to develop inclusive scholarship that had direct applications within and without the academy. Nellie Y. McKay, Barbara Christian, and I were collaborators and friends until their deaths. My friendships with Susan S. Friedman and Stanlie James continue to this day. Though Barbara Smith and I did not form a close friendship, her coedited volume *All the Women are White, All the Blacks are Men, but Some of Us are Brave* included one of my course syllabi and helped clarify and contextualize my personal situation. This is but one of many such stories I could tell about finding a support system that helped me avoid schizophrenia and fragmentation.

Since the seventies, I have been identified and I have identified myself with women's studies. In 1994, I accepted a joint appointment in English and women's studies at Emory University. When recruited, I was assured that my teaching and research would be paramount, but all too soon I found myself the director of the Emory Institute for Women's Studies and later the chair of the English department. Again, I was among the first and the few women of color to have such responsibilities. And again, my network of friends helped me turn tears into laughter, anger into positive energy. I was able to lead the women's studies program in its transition to department status and to hire its first tenure-track faculty. I have chaired dissertations for women's studies PhDs who are making strong reputations in the field. I have participated in NWSA conferences, and I am well-published in the discipline. I helped convene the first national conference on the PhD in women's studies and I regularly serve as external reviewer for women's studies programs and departments.

But through it all, I know that I have never been totally accepted as a "real" feminist. Graduate students are quick to tell me that they appreciate what I do and have done, but they also speak strongly about the need for "truly" interdisciplinary, more obviously "theoretical" and real "women's studies PhDs" to teach and to lead women's studies. Given the prevailing definitions and predominant interests of those they admire, I agree that I don't fit their models any more than I fit the mode of women's studies in the 1980s. I have refused to self-identify as feminist, womanist, second-wave, or any other categorized invention. "I am what I am, and I do what I do" has become my mantra.

During my sojourn in the field, who I am and what I do have changed—a bit. I think that, nowadays, the first things most people notice about me are my brown skin and my gray (sometimes red, brown, or even blonde), naturally curly short hair. Being recognized and categorized as an African American woman is not new, but being "not young" is a perplexing, irksome thing that I'm still trying to get a grip on. Being seen and categorized by race and gender is a reality that I had come to accept much earlier in my life. Today, as people discover my name and my professional status, they add more categories and assume more attributes. They "know" me before I even open my mouth: I am a tenured professor holding an endowed chair in English and women's studies at a prestigious university—a position they assume that I probably got by being a not young, African American woman who was probably an affirmative action baby. Clearly, I was not trained in women's studies and thus I must be limited in my theoretical perspective and analytical skills. Maybe I have been helpful as a foremother, but as some women's studies students and younger faculty have hinted, I've served my purpose, and the sooner I relinquish my tenure line and high salary to the newest wave of women highly trained in theory and devoted to making women's studies the respected discipline it should be, the better.

It is probably this latter situation that has finally made me feel at home in the fold of a growing but relatively unacknowledged contingent within women's studies. The woman who spoke those hurtful words about being lumped with black studies has long ago retired, and so too have an increasing number of those with whom I laughed, cried, fought, comforted, supported, and grew up. Too many have died. Many colleagues have changed their appointments to other departments or made different issues the center of their immediate concerns. Many of us who remain have changed our research interests and are teaching fewer graduates and more undergraduates. We have abdicated leadership of women's studies curricular foci for service on university-wide or national committees and issues outside the academy. We are running humanities centers, serving as deans and provosts, and mentoring applicants for international research awards and admission to graduate or professional schools. We are developing programs in peace, sustainability, health, and literacy. Almost always, we continue our support of women's studies and women's aspirations and when asked, we give our advice. But as our bodies have grown larger and gravity pulls us earthward, we are also trying to deal with the declining health of parents and our own changing physical realities. We are mourning the deaths of colleagues and loved ones. We are enjoying our grandchildren and youth generally as that which our past has made—the actors in our future.

Today as I work with Beverly Guy-Sheftall and Stanlie James on a sequel to the first black women's studies anthology *All the Women are*

White, All the Blacks are Men, but Some of Us are Brave, I am convinced that to be in "black women's studies" is to be, as our volume is titled, *Still Brave*. Today, as I work with colleagues new and old to celebrate the fortieth anniversary of the San Diego State University Department of Women's Studies, I am also commemorating definite changes in my old and my newer colleagues' attitudes about difference and cooperative relationships. A few years ago, at an NWSA conference, Carol Perkins and I attended the only session of which I have been aware that focused upon aging women's studies folk. I have talked with others of my generation (and some who just feel as if they were of my generation). I've learned from Judith Fetterly and Cynthia Enloe, from Johnnetta B. Cole and Valerie Smith, from Bonnie Zimmerman, Pat Huckle, Jackie Jones Royster, Jean Fagin Yellin, and many others about the new fears, frustrations, excitement, and pleasures that come from being eligible for social security and retirement. I am seeking a word to describe us—crones? bitches? foremothers?—but so far I have none better than our given names. That may be just as it should be. The details of my defining moments in women's studies are personal. But I know that most, if not all, of the women of color who participated in the early days of women's studies have had similar experiences. As I write this memoir, I know they will see themselves in many of my experiences. I know, also, that too many of those just entering women's studies are experiencing similar situations from the position of a different time and cultural context. I have the audacity to hope that as I share my memories, those coming after me will find somewhere in them the positive energy I found in the words of earlier women's writings.

WORKS CITED

Christian, Barbara. "But Who Do You Really Belong To—Black Studies or Women's Studies" (1989). In *Still Brave: The Evolution of Black Women's Studies*, edited by Stanlie M. James, Francis Smith Foster, and Beverly Guy-Sheftall. New York: Feminist Press, 2009. 86–91.

Quarrels into Ploughshares: Feminism and Race

Hortense J. Spillers

IT WOULD BE ACCURATE TO SAY THAT I backed into a series of essays that I never intended to write, all of them related to the feminist movement as it unfolded in the decade of the 1980s. But regarding those years from the vantage of the new century, it is as though things turned out exactly as they should have. It was not a secret for very long, if at all, that the near-simultaneous establishment of black studies and women's studies in the US academy would split this historic alliance right across the midriff of black women academics; no other constituency of the new academy, brought to stand around 1966, would be quite affected in the same way, and this shock of recognition appears to have alighted on an entire collective of historical subjects all at once rather than on a privileged visionary actor in splendid solitude. There we were, I recently explained to a class in feminist theory, trapped between two well-defined sociopolitical entities—actually, not so different from the current synthesis—and no clear way to negotiate a coherent and becoming response to a position that was not named. What to do? This writing, solicited by an old and persistent friend, marks an attempt to articulate that awakening that has disturbed my rest for the last three decades. Feeling noways tired yet, how little did one know it would last so long!

To name a moment of origin here (even though I will posit one, despite the denial) is rather like implementing an act of fiction—who can say how, when, where, why an impulse starts up? An itch on the brain, or the jump of the left or right eye, just under the bottom lid, and what it portends of what must be headed down the pike that your somatic organization is already registering it? Getting you ready to do something you have no idea you will be able to stand? Or perhaps not. But in any case, our bodies have far greater intelligence, we learn, than we would allow, although the origins of this story are embedded in an actual phone call. I remember receiving it—in the old days, back in the twentieth century, when we took every blast of the telephone, and answering machines belonged to the offices of CEOs—in the kitchen of my faculty house at Haverford. Carole Vance was on the other end, calling to invite me to Barnard College's well-known "Feminist and Scholar" conference series, this one, the ninth, to be devoted to an exploration of female sexuality. I cannot recall if I accepted the invitation right away because black women, chary of phone calls like the one I perceived this to be, were talking among ourselves about our token position at feminist conferences and how we should refuse to cooperate in it. But such decisions, taken before the fact, were usually hard to sustain and even harder to justify, inasmuch as feminists across the color spectrum all claimed to be devoted to anti-racist practices; not participating would not help that. In any case, the person with whom I was speaking, the future editor of *Pleasure and Danger: Exploring Female Sexuality*, seemed implicitly aware of the fragile moment that the movement had entered, but in her own courteous way did not seem prepared to take no for an answer. "Interstices: A Small Drama of Words" not only defined my contribution to "Feminist and Scholar" number nine, but also propelled me toward a project and commitment that I would pursue well beyond the occasion.

Anger has its uses, but I will not easily acknowledge that I have had and still have my share of it. In fact, a manuscript that I might write someday, still, was struck from the drawing board because the persona behind it was just too furious. But that gets ahead of the story.

The Barnard engagement, in turning my attention to another topic, one in which the investigator could not exactly stay neutral, brought me face to face with the politics of gender in the African American community, where the matter had been put off—indeed, cancelled—in the name of unity. We had urgent things to do, we said, and little of it had to do with gender, but one looked askance at that idea as it came out the mouth. It was clearer and clearer to me, however, that this side of my parents' generation, the problem of "intramural" equality between black men and women was something of an elephant in the room, especially given the powerful impact of the romance of Black Nationalist machismo on the African American psyche. Getting into this swirl of wish and desire, real things and illusion, was going to bring on a genuine headache that I would have preferred to avoid. In other words, when I opened this door, in 1982–83, and *stopped*, rather than peeped in, things looked a mess, precisely because we were in the very midst of change! The difficult reconciliation was the fact that change, when it happens at all, occurs in dribs and drabs, or to put it nicely, by increment. Between "Interstices" and the new century, I would have to learn greater calm, if not patience.

The problematic that I wanted to identify and name in my Barnard essay and many of the ones that followed was that of recognition. It will be objected that this thematic demarcates the universal human, which might well be the case, and therefore, all the more reason that it would appear before me as a *particular attitude* of a more general problematic. We know now that the situation of the African American women's community in its cultural, political, historical, and social dimensions inspired intersectional theory, or the convergence of race, gender, and class analyses, but the hidden or obscure constituents of this positionality are not the ones that openly declare their riddle. Rather, they assume the more evasive and sporadic puzzles and haltings that come and go with virtually subjective urgency—that is, the doubly intramural threat that falls out as a formidable muteness in the confrontation between "lookalikes." In other words, African American women as historical subjects are *like* African American men, qua black people, while they share a status with white women, qua women. The final inflection of this subjective calculus is perhaps the most difficult one to bring to light: African American women's relation to one another.

In this cross-hatch of motives, black women, at least from the point of view of the newly enforced civil rights practices, were lost in the transit from one to the other. What I wanted to do was capture the yawing motion in between, in which case legislation is powerless to intercede: for instance, you cannot take a "brother" to court for cat-calling you or a friend, or who makes you the object in song and verse of the lowest human image and idea that he is capable of concocting in his adolescent brain, any more than you can haul before a magistrate your white women colleagues, who, when called upon to project a "progressive" view of social relations, are mired in "(white) women and black (men)" like a broken LP and of an analogous technological vintage. This practice was so persistent a feature of the new stage of relations that it yielded a piece of proverbial folk wisdom, genially invented during the "battles" to win the "war": "All the blacks are men, all the women are white."

Just so, you cannot lock up a "sister" who "loves" theory as long as it emanates from somebody's mouth other than another black female one. These instances of engagement—beneath the radar of law and quite beside the point of judicial and public personality—hinder any easy apportionment of heroes and demons. We are nonetheless bent on solutions—at least an improvement on the question—even if this requires the revision of outmoded conceptual tools. The peculiar contribution of postmodern theory, in full throttle backlash at that precise moment, was to conceptualize out of contemporaneity not only the potential force of a corrected emancipatory protocol, but also to delegitimate and excise whole precincts of feeling that necessitated reconsiderations of the ethical imperative. In short, one was about to be intimidated into a tonguelessness as old as Philomela's. Perhaps it will be clearer, via these fictions of actual life, why, by 1996, some people were pretty pissed off.

To claim that the work that the investigator here was trying to perform was relatively unprecedented will sound boastful, but the truth of it is far narrower, more pointed, and quite a lot harder to explain than it seems. The assertion is *not* claiming that African American women in their historical vocation had not accumulated a respectable quantity of self-referential and socially responsive projects by the late twentieth century, but, rather, that their critical and theoretical engagement with intellectual technologies had been severely circumscribed by the very nature of the historical case (and what *was* the historical case?). Who is "she" as both a subject and an object of contemplation *in writing* and, as Nahum Chandler asks, as a "subject for thought"? As far as I can tell, no generation before the baby boomers had put this question to black women, even though W. E. B. DuBois's subject of "double consciousness" and Alain Locke's prime mover of the "New Negro" had both launched this problematic in implicit relation to African American manhood. The game here, then, was to catch up in all the directions and not only to advance the question, but perhaps to revise it to the degree that gender and sexuality might then be rethought as a *not*-given, becoming, instead, a historically ordained punctuality—something that history plays around with.

Long before these researches appeared, Simone de Beauvoir had famously noted that "One is not born, but rather becomes, a woman." But in truth, nearly three decades later, this historic assertion could not have been taken up simply as a grant of theoretical sanction to global communities of women, alien to a putative entity called the "European Union," and perhaps least of all by women-as-existents located in a post-slavery political synthesis. Despite the universal posture and appeal of de Beauvoir's classic work, its field of reference could not be extended to a broader application of meaning precisely because of racialized perceptions of identity peculiar to the modern world and, in the case of African American women, their general assessment of the uses and resources of feminism. While no single individual can justifiably contend that all of any totality believe any one thing, I do think that black women in certain quarters have entertained serious doubts over time about the efficacies of feminism and the women's movement. It was not unusual to hear it said in the eighties that if only racism would "go away," then black women could very well take care of the rest of it—as in "dealing" with their men—or even that, given black women's quite remarkable "strength" in the face of Everything, they really did not "need" a women's movement like women in the dominant group did. No investigators were more diligently concerned to probe such claims than Barbara Smith, bell hooks, and Michele Wallace. As a result of these thinkers, as well as a number of others, feminist work emerging in the academy of the eighties and nineties was pressured soon enough to respond to projects that tended to shift the debate from center to margin.

To have been involved in what was essentially a revolt *within* the academy meant a willingness to take risks, insofar as the most inveterate interlocutors of the established canons of scholarly writing and practice in some cases not only held the new researches in contempt, but often enough evinced no interest in them whatsoever and little or no inclination to understand why or how such ideas had been engendered in the first place. The level of self-righteous incuriosity in some academic circles is really quite astonishing, as common as it remains. One did not expect it here and consequently was caught rather flatfooted when there turned out to be "shootin in dem dar hills." In its guise of intellectual hostility, racist sentiment assumed an especially virulent brand of malice that marks a special chapter in the history of higher education in the United States between the mid-seventies and the turn of the millennium. But one quickly acquired certain skills of survival, among them obedience to an implicit caveat: keep your head down, and by all means keep moving! For women without helpers or mentors, lookouts or redoubts, this was not bad advice. The absence of models here or narratives to throw light on this particular landscape and its treacherous ground was painful, but no matter. We became the narrative we were looking for, as the occasion itself could be seized to advantageous ends.

The establishment of black studies as an interdisciplinary curricular object in the context of predominantly white institutions put "race" on the table, often in heroic accents and hagiographical modes of response. Breaking through the inherited modalities *and* the emergent ones took on urgency because the latter tended to overlook the problem of gender, indeed, to excise it. Because slavery and its impact on the entire Atlantic world are so consequential to Western development, history bleeds into the study of literature. Starting from the mid-eighties, my own cross-disciplinary interests in both black studies and women's studies meant that my way of looking at things traversed both orbits. For example, a central chapter in the making of the US nation-state, the "tragic mulatto/a," was both a literary and historical question for African American as well as for American literature. But it seemed that historical certitude had foreclosed on its reappearance as a genuine puzzle. To my mind, something akin to it had occurred regarding the problematic of slavery so much so that there seemed nothing new to discover, especially in light of the distinguished historians' marque that had accorded preeminent status to slavery studies for at least two generations. In short, if a non-historian were going to breach this formidable threshold, then she would be wise to do so in fear and trembling. But the urge to speak and to speak critically in an apparent discursive vacuum meant that one did not have the luxury to do too much of either.

Stylistically and with regard to method, the outcome might be described as "wild" theory: the procedures of the writing do not profess or intend to belong to any particular school of practice, but, rather, mimic certain tendencies that would mark them according to contemporary categories of alignment, primarily the refusal of closure at the level of the sentence. In this instance, the basic unit of composition is not the paragraph, as we imagine criticism conventionally proceeding, but the agonism or struggle is redirected into the *line*—both of the period and the reasoning—wherein I perceived that so much damage had been done to black personality. Therefore, one was attempting to "break the line," to echo Pound at a very different location, and to write a new one that opened up declarative possibilities beyond the traditional assurances that would brook no interference. To that extent, stylistic consciousness, even a level of attention that might translate into anxiety, takes on a political character, as I understand it.

What we must grasp about the critical and theoretical engagements of black academicians writing in the late century is precisely this anxiety of attention to the long venerable ages of Western scholarship that had sealed up the epistemological and ontological outlook of black life and thought and its ramifications as a done deal. To speak, then, of "epistemic violence" is not an otiose search for a fancy name, but, rather, illuminates the actual harm of the dominant word in its "civilizing mission" that has often enough "unmade" the world of the other Others. At the same time, one was *in* the academy and *of* its "tribes." Generally speaking, the deconstructive urgencies that characterized continental thinking in the postwar period seemed to sweep across the Atlantic as the conceptual "answer" to what was otherwise a left/youth movement, with global implications. Oddly enough, such accents seemed especially appropriate to the putative "outsiderly" status of the academy's new actors.

The topic of slavery, in its time-honored appeal, reappeared as a *literary* thematic, partially related to the influence of Darwin Turner's annually-convened Institute of Afro-American Culture, held at the University of Iowa. The institute in turn provoked new researches on the slave narrative in the 1970s, which work advanced it as a proto-typical generic formation that engendered successive generations of prose narrative as a staple of black American literary tradition. This rather radical shift of domain from the historian's purview to that of the literary critic's brought about interesting spatial and conceptual relocations of the study of the slave narrative as well as critical inquiries into the institution of slavery itself. For instance, "Slavery and the Literary Imagination" was adopted as the theme of the 1987 meeting of the English Institute at Harvard University. In an essay written expressly for that occasion—"Changing the Letter: The Yokes, the Jokes of Discourse, or Mrs. Stowe and Mr. Reed"—I attempted to recast the slavery debate as a crisis in terminology that would enable the descendants of the enslaved to return to the problematic in anticipation of this difference. By confronting slavery as an unrelenting regime of terror that lasted at least two centuries across the life of the New World, the investigator could find no plateau of respite or reprieve from the frisson of fear that its descriptions induced. To that extent, the topic of slavery might be considered a still live wire of affect and intimidation.

But if we could conceive of this material and historical phenomenon as an instance of the play of signs as well, then we could lay hold of a strategy of mediation from which to examine its premises and practices. In other words, words, words, words about slavery made it, in effect, possible to contemplate, and it seemed to me that such a translation was exactly what Ishmael Reed's *Flight to Canada* had accomplished. In that way, slavery as a terministic regime became a kind of antidote to the poisons of its actual excesses that had no reason whatsoever not to go on, except that its human subjects, in an often fatal determination to change history as they had inherited it, coaxed its end. I had not thought before of literary criticism as a sort of prophylactic device, wielded against an infectious archival dissemination, but it seemed to me that here was one of its general uses that did not ward off the "real" world, as suspicion of criticism often posits, but, rather, aids in specific instances to navigate through it.

Going farther onto the historiographical and literary terrain of slavery's practices, I sensed this historic enormity as both the consequence of everyday practices (its diachronic dimensions) and a massively fortified structure of overarching political and economic apparatuses (its synchronic dimensions) that constitutional principles not only did not avert, but also handsomely complemented and rewarded insofar as the stately march of "private property" and its "freedom to use" and its vaunted liberty had broken through the protocols of primogeniture, or the orderly processions of inherited wealth in the placement of the first-born son. This was America, and "anything could happen in it" is precisely the fiction that came to be inscribed along with the laws of the "strong man" that sanctified the idea. In short, though slavery might have evolved, as some historians convincingly argue, its social and political logics took hold and proceeded astraddle the contestatory ground of democratic and republican aims. In the convergence of synchronic and diachronic themes, democratic and republican premises, slavery therefore had to traverse public and private interests that would draw gender into its folds not as a second thought to race, but as a fundamental aspect of its entire installation. Quite remarkably, however, gender under slavery's auspices assumed a highly nuanced character, skillfully calibrated to the rationalizations of profit margins and markets. On the one hand, there were the protocols of gender as they orchestrated the behavior of the patriarchal family attached to the interests of the dominant class; and on the other, the supra-familial claims of private property, authored by the same class, that manipulated gender arrangements through an extra step—that is to say, their becoming rankly malleable and porous. In this case, gender takes on a transparent degree of economic fungibility insofar as male can become female, or function as female, female, male, as conditions dictate. Where slavery reigned, gender, for all intents and purposes, did not practically exist for the bonded human being who slid over into the status of "thing."

In "Mama's Baby, Papa's Maybe," I wanted to name precisely this double operation as an inchoate notion that had suddenly sprung into the full blast of day: the status of the feminine/female generated different stakes for women according to racialized ascriptions of class, subtended by law and public policy. And therein lay the fundamental reason why, in the contemporary period, African American women had come to hold contrasting views of the feminist movement from those of Anglo-American women. What had happened historically was freighted with ontological implications—black women needn't be "women" at all, having no inherent right to such status. Their vulnerability to exposure, or their exclusion from whatever benefits accrued to patriarchy's protective engines, spoke voluminously: 1) it signaled the consolidation of the dominant class by walling off the intellectual and social energies of white women in the reductive frame of activity that would be later identified as the "cult of true womanhood"; 2) it melded the fortunes of African American males and females in a robustly race-based determination of human value, which gesture not only eliminated black subjects from the competitive energies of the modern world, but denied their human subjectness in the most general sense; and 3) it illuminated patriarchal status as the material embodiment of a constitutional perfection—the power of the law, the author of the law, and its reflection. Nothing had quite yet dispelled the long shadow that slavery's practices had thrown athwart the future. Here was a "situation for feminist inquiry," but the latter had invested the energy of its gaze elsewhere.

As a result, I set out to write an entire series of essays devoted to what I think of now as a ground-clearing exercise that would bring into view the interstitial and obscure historical character of African American women's discursive and critical positioning. "Mama's Baby,

Papa's Maybe" and "Changing the Letter" were among the series that included "An Order of Constancy: Notes on Brooks and the Feminine," "Notes on an Alternative Model—Neither/Nor," "'The Permanent Obliquity of an In(pha)llibly Straight': In the Time of the Daughters and the Fathers," and "Black, White, and in Color, or Learning How to Paint." In every instance, I thought of the writing as a "note," or a notation that would serve as a kind of placeholder—in other words, a stake in the ground that would mark out a plot to be worked and elaborated to the full in the future. But the route to something more definitive is always tied up with living itself, so that there is never any such thing as what we hope for—"work," on the one hand, divorced from the dreadful mundaneness of the everyday and its terrible failings and mishaps, and "life," on the other; in effect, what one is negotiating is a rather enormous mess, draped out as moments in the now. How you get a future out of such fleetingness rightly puzzles me, inasmuch as the philosophers didn't solve it either.

As I attempt to place myself "back there" and in the imaginative frame of mind out of which the work of those years was produced, the reel of my recollection unfolds nothing heady, or necessarily anything of archival interest—I know that I was in a hurry and in occasional revolt against the beloved country, seemingly hell-bent on electing who, to my mind, was usually the wrong guy for president. (Once upon a time, I was so annoyed about the new chief executive that I weaned off TV for eleven years! I made it back just in time to take in the Thomas–Hill debacle live and in color.) Multiple impressions seem to run off a mother-vein that had nothing at all to do with these writings or feminist commitments and disappointments or anti-race struggles, but now that I think about it, everything to do with the future and the largest stakes: I had not taught *Paradise Lost* in more years than I could remember when, one day in a Haverford classroom, having taught the epic to a junior class of majors, we'd come to the last day of our study of Milton and the end of the poem. Reading out loud the passage of the expulsion of the first couple, I suddenly stopped at: "The World was all before them, where to choose . . ." and for a beat could not continue, for fear of crying, embarrassing myself. I've always suspected, though, that no one noticed because the preceding end-stop line conveniently allows a pause. Days before, my brief marriage had ended in the most familiar of ruins so that Milton's "solitary way" and the unfolding panorama of the phenomenal world were not in that instant only an impressive and adventurous fiction in iambic rhythms, bled over from the seventeenth century, but were also a version of the stunning (and ordinary) fall that was always going on. One's writing against it—the confrontation that you are just as likely to lose as win—is the risk that one cannot refuse to take. If I'm not mistaken, feminist work of the last three decades—with so little to guarantee its perdurability—is precisely the game of risk that a generation chanced. We have not always agreed, have not always been pleasant, but despite all that, you have to admire it!

What I Have Learned as a Chicana Professor, or, "En Bocas Cerradas no Entran Moscas"

Tey Diana Rebolledo

RECENTLY A STUDENT IN MY CHI-cana literature class asked to interview me for her American history class at the University of New Mexico. The assignment was to interview someone who "had lived through the sixties." I certainly guess I qualify since I was born in 1937. When she came to my office, she asked me what I knew of the Chicano Movement and if I had participated in it. I told her my *veterano* stories of participating in the grape and lettuce boycotts of the United Farm Workers, of the dramas we used to stage in the supermarkets, asking people if they knew where the grapes and iceberg lettuce came from (California), why we were boycotting them (in support of the United Farm Workers and fair wages for Filipino and Chicano farm workers), and asking them not to buy the products. Of course, we never bought grapes or lettuce ourselves, and we asked restaurants not to buy them. To this day I still don't drink Gallo wine (Gallo wine-makers were one of the last holdouts). I told her how César Chávez came to Portland, Oregon, where I was living, and how my young daughter and I marched with him, how we sent money to the United Farm Workers Union. I told her how I had returned to graduate school at the University of Arizona, majoring in Spanish, and learned about Chicano literature from a lecture that Dr. Arturo Madrid had given there on Oscar Zeta Acosta's *The Autobiography of a Brown Buffalo*, and about my friend and co-student Margarita Cota-Cárdenas's poetry reading. At that lecture and at that poetry reading I recognized that there was a body of literature called Chicano literature.

I talked about the violent demonstrations against the Vietnam War in Portland, about the support for the civil rights movement, and about how the feminist movement made me rethink my life (I got divorced and returned to graduate school). The more I talked, the older I felt. She looked at me in astonishment and asked, "Did this change your life?"

"Absolutely," I replied. And added, "It was also a lot of fun."

She let out a big sigh and said, "I wish I had lived then."

Indeed, those were heady times, with many life-altering changes and also with many struggles. In the early 1970s, as a single mother, I went to the University of Arizona, studied Latin American literature, took probably the first class that was given at the university on Latin American women writers, and wrote my dissertation on a Mexican woman writer (Rosario Castellanos). I got several jobs at big universities and read Chicano literature at the moment it was developing. At conferences I would seek out Chicano/a books and writers. I would also talk to colleagues interested in the Chicano movement. When I began teaching at the University of Nevada, Reno, I began slipping Latin American women writers and Chicana writers into my general classes in Spanish and into my classes in Latin American literature. Of course, until then none of us had been trained in Chicano literature; it was more of a living experience. Several colleagues, my dissertation director Eliana Rivero, and I applied for a NEH grant to collect materials on Chicana writers and to write a critical book. We were turned down. It was one of the first times (but not the last) that we were asked if Chicana writers were any good. In 1984, with the help of the women's studies program and the Southwest Institute for Research on Women (and Myra Dinnerstein and Jan Monk, thanks guys) at the University of Arizona, Eliana and I reapplied and received a NEH grant. The result of that work was one of the first anthologies of Chicana literature, *Infinite Divisions: An Anthology of Chicana Literature*. By all indications the anthology is still widely used today.

Gaining credibility as a scholar in Chicano/a studies is another story, though, and it, too, has been a long struggle. However, it has been a struggle actively supported by students, coworkers, colleagues, and others both inside and outside the Chicano community. And so I think I do not write merely about what I have learned as a Chicana professor, but rather about what my generation (as few of us as there are) has experienced during these last thirty or so years. And I believe that the experience is not ours alone as Chicana/Latina professors, but also the experience of black and Native American scholars. We have been fortunate to have a cohort of teachers, writers, and artists who have struggled *juntas, que nos conocemos* (who know each other), and who together have helped establish and amplify this literature which records our shared experiences, experiences that are at once similar but at the same time different.

Over the last thirty-five years as a teacher at diverse universities, I have learned that students, not just Chicano/a students, are hungry to know of the lives and dreams of ethnic writers. Students love the readings we do in class, from classics of Chicano/a literature (yes, we do have classics!) to Chicano/a autobiography. In my classes, perhaps 90 percent of my students are of Hispano origin, and this is the first time many have seen their experiences reflected in their readings (well, maybe not the very first time; they might have read *Bless Me, Ultima* by Rudolfo Anaya or *The House on Mango Street* by Sandra Cisneros in high school). It is not unusual for students to comment that such and such a character is like their aunt or their grandmother or even themselves. And they like to try their hands at creative writing to complement their readings. (I usually have a creative component in the class.) In the autobiography class they read, they write their own autobiographies, and they cry. Sometimes the books we read are much too close to their lives, in terms of the struggles against racism, poverty, sexism, classism: here I am thinking of Helena María Viramontes' *Under the Feet of Jesus* and Demetria Martínez's *MotherTongue*.

As a Chicana professor, I have learned that you have to prove yourself, over and over. I remember that when I first came up for tenure I was asked to provide a list of the number of subscribers to each journal in which I had published. This was, I think, to prove that Chicano literature was a scholarly field. I complied with the request, indicating also the institutions that the readers represented, but went a bit further. I investigated the number of subscribers to the scholarly journals in which our esteemed French medievalist published. Imagine that the readers of Chicano scholarly publications substantially outnumbered the readers of the French medievalist's journals!

As a Chicana professor I have learned that you cannot be quiet. You constantly have to remind your department, your colleagues, and particularly your administration that you are a viable and important presence in the university. You need to continue to communicate with this diverse community even if you are a shy, retiring person. It helps to put on national conferences that attract lots of other scholars and students and that have interesting and provocative titles. If you can create controversy during these conferences, so much the better. In other words, a public face is important for communities within and without the university. In one 1986 conference at the University of New Mexico, "Reconstructing the Canon; Chicano Writers and Critics: A Symposium on American Literature," we paired a Chicano/a critic with a Chicano/a writer in a number of consecutive events. One of the students who attended the conference series and who is not a Chicana recently told me that the conference had been a turning point in her life. It was a moment when she opened her mind and thinking to different perspectives, to other ways of being. I am constantly asked for the poster of the conference where we inserted Chicano texts into a shelf filled with books of canonical American literature. It was our response to being asked "if Chicano/a writers were any good."

I have learned that we must continue to work toward inserting Chicana and Latina works into our educational process. I remember well that when I was in college in the 1950s, the so-called canon in Spanish was a very small-minded and limited one indeed. We read many undistinguished works by nineteenth-century male writers (many of which are no longer taught in any courses), a few select sacred texts (including, of course, *Don Quijote*), and in advanced litera- ture courses only a few women: the Mexican poet and feminist Sor Juana Inés de la Cruz, the Chilean Nobel Prize winner Gabriela Mis- tral, and the Argentine poet Alfonsina Storni. There were none of the political and social texts these women had written on the position of women, their struggle as writers in a male-dominated society, or their poems of passion and desire. These strong and resistant poems were generally not included in the anthologies of Latin American literature edited by men; perhaps in the 1950s they were considered too incendi- ary. Later, when I taught a course on Latin American women writers at the University of New Mexico, I was asked by a male colleague why I felt I had to teach such a course. I asked him how many women he included in his survey of Latin American literature. "One," he said, "Sor Juana." "That's the reason," I answered. With this sort of resis- tance in a literature already considered to be part of the canon, you can imagine the resistance to a "new" Chicana/o literature.

Although we have made some headway in inclusiveness in the liter- ary canon, the struggle is not yet over. Now we struggle to include both Chicana and Latina writers into Latin American literature courses, American literature courses, and American studies courses. And, unfortunately, we continue to be asked the same questions: Why? Are they any good? I have learned that you cannot let yourself or your discipline be belittled or put down, and you must be prepared for small thinking, for the insidious remark, for the lofty put-down. And you must do it wisely, intelligently, and creatively. Moreover, as critics and scholars we need to "have the courage to persist and maintain lines of inquiry that are not mainstream" (Rebolledo, *Chronicles* 33).

I have learned that you must continue to dream. I have written elsewhere about my dreams of inclusiveness of Chicana scholars and writers at all levels of the profession. Additionally, the creativity of Chicanas has been elaborated by Chicana artists who have long had a symbiotic relationship with writers, working together to insert Chica- nas into subjectivity and exploring a Chicana aesthetic. As I asserted in my book *The Chronicles of Panchita Villa*, "the contemporary Chicana subject remains in a pondering, contemplative, ironic questioning mode" (71–73). I am sure that the Chicana professors and students I know are still in that same space today. These dreams have been aided by the fact that many Chicana writers and scholars *no tienen pelos en la lengua*, are not afraid to speak up and to speak out. This is not an easy thing for Chicanas to do when, as children, we are cautioned to be respectful, to be seen and not heard: we are told, *"En bocas cerradas no entran moscas"* (flies don't enter a closed mouth), a *dicho* that any Chicana would recognize.

It has been a long haul since Gloria Anzaldúa, Sandra Cisneros, Ana Castillo, and others explored and commented on that silence we had been subjected to for so long in order for Chicana writers to voice all those hidden disappointments, traumas, and desires. Anzaldúa called us *deslenguadas* ("without tongues," unable to speak). As Lucha Corpi wrote about the paralyzed voice, "I learned silence, painfully, slowly, as one learns to write, stroke by stroke until the letter's form and sound is etched on the whiteness of the paper, and voice uncovers its reason for being" (150). In a more violent image in a recurring nightmare, Corpi continued, "I couldn't begin to describe the horror of it all. This time it was a man, and he sliced my tongue . . . What clearly frightens me most is that I didn't fight him. I let him maim me. He took away my tongue. My tongue!" (127).

Pat Mora describes the silencing of Chicanas in this way:

> *Virgin mothers.*
> *Women of closed*
> *uterus. Women*
> *of closed*
> *mouths. Women*
> *of covered*
> *hair. Women*
> *of cloaked*
> *bodies.*
> *Who crush*
> *víboras. Women*
> *who crush their*

own tongues.
Silent women.
Altered women. (66)

The silences here are not only verbal but also sexual, and Mora calls on us to "Alter / the Altered women" (66). She calls upon us to utilize the sensual snake image and to become "loose-tongued women. Open-mouth women. Open women" (66).

Over and over, that learned silence, that learned passivity has been breached. Mora counsels us "Oye: Sometimes raising the voice does get attention" (77). More recently, Sandra Cisneros shouted gleefully, "By all accounts I am / a danger to society. / I'm Pancha Villa. / I break laws, / upset the natural order, / anguish the Pope and make fathers cry. / I am beyond the jaw of law. / I'm *la desperada*, most-wanted public enemy. / My happy picture grinning from the wall" (113–14). She concurs with Mora about raising the voice and creating an *escandalosa malcriada* image of the Chicana, writing,

I'm an aim-well,
shoot-sharp
sharp-tongued,
sharp-thinking,
fast-speaking,
foot-loose,
loose-tongued,
let-loose,
woman-on-the-loose
loose-woman. Beware, honey. (114–15)

As can be seen, for the last forty years (has it been that long already?), Chicana writers and scholars have been persistently opening up a space to define themselves. Today to be a bad girl, a *malcriada*, seems to be "in." Chicana writers are letting it all hang out. No longer is it a secret to be sexual, to be lesbian, to be vocal. But it has been a long time coming.

Several months ago I went to a panel discussion for a Chicana art show titled "Bad Girls: Las Hociconas." Both the show and the panel were precisely about silence, voice, and the power to speak; about taboos, about sex, about violence, about our other selves. The women who were included in the show clearly see themselves as *malcriadas*, bad girls who are speaking up and seizing their voices. The panel was a contestation and a dialogue with an incident in 2001 when a show in Santa Fe, "Cyber Arte," attracted a good deal of controversy because of a digital painting by Alma López depicting the Virgin of Guadalupe in a rose-covered bathing suit, and standing in a way that not only displayed her body but also her power. At her feet, the angel holding her up was portrayed bare-breasted. This small piece generated physical and verbal threats against the artist and the curator of the show, Tey Marianna Nunn, and condemnation by the archbishop of Santa Fe and others. Many academics and community members, however, defended the show and the artist's right to portray the Virgin of Guadalupe icon as a powerful woman. In the current "Badgirls" show, then, eighteen artists displayed provocative works challenging traditional notions of womanhood, saying "that there is a Chicana badgirl in every one of us, speaking truths, visions, hopes and criticism necessary to greater individual integrity and to the acceptance of seemingly irreconcilable differences within our own selves, and thereby our families, our communities" (Pérez 5). The show is the culmination of a long-running commentary that has been at the root of Chicana feminism: how do Chicanas of all ages, social ranks, and geographical locations learn to find their voices, speak up, and fight back? As one of the co-curators noted, "Chicana badgirls, *hociconas*, big mouths, loud mouths, women who talk back. They're the ones who won't stay quiet, who won't make nice, won't pretend everything's okay when it's not. Badgirl *hociconas* don't behave in a world of double-standards, whether these be men over women, heterosexuals over queer folk, haves over have nots, 'white' people over those 'of color,' and so on. They shouldn't" (Pérez 3). It seems, then, that these long years of Chicana feminist writers, critics, and artists have taken root, deep deep root, spread the seeds, and are producing a harvest of creativity, determination, and above all, voice.

Over the years, I have learned that it is good to have colleagues, partners, children, friends, and family who support your efforts and believe in your causes. It helps if they are *malcriados/as* also. As I said in my "Chronicles of Panchita Villa: Episode Two" essay, "I would like to acknowledge all my revolutionary co-troublemakers who function on the theory of Bad Conduct, who resist tradition and easy answers, who want to revolutionize the world to make it more just for all its people, who desire a system of knowledge and learning that is truly egalitarian and who support teachers, texts, and critics who represent the other. I acknowledge those troublemakers who are not afraid to question established systems and who are on the edge of the wave of new learning. These are the colleagues who understand that revolution is the only real road to learning. And especially, I want to acknowledge Sor Juana, who questioned and who clearly understood that language and knowledge are tools in the stairway to the pyramid of the mind" (22–23).

Finally I have learned that you not only have to find your own voice, you must also listen to it. As Pat Mora has stated in her "Cuarteto Mexicano," "Oye: Never underestimate the power of the voice" (77).

WORKS CITED

Cisneros, Sandra. *Loose Woman*. New York: Alfred A. Knopf, 1994.

Corpi, Lucha. *Delia's Song*. Houston: Arte Público, 1989.

Mora, Pat. *Agua Santa. Holy Water*. Boston: Beacon Press, 1995.

Pérez, Laura. "Con o Sin Permiso (With or Without Permission): Chicana Badgirls: Las Hociconas," in *Chicana Badgirls: Las Hociconas. Exhibition Catalogue*. Albuquerque: 516 Arts, 2009.

Rebolledo, Tey Diana. *The Chronicles of Panchita Villa and other Guerrilleras. Essays on Chicana/Latina Literature and Criticism*. Austin: University of Texas Press, 2005.

The Psychoanalyst,
the Sociologist,
and the Feminist:
A Retrospect

Nancy J. Chodorow

IN THE SPRING OF 1969, I WENT TO MY first conference on "women's liberation." I was twenty-five and a budding social scientist about to switch from anthropology to sociology, with an (already psychologically overdetermined) interest in child development and the relations of psyche and culture. I had made it my business intuitively to choose an undergraduate field—anthropology—in which there had been an unusual number of prominent women and in which I could actually work with women professors. Moreover, my own subspecialty, psychological anthropology, had investigated the psychology of gender in culture, especially through the work of Margaret Mead. For many years, however, no social science, including psychological anthropology, had focused on or problematized women or gender. As for numbers of women of my generation, the women's movement exhilarated and propelled me into awareness.

The following fall, during the first semester of my graduate studies in sociology, I wrote what would become my first published paper, "Being and Doing: A Cross-Cultural Examination of the Socialization of Males and Females." At this time, American feminists had begun to conceptualize and document sexism in political, economic, and familial institutions. Sexism was external, and although the personal was political, this meant that feelings were caused by external forces, not that we needed to investigate their internal constitution and creation. Yet "Being and Doing" located the origins of male dominance not externally but internally, in men's dread of women and fear of their own femininity, and it suggested that men's and women's bisexual identifications were asymmetrical, the man's more threatening. I contrast women's more easily attained feminine identity, based on "being," with men's constantly challenged masculine identity, based on "doing," and I describe a "self-perpetuating cycle of female deprecation" in which mothers transmit to daughters their own anxieties and conflicts about femininity (41). At a time when few women did so, and when feminist theory was not on the map, I claimed space as a theorist, and I worked from within a paradigm, psychoanalysis, that has always provided a challenge to sociological thinking.

This first publication of mine anticipates many of the themes found in subsequent psychoanalytic rethinkings of femininity, as well as constituting a protomodel of my own later work. My argument here, as in many of my writings, begins with a single, self-evident, taken-for-granted but previously unnoticed or unstudied feature of the psychic or cultural world and elaborates the consequences of this fact from within. In what would become characteristically Chodorovian fashion, I unabashedly invent theory, putting together observations from different studies and drawing upon evidence and (sometimes apparently contradictory) theories from a variety of fields.

In "Being and Doing," the self-evident observation is that male dominance seems to be universal. I ask, how can we account for this? In my next publications—"Family Structure and Feminine Personality" (written in dialogue and dividing the territory with Shelly Rosaldo, who wrote on social structure, and Sherry Ortner, who wrote on culture), "Oedipal Asymmetries and Heterosexual Knots," and *The*

Reproduction of Mothering—I begin from the fact that women mother, a completely self-evident, taken-for-granted fact that at the same time had been theoretically and clinically unremarked. In "Heterosexuality as a Compromise Formation," I observe that heterosexuality has been taken for granted as normative, not only culturally but within psychoanalysis, and that it has therefore not been studied. I ask, what if we treat heterosexuality as problematic, as we have done with homosexuality and the perversions? In *The Power of Feelings*, I begin from basic psychoanalytic observations: the documented existence and effect of dynamically unconscious mental processes, thoughts, and feelings, and the finding that meaning comes from within as much as from without. I argue against assumptions found in feminist poststructuralism, cultural studies, and social science, that people (gender and sexuality) are shaped culturally and discursively from without rather than creating their own psyches (their own gender and sexuality) from within.

Just as with the classical writings on female psychology, there is some implicit autobiographical input in my first contributions. I do not think that without a personal analysis, a strong mother and maternal lineage, and early experiences of finding myself a cultural outsider, my writings would have the emotional and affective solidity and resonance that they possess. Yet, in spite of being a member of the feminist generation who believed that the personal was political and knowledge perspectival, that the female scholarly "I" should replace the male objectivist view from nowhere, my writings (at least until well into the 1990s) do not begin from a female experiential voice. My voice seems characterized rather by clarity and confidence, even by a certain courage: "This is what I think, there is no other way I can think, all I can do is present it to you, as directly as possible." When I first presented "Family Structure and Feminine Personality" to a group of feminist English faculty in the Boston area in 1972, I was accused of being too confident and of "writing like a man": how could I begin so directly, "I propose here a model . . ." (45)? I was shocked, in 1978, upon first encountering *l'écriture feminine*, to find that French feminists like Irigaray and Cixous believed that traditional language and modes of argument were phallologocentric.

My voice, perhaps, echoes those no-nonsense, traditionally Western, pioneer lineage women with whom I grew up, or my Jewish New Yorker mother, all of whom had been professionals—teachers, librarians, social workers, scientists—before marriage, women of that pre-feminine mystique 1890–1920 birth cohort with higher education and more professional participation than those who came before or after them. Perhaps in my voice there is also a paternal identification—hence, writing like a man: my father, a professor of physics and applied physics and Silicon Valley pioneer, once told me that while he was not a great theoretical physicist, he had a special capacity to see linkages—connections among disparate scientific insights—in ways that enabled him to conceptualize comprehensively, leaving nothing out, how these might all be put together to work perfectly in a new instrument or process.

A traditional stance toward voice continues, as I resist those postmodern locutions and wordplays that became so prominent in academic feminism and the humanities and that have entered into relational feminist writing. I have written that the difference between women psychoanalysts of the second and third psychoanalytic generations and feminist psychoanalysts of my own was that for us the theoretical was personal: we evaluated psychoanalytic theories of femininity against our personal experience. But it is not the case that I brought in personal experience, or shifted voice, in making my theoretical arguments. Thus, even as I begin from experience, from a freedom to challenge, and from a sense that knowledge is perspectival and derived from power, I have found myself on the classical-modernist side, or somewhere in the middle—in psychoanalysis as in feminism—of a divide about evidence and language.

My work has always received attention somewhere, but often belatedly, and not necessarily from its intended audience. *The Reproduction of Mothering* was immediately recognized and lauded within the feminist humanities, ambivalently accorded admiration but also widely criticized in my then exclusive field, sociology, and only noticed within psychoanalysis many years later. Articles that became classics, widely reprinted and cited, were originally rejected or subject to withering critique by reviewers for journals.

Since this question of hybrid-margin-cusp is so central to my identity and work, I will expand upon it for a bit. When I was honored in 2004 by the program that enables academics to be trained in the American Psychoanalytic Association (CORST: the Committee on Research and Special Training), I titled my talk, "Why It Is Easy to Be a Psychoanalyst and a Feminist, but Not a Psychoanalyst and a Social Scientist" (I joked that I almost called the talk "From Margin to Margin and Back Again"). There, I described the experience in 1979 of simultaneously receiving the Jessie Bernard Award for *The Reproduction of Mothering* from the American Sociological Association and being in a symposium on the book (later published in *Signs*) in which Judith Lorber observed, "When I read *The Reproduction of Mothering*, I found to my disappointment that it is primarily an exegesis of psychoanalytic theory and therefore, in my eyes, a lesser contribution to the sociology of gender than Nancy Chodorow's earlier, short pieces" (482), and Alice Rossi said, "I was not prepared for so extended an exegesis of psychoanalytic theory past and present . . . what constitutes 'evidence' in Chodorow's book[?] . . . does her central insight require the burden of so much psychoanalytic theory?" (493; Rossi also took me to task for my radical anti-biologism). Only Rose Coser enthusiastically supported my use of psychoanalytic theory in the work.

For years afterward, in sociology meetings, I would wander into session after session on gender, feminist theory, or mothering, only to hear someone saying, "We can take seriously five different understandings of women's mothering [or sexual inequality], but Chodorow's individualistic psychology is not one of them." A former student, Michigan Professor of Sociology Karin Martin, remarked, when we were at a UC-wide academic-psychoanalytic conference, "Have you noticed, Nancy? All the feminists here, except you, are in the humanities, and all the social scientists, except you, are men?" Just before I left academia (an early "retirement," in order to move east and begin a full-time clinical practice), my department chair graciously invited me to offer a final seminar, "Chodorow: Theorizing and Theory," on my own work. The department graduate assistant, upon hearing this, said to me, "I hope you're doing something that the students want, not just Freud!"

I have to acknowledge some truth to my sociology colleagues' critique and unease. Even as I have drawn upon many theories, my "field" has always been, basically, psychoanalysis. I have always been interested in the complexities of individuality, and I think that the absence of serious attention to individuality as a field of study in its own right is a great lack in the academy. I've never studied groups, institutions, organizations, stratification, collective behavior, or any other typical sociological topic, and I don't do research. I came to feminism in the first place partly because it called for an understanding of the psyche, along with culture, society, and politics, and my feminist friends welcomed my interests and knowledge.

While my sociological colleagues were excoriating my individualistic psychology, colleagues in the humanities—in literary criticism, philosophy, and political theory—were writing books and dissertations based on my work. My focus on the mother–daughter internal world and its sequelae opened new vistas for understanding women authors, women characters in women's novels, and imagery, metaphor, and characteristics found in women's writing. My characterization of the female psyche, in terms of relation and connection, and my noting the defensive denial of connection and dependency in men, served as a basis for thinking in moral philosophy and epistemology and for critiques of normal science, classical political theory, and so forth. For many practitioners of these literary and textual-theoretical academic feminisms (at least until the poststructural and Lacanian turn), my work was almost idealized (when it wasn't criticized for its psychoanalytically-inspired "difference feminism," "universalizing and essentializing," or purported homophobia and class prejudice). It was certainly considered a founding feminist theory.

When at thirty years of age I finished the dissertation that became *The Reproduction of Mothering*, a daughter but not yet a mother, a psychoanalytic sociologist whose first intellectual love had been psychological anthropology but not yet a psychoanalyst, I had had, as a feminist, during its writing, the dubious benefit mainly of the sharp critique and dismissal of psychoanalysis found in de Beauvoir, Friedan, Millett, and others. I could also draw upon a few psychoanalytic feminist books and articles that appeared from 1971 to 1978, during the period from beginning the dissertation to book publication.

Thinking about context is important for psychoanalysis as well as for feminism. As we look back over the development of psychoanalytic thinking about women, and the place that my own work, along with that of other feminists, played in psychoanalysis itself, we can recall what Fliegel calls "the [40-year] quiescent interval" in thinking about women (17), an interval brought to an end by psychoanalytic feminism, and then, almost in response, psychoanalysis. These changes did not simply emerge from within psychoanalysis, through the disconfirming of hypotheses and "normal" scientific progress. Rather, theorizing and critique mainly from without came slowly to be accepted from within, leading to major breakthroughs in understandings of gender and sexuality, changes in psychoanalytic attitudes toward mothers, and increased attention, revaluation, and depathologization of "pre-Oedipal" levels of functioning. In addition, feminism as a social and political force propelled greater numbers of women into the professions, and psychoanalytic institutes began accepting more women candidates, so that women now (or once again) form a strong presence in American psychoanalytic societies.

In a preface to the second edition of *The Reproduction of Mothering*, I sought to restate the book's basic contribution, which was not so much its feminist politics as its theorizing the psychology of women and maternal subjectivity, as I put it: "The enduring contribution of the book . . . is in its understanding of important aspects of female development and the female psyche . . . the mother-daughter relationship and how women create and recreate this relationship internally" (1999b, vii). This specific project had wide impact, anticipating and providing groundwork for feminist self-in-relation theory, theories of women's voice and morality, relational psychoanalysis, and other critiques of classical psychoanalytic theories.

Throughout, even as I am critical, I draw capaciously from previous psychoanalytic writing. I do not summarily dismiss any of Freud's claims. Partly, I am a serious theorist; partly, I am a dutiful, if challenging, daughter (just as, in arguments with my father, I was always careful to be rational and articulate rather than emotional, citing facts and grounding arguments). This is one component of my work's strength: the theory is complex and elaborated. But there is little feminist outrage. The theory may have been radical, but the writer was not.

I am only intemperate and overly dismissive, as I note in my 1999 preface (and as Rossi had rightly noted earlier) about biological explanations for maternality: not yet a mother, swept up in 1970s' feminism, I leave no room at all for the possible influence, however clinically and developmentally individual, of libido, lust, physical maternal passion and desire, or for the demands for psychic representation and fantasy of bleeding, breasts, arousal, pregnancy, and lactation (it would be no surprise to a psychoanalyst that I seem to have been from the beginning more intemperate in regard to theories about the body than about anything else that contributes to psychic life).

As I also remark in the preface to the second edition of *The Reproduction of Mothering*, the call for shared parenting at the end of the book gives short shrift to the very psychic developments—maternal passions, desires, and capacities in women—that the book documents. The account should have led to thinking about policies that would recognize mothers and enhance the mother–child relationship, providing family supports, parental leaves, and so forth, but the shared parenting call—as with other feminist claims about no gender differences—could be used instead in fathers' rights movements and in family policies, like workfare, that implied that any caregiver would do. I have written, in "'Too Late': Ambivalence About Motherhood, Choice, and Time," about how this call has come back to haunt me, how patients, students, and young colleagues claim, using it along with other feminist and culturally rationalized defenses and tropes against exploring intrapsychic conflicts and ambivalence about motherhood, that they will not have children unless their husbands agree to do half the childcare.

The main outcome of my thinking in the book was professional development rather than more writing: I concluded, quite rightly, that I had gone as far as I could in thinking about the psyche from within, rather than about the contours of theory from without, without clinical experience and psychoanalytic training, which I began in the mid-1980s. In anticipation of applying for this training, and perhaps in a tacit search for the professional reproduction of mothering, I undertook in 1980 an interview study of early women psychoanalysts. I wanted to hear, from these women themselves, how it came to be that there were, compared to other professions, such a large number of women psychoanalysts among the second and third generations (those analyzed by Freud, Ferenczi, Abraham, and others of the first generation and those analyzed by their analysands). I wondered what it was like for these women, and, especially, how they came to understand and internalize Freud's theories of femininity, which were such a challenge and insult to women of my generation.

As with my theoretical work, I seem even in this historical and sociological project presciently to have made problematic the heretofore unnoticed and taken-for-granted. In 1980, when I began the research, there was little published work on female psychoanalysts. Within ten years, over twenty-five biographies and autobiographies of individual early women analysts had appeared, as well as several studies of women as a collective presence in the post-Freudian period. Today, we find plays and films about these women.

In this research, I learned of the family culture of psychoanalysis—the analytic couples and parent–child lineages that are still with us and that give psychoanalysis something of a craft and guild character. I described, in implicit and explicit contrast to what I saw in the academy, what I called the several "hats" that psychoanalysts can wear—clinician, teacher, theoretician, writer, institutional mover and shaker—which, along with the sense that psychoanalysis required both a kind of knowledge (about children, families, feelings, the psyche) and stance (listening, empathy, careful attention to the other) that women were particularly likely to have, allowed women not only to participate but to gain recognition and eminence. Unlike in psychiatry or any other medical, scientific, or academic field, recognition and advancement in psychoanalysis came in the first instance from clinical acumen rather than from research or writing—it is as if you built your skills in the academy initially from teaching rather than writing, and that later on, you could write and get recognition based on your teaching immersion and skills.

The field, then, recognized that part of its practice in which women, balancing family and work, were as likely to participate as men (for years, I noticed how passionate analysts were about their clinical work, whatever else they did professionally, in contrast to the standard academic attitude toward teaching: when you ask someone how they are, they are likely to report with relief about an upcoming sabbatical, or the beginning of the summer—whatever gets them away from the classroom or lecture hall).

On the matter of the theory of femininity, which was of equal concern to me as the question of what facilitated female participation, my encounter with my interviewees was perhaps the first step in my own move toward rethinking and revaluing the theory. In the reflexive paper "Seventies Questions for Thirties Women: Gender and Generation in a Study of Early Women Psychoanalysts," I came to see for the first time that the views of my own feminist psychoanalytic generation, while partly based on progress in knowledge and theoretical advances, were also partly a product of our own generational location and (lack of) life or clinical experiences.

Most stunning, in contrast to feminists and psychoanalysts of the second-wave generation, for whom it was axiomatic that the theoretical was personal, few women of the second and third generations seemed explicitly—as Freud had invited them—to "enquire from [their] own experiences of life" (135). These women had been, after all, independent and strong enough to get themselves into medical school and perhaps from the US to Vienna in the 1920s and 1930s, were political and cultural radicals, aided in anti-Nazi work in the 1930s. One, Henriette Klein, claimed to hold a "secret" theory that challenged penis envy; others said that what Freud said about women was nonsense. But in terms of the personal and the theoretical, my interviewees were perhaps best represented by Margaret Mahler, who claimed that "it didn't go through my brain" to consider Freud's theories in relation to her own life, or Jeanne Lampl-de Groot, who claimed that there was nothing autobiographical in her 1927 observations about the daughter's attachment to her mother, that these came entirely from her work with patients.

"Seventies Questions for Thirties Women" makes problematic the different views on femininity that women of different generations and trainings can hold. It brought my feminist social scientist's eye to perspectives on femininity held by practitioners and added generation as a feature of specificity to feminist understandings of differences among women: when you interview people, you realize that, depending on someone's generation, country of origin, professional background, own mother and family, and personality, she will have her own individualized view.

This individualized perspective came most radically to the fore in my writing and thinking as a result of psychoanalytic training and practice, in what I called the perspective of the clinical individual. As all clinicians know, the individual is immersed in bodily, sexual experience and in affectively charged, psychically organizing (and disorganizing) unconscious fantasies about internal self and other, but psychoanalytic theory, at the same time, tends to generalize and often universalize in its theories—you are an ego psychologist or a relational analyst, a Kleinian, a Winnicottian, a Kohutian, a Bionian, a Lacanian, and you see your patients through that theoretical lens. I noted clinical individuality first in *Femininities, Masculinities, Sexualities*: my plurals themselves challenged psychoanalysis, which had always written about "the girl," "the boy," "the woman," "the man," "the mother," "the father." Even in Freud, I argue, there is no single clinical femininity, masculinity, or sexuality, and along with him, we have conflated a singularized normativity with clinical plurality.

I make a similar argument about sexualities. In "Heterosexuality as a Compromise Formation," and later, in a 2000 preface to Freud's *Three Essays on a Theory of Sexuality* and "Homosexualities as Compromise Formations," I note that Freud's texts provide grounds for a gender-bending view of sexuality, in which everyone is masculine and feminine, heterosexual and homosexual, and where any single object choice or identity is seen also as a defense or a "tyranny." I note that no one is "gay" or "straight," that each person's erotism is individualized, particularized, and made up of many constitutive ingredients—of fantasy, bodily eroticism, identity and identifications, superego admonitions, filterings of culture and politics, and many other things.

My thinking about clinical individuality culminated in *The Power of Feelings*. Addressed to both psychoanalysts and academics, the book, once again, derived from a simple observation: of the several women and several men patients I had treated, each person's psyche was unique. What psychoanalysis gives us is a universalized account—an account of the psychobiology of being human—of the functioning of the human psyche, much as, say, cognitive psychology gives us a universalized account of cognition, perception, and so forth. I locate the center of this functioning in the creation of personal meaning, meaning best described as created through transference, fantasy, introjection, and projection. "Experience," whether embodied and biological, cultural and social, interpersonal and familial, is actively created and individually filtered through these affective, unconscious meaning-creating capacities and the internal, affect-laden fantasies about body, self, and other that they create. Each of our many theories helps to explain these elements of psychic life in some individual some of the time.

Psychoanalysis, I suggest, argues against determinism. In a dialogue with psychoanalysis, I argue that universalized developmental theories based on the *content* of unconscious fantasy or affect—the universalized accounts we have of gender, for example, or of the necessary interpretation of the body, as in the later (but not the earlier) Freud, or of *Oedipus*—exhibit a misplaced concreteness. What is universal is the demand, because of the powerful salience of bodily experience, or the powerful salience of early family experience, or the powerful salience of being labeled and treated as female or male, that these experiences be given psychic and fantasy representation, but the particular representation that they are given will be set in the context of the individual's overall psychic makeup and functioning. When we call something "Oedipal," or "feminine," or "oral," it is because we have discovered prevalent *patterns* that characterize the ways that people respond to these meaning-creating demands. When we universalize these, we take away from the activity of the psyche and from clinical individuality.

One result of my clinical experience, then, was to enable and require me to rethink the psychology of women, especially two particular characteristics of the thinking that went into *The Reproduction of Mothering* and related early work. First, the book falls into a tendency (though I am careful not to universalize) to create a generalized theory. I wrote it in the era of universalistic theory (structuralism, functionalism, Marxism) as well as of classical universalizing psychoanalysis; we had no postmodernism or poststructuralism to temper our grand theoretical visions.

On this matter of my generalizations, I was, in contrast to some of the classical theories, like universal penis envy, largely right: it is certainly the case that for virtually all women, the internal and external relation to the mother is developmentally central. The experiences of puberty, menarche, breast development, the potential for pregnancy and motherhood, pregnancy, childbirth, lactation and motherhood themselves (including adoption or co-mothering a partner's child), are also important in virtually every woman's development. My own solution here, developed in *The Power of Feelings* and elsewhere, was to think in terms of patterns of development and psychic femininity: the intrapsychic and intersubjective reproduction of mothering that I describe is certainly a prevalent pattern, but it needs clinical specification for each individual, put in the context of her entire internal life. We will not find it in all patients, but it helps us to have this pattern in mind and to know that for many women a projective and introjective filtering of the mother–daughter relationship will be centrally constitutive of their sense of female self and femininity.

Secondly, as a product of 1970s' feminism—deeply critical of the biological determinism found in Freud and without clinical experience, not yet myself having given birth, nursed, or mothered—I went out of my way to deny any importance to the reproductive body and was extremely leery of according the body any determinative role. I gave the body in general (including real sexuality—passion, desire, arousal—which I only took up in my writing in the 1990s) rather short shrift. In my more recent thinking, I reclaim the reproductive body and drives. Even if these are not biologically enacted in an actual pregnancy, I suggest that this biology demands psychic representation.

I began my graduate work in 1969 with an intuition that psycho-analysis gave us a primary vehicle for understanding gender and its discontents. Forty years later, clinical (as well as life) experience has deepened and transformed my understanding of men and women, masculinity and femininity, sexuality and desire, and, more generally, of psychic life and how we study this. The lens that best captures what clinical experience has given me, that of clinical individuality, is a lens generated by experience, by "listening to" patients rather than "listening for" instantiations of theory. My recent writing returns me to my roots: I write mainly theoretical articles on psychoanalytic process and therapeutic action, as I continue to form and formulate my own clinical identity and to try to understand the pretheoretical, taken-for-granted assumptions that underpin clinical work.

WORKS CITED

Chodorow, N. J. "Being and Doing: A Cross-Cultural Examination of the Socializa-tion of Males and Females" (1972). *Feminism and Psychoanalytic Theory*. New Haven: Yale University Press, 1989. 23–44.

———. "Family Structure and Feminine Personality" (1974). *Feminism and Psychoanalytic Theory*. New Haven: Yale University Press, 1989. 45–65.

———. *The Reproduction of Mothering*. Berkeley: University of California Press, 1978.

Fliegel, Z. O. "Women's Development in Analytic Theory." In *Psychoanalysis and Women: Contemporary Reappraisals*, edited by J. L. Alpert. Hillsdale, NJ: Analytic Press, 1986. 3–31.

Freud, Sigmund. "Femininity." *New Introductory Essays on Psycho-analysis*. Standard Edi-tion. London: Hogarth Press, 1964. 22: 112–35.

Lorber, Judith, Rose Laub Coser, Alice S. Rossi, and Nancy Chodorow. "On *The Repro-duction of Mothering*: A Methodological Debate." *Signs* 6.3 (Spring 1981): 482–514.

Critical Connections in Religion: An Intellectual Autobiography

Rosemary Radford Ruether

Mᵧ INTELLECTUAL JOURNEY HAS been deeply shaped by certain concatenations of relationships that were part of my family and early development. I call these "connections," rather than "crises" or "turning points," because they have to do with certain patterns of relations, rather than with one or two "shocking" moments that "turned my life around." I have experienced my life much more as evolving and spiraling in larger circles, rather than as taking sharp turns. Nor can I identify one person who was decisive, so much as many family members, teachers, and mentors who together helped shape my own processes of thought and development.

In this intellectual autobiography, I will focus on three concatenations of relationships and events that were the seedbeds for my process of development. The first of these I call, broadly, "ecumenism," having to do with how family relations shaped my religious identity. The second of these I call "racism and social justice," and the third "feminism and reproductive rights."

Ecumenism

I grew up in a family that was simultaneously Roman Catholic and ecumenical. I have expanded but maintained that combination. My mother, Rebecca Ord Radford, was the decisive figure here. She was a Roman Catholic of English and Austro-Hungarian extraction who was born in Mexico in 1895 and grew up in San Diego, California. She took her religion seriously, with regular prayer, daily Mass, and serious readings in religious classics, such as the writings of Meister Eckhart. But she had little patience with what she saw as "vulgar Catholicism"—that is, superstition or clerical authoritarianism. When a nun or priest gave me the impression that I should regard myself as having fallen into "serious sin" because I had eaten a bite of hamburger after midnight on Friday or missed Mass on a "holy day of obligation," my mother would dismiss such views with a wave of her hand. For her, it was good to fast on Friday and go to Mass on Sunday, but one should not turn such obligations into onerous guilt trips. If one had to miss occasionally because of other demands, it was no big problem. My mother passed on to me a sense that the Catholic tradition should be taken seriously, but should also be thought about critically and practiced freely.

In high school I aspired to be a fine artist and enrolled in a life drawing class at a university near my school. On one occasion I was walking through the corridors of my Catholic high school with my portfolio of drawings from the class when the nun-principal of the school happened to encounter me and asked to look at them. I readily opened the portfolio and was surprised when the nun was shocked by the fact that I was drawing adult male and female nudes. I simply felt amused at this consternation, since I assumed that drawing the nude body was how one learned to draw the body. I hastened home to tell my mother and older sister of this experience and was confirmed in my view by their laughter at this nun's parochialism.

In retrospect, I would have to say that there was a certain class and cultural bias in my mother's view of the priests and nuns of the American Catholic Church. She saw many of them as "Irish peasants" and hence lacking in sophistication. By contrast, I remember her making great efforts to attend the lectures of a French theologian from the Sorbonne in Paris, who, for her, represented "intelligent" Catholicism. But this cultural bias, more implied than imposed in our household, gave me early permission to think for myself in religious matters. The ghetto mentality of many Catholics growing up in the United States in the 1940s and 1950s was largely absent from my experience.

This sense of belonging to a larger world rather than a "ghetto" Irish American Catholicism was reinforced by the religious diversity of my family. My father was an Episcopalian whose family roots in that church went back many generations. The Radford family church was Trinity Episcopal, about two blocks from the family home in Georgetown (Washington DC). I grew up with the story that my grandfather, William Radford, a Civil War admiral, had belonged in the 1870s to St. John's Episcopal, the oldest historical Episcopal church in Georgetown. One Sunday the rector rose in the pulpit to lambaste those who allowed their daughters to dance past midnight into the Sabbath. The admiral took this as a criticism of himself. He rose in his pew, gathered his family around him, and walked out of the church, joining Trinity church instead. Whenever I walked past St. John's as a child, I wondered if the leaders there still remembered our family's repudiation of them some seventy years earlier!

I doubt that they did, but the memory of this event retold in family history carried a message. Going to church is a respectable thing to do, but the clergy should not interfere in people's private life. My father's Episcopalianism seemed to me more of a social and class identity than a deep religious experience. He usually attended church on Christmas and Easter. Although my sisters and I were raised as observant Catholics by my mother, she did not assume that we would never darken the door of a Protestant church (the typical assumption of Catholics at that time). Sometimes I would go with my father to his church, on those few occasions when he went. Thus I grew up with the assumption that my father's church was to be respected, but in terms of seriousness of commitment there was not much contest between my mother's and my father's religion.

My favorite uncle, David Sandow, the husband of my father's sister, was a Jew whose religion was more of a culture than a personal practice. Once when I was a child, my mother told me that he had considered becoming a Catholic and attended some catechetical classes with Monsignor Fulton Sheen at Catholic University in Washington DC. But he decided that he could not take this step away from his own tradition. I remember feeling a spontaneous pride in his decision. "Good for you, Uncle David," I thought. Since the regnant assumption of Christians at that time was that Jews should become Christians "to be saved," I cannot quite account for this spontaneous response on my part. Somehow I had already absorbed the assumption that my uncle's Jewish identity was integral to who he was and that he shouldn't give it up.

Uncle David and his wife, my aunt Sophie, had no children of their own. For me and my two older sisters, he was a surrogate father during the years when my own father was away in France during World War II. A lover of music and a skilled painter, he trained my older sister in voice and tutored me in my interest in painting. I learned to know the paintings of the National Gallery by heart through numerous visits there with him. Thus it is to Uncle David that my sisters and I owe a lifelong love of music and art. On my wall in my house today hangs an oil portrait of him and one of his own paintings of an old rabbi.

My great-aunt, Sophie Radford, one of the daughters of the admiral, was married to a Russian diplomat and lived for many years in St. Petersburg. She was a writer and playwright who published books and articles on Russian folk literature. She also published a history of her own father, Admiral Radford, in 1920. Her husband was Russian Orthodox, and she became partial to this tradition, as well as to spiritualism. When both her husband and her son died suddenly, she cultivated spiritualist contact with them and published her experiences in *There Are No Dead* (1912). Fluent in Russian and French, Sophie tutored my oldest sister, Manette, in French. This relation to our great-aunt gave my sister a lifelong love of both French and Russian Orthodoxy. Manette went to the French university Montpelier, in 1948–50. Later, when she moved to San Francisco, she preferred attending an intimate Russian Orthodox liturgy and took me there when I was visiting her.

To these diversities of religious traditions of my childhood and young adult life should be added the Quaker tradition. When my mother and sisters moved to La Jolla, California, after my father's death in 1948, we became close to several of my mother's oldest women friends from her youth in San Diego. They were cultural and social leaders in the area and had chosen to attend the Friends' meeting in La Jolla, appreciating their pacifist stance. These women engaged me to teach art to poor Mexican children served by the Friends' community. As a result, I began to attend the Quaker meeting on Sunday as well. I also continued to attend Mass with my mother, finding that these two forms of worship complemented each other admirably.

Thus, I grew up with the assumption that different religious traditions, within Christianity and beyond, were complements rather than rivals to be judged as good and bad, better and worse. Indeed, it was perfectly appropriate to cultivate several traditions at the same time, Catholic and Episcopal, Russian Orthodox, and the Society of Friends. Each tradition enriched the other. Since my youth I have added further explorations of other religious traditions, a habit that led me to one of my earliest projects.

By the end of World War II, I was fully aware of the Jewish Holocaust in Europe and the injustice of Christian hatred of Jews, a sensitivity fed by my relation to Uncle David. In the 1970s, I began to explore the religious roots of anti-Semitism in Christianity. This research resulted in my early book *Faith and Fratricide: The Theological Roots of Anti-Semitism* (1974). This work brought me into contact with religious Judaism but also eventually led to questions about the relationship between Western Christianity's supposed repentance of anti-Semitism and its uncritical support for the state of Israel.

My concern with injustice in the Middle East additionally led to dialogue with Palestinians and the Islamic world. My husband, Herman Ruether, has also made Christianity's relationship with Islam a key part of his personal and scholarly life, so together we have long been involved with conversation with Muslims, both on religion and on politics. For many years, we attended lectures and events at the Islamic College in Chicago and worked with the Palestinian Human Rights Campaign, where we met Jews, Christians, and Muslims working together for justice as good friends.

For more than twenty years, my husband and I have also been involved in Christian–Buddhist dialogue. This was initially shaped by the invitation of my former teacher, John Cobb of the Claremont School of Theology, to participate in the Buddhist-Christian dialogue group that he developed with Maseo Abe, a Japanese Buddhist. This conversation has led to some deep friendships with Buddhists like Rita Gross, an American convert to Buddhism and author of *Buddhism after Patriarchy*, and Sulak Sivaraska, a Thai Buddhist who is one of the founders of socially engaged Buddhism. In all these explorations of other religious traditions, I have felt deeply enriched and have developed a greater understanding of my own Catholic Christian tradition.

Racism and Social Justice

My commitments to anti-racism and social justice developed in the 1960s, primarily through a family friend and through my connections with college chaplains. These commitments were not particularly fostered by my immediate family context. My father was a Virginian who assumed a certain paternalistic relation to blacks that was part of southern society. Years after he died, I came across a piece he had written about a black childhood playmate who was the son of the family cook and the master of an adjoining plantation. His father occasionally brought the son cast-off shirts. My father recounted how he had to learn, as they grew up, that he and his playmate belonged to different worlds and could no longer be equals as friends.

My mother grew up in Mexico, and had a deep sympathy for Mexican immigrant women and their struggles to survive in San Diego. When we moved to La Jolla, she often extended quiet aid to these women, harboring them for periods of time in her house and finding them jobs. I would often return home from school to find my mother and a Mexican woman friend, having finished some household chore, enjoying conversation in Spanish around her kitchen table. However, she never knew blacks as friends and was uncomfortable with them in other than servile relationships. Even with Mexican immigrant women, her relation was more as a *padrona* than an equal.

However, several of my mother's closest friends (the ones who attended the Friends' meetings) more openly critiqued racism, militarism, and social injustice in American society. My mother's oldest friend from San Diego High School, Helen Marston Beardsley, daughter of San Diego city father George Marston, was one of the founders of the Women's International League for Peace and Freedom in the 1920s. When I was in high school and college, Helen Beardsley was very involved in supporting resisters to the Vietnam War within the military and also in picketing grocery stores in support of the farm workers' efforts at unionization. She often took me along on these political activities. Thus my education in social justice really began with my mother's friend, Helen.

In the early 1970s, President Richard Nixon was revealed to have compiled an "enemies list" of Americans he regarded as adversaries of his policies. Helen Beardsley's name was on it. I still remember my mother and several friends talking and laughing together about this. They exclaimed to one another, "We are so proud of Helen. She made the enemies list!" My mother and her friends exhibited an interesting relation to liberal causes. While undoubtedly members of old-line WASP elites, they favored the civil rights and anti-war movements. They were not surprised when their children went off to Mississippi in 1965 to work for civil rights. Indeed, Helen Marston Beardsley herself had left her elite San Diego family in the 1930s to work for racial justice with the Highlander School in Kentucky. She was almost run out of town in a rural area of Kentucky for creating an interracial school.

For these reasons, my mother showed no particular surprise when in 1965 I asked her to care for my three small children while I spent the summer working for racial justice in Mississippi. This summer trip to Mississippi was organized by the chaplains at the Claremont College where I was a graduate student from 1958–65. The chaplains increasingly drew students into anti-racism work and in 1965 took a delegation from the colleges to work as volunteers with the Delta Ministry in Mississippi. I was one of those volunteers.

That summer in Mississippi was a crucial turning point in my social and intellectual development. For the first time, I glimpsed the United States from the underside, from the perspective of poor black people in the United States. The face that I saw was violent and frightening. Our delegation was housed at Beulah, the campus of a former black college that was the headquarters of the Delta Ministry. A variety of projects were under way there in the summer of 1965. Housing and farming cooperatives were being developed. A voter registration drive was under way to win full voter rights for blacks long denied the right to vote in Southern states. The Mississippi Child Development Project was organizing preschool education for poor black communities under the national promotion of Head Start programs to prepare underprivileged children to enter first grade.

I committed myself to working with this Head Start project. A black woman colleague from Brooklyn and I traveled throughout the state for several weeks visiting these programs, which were mostly lodged in rural churches. We both were very aware that even to be traveling together in the same car exposed us to danger in Mississippi in 1965. We kept our eyes open for white men in pickup trucks with shotguns across the back window, a common phenomenon in the rural South.

During our travels we heard that the Ku Klux Klan was besieging Bogalusa, Louisiana, because of its resistance to racial segregation. We decided to cross into Louisiana and visit this town. There we found a mostly black town literally under nightly siege. The churches had organized counter-vigilante groups, the Deacons for Defense, that stood watch each night to protect the neighborhoods from the Klan. My friend and I attended a rally for the Deacons at a black church and later sat around the kitchen table of one of the families involved in this struggle, listening to their stories. They also graciously put the two of us up for the night.

As we continued our survey of Head Start programs in Mississippi, we became aware of how much the consciousness of even the four- and five-year-old kids in the program was shaped by the experience of racial violence. The children often painted dark, foreboding pictures. The teachers asked the children what they were painting and wrote their narratives on the pictures. I copied a number of these narratives, which often told of being driven out of town or being lynched by violent whites, and of the decision of some family members to immigrate north for better opportunities.

Our headquarters at Beulah were also touched by this threat of violence. One night hooded Ku Klux Klansmen drove through the campus randomly shooting at the windows of the buildings. Thereafter we stationed a nightly guard to watch for such incursions. If we saw anyone approaching, we were to ring a loud bell, warning the residents to get under their beds and away from windows. These experiences in 1965 gave me a graphic sense of living in racist America as a war zone. One had to assume that the local white elites, especially the police, were one's enemies who might at any time pull you over to the side of the road, beat you up, and even kill you when they realized you were there for civil rights work.

In the midst of this work, the racial prejudices of my own family revealed their questionable face. My father's maternal clan, the Armstrongs, was a Mississippi family who settled in the state in the 1820s. I had grown up with my father's stories of visiting the Armstrong antebellum plantation house, which was reputed to be haunted by family ghosts from the Civil War era. My father claimed he had heard piano music from a former music room (where there was no longer a piano) and saw the figure of a woman in white walking in the cemetery. Curious to visit this family house while I was in the South, I made arrangements to drive to the rural area outside of Columbus, Mississippi, where it was located.

After some wrong turns, I found myself on a country road almost entirely surrounded by dense trees. What had been plantation lands had been allowed to return to forest over the years. Blacks in the area pointed me to the Armstrong home. As I made my way on the road, I noticed a car behind me sporting the Stars and Bars license plate of an unrepentant Confederate. In the car were my father's two cousins, Lady and Cara Armstrong, both in their seventies. They were expecting me and took me into the house, showing me family pictures that lined the wall.

I noticed that they often spoke as if they themselves belonged to the Civil War generation, although they must have been born in the 1890s. They pointed to one side of the house that lacked a porch and noted, "We had intended to put a porch on this side of the house, to match the porch on the other side of the house, but then the war came, and we never did build that porch." They spoke of "the war" as if it were a recent event. I found out that the reason the sisters had been driving in the car behind me when I arrived was that they had just returned from voting against the civil rights voting bill that I had been working on the other side of the state to get passed. Two elderly brothers who also lived in the house had similarly gone to vote against the bill, and one had had a heart attack and died. The other brother had retired to the "men's quarters" of the house and was not disposed to meet guests. Thus, I had arrived at a moment of crisis.

I wondered if the Armstrongs knew I was in Mississippi with the civil rights movement. At one point, Cousin Cara turned halfway up a staircase to the second floor and said calmly but pointedly, "If any of these civil rights workers come around here, we're going to drive them right off this earth." In my mind's eye, I imagined her on the edge of a crowd that was lynching someone, wearing white gloves. I realized the elderly sisters knew exactly why I was in Mississippi. Because I was "family," they were being polite, but I had received a fair warning. As I drove away from the antebellum plantation house surrounded by dark forest and into the sunlight, it occurred to me that I had indeed seen the family ghosts. They were these two elderly sisters, and the brother mourning in the men's quarters.

This experience in Mississippi in the summer of 1965 has been crucial for my ongoing life process of concern for the victims on the underside of race and class privilege, not only in the US but throughout the world. I have been involved in many other social struggles since that time, on behalf of the Nicaraguans during the Sandinista years and beyond, and also on behalf of the Guatemalans and El Salvadorans struggling against the US funding of oppressive dictators. I taught in South Africa at the end of the apartheid era and have been many times in Palestine as conditions there have steadily worsened for the Palestinian people.

Although I have spent much time reading and seeking to understand many situations of social injustice through book learning, I have continued to feel strongly that you cannot really understand a situation unless you stand for some time in the shoes of the victims and see what it feels like to live on the underside of dominating power.

One also needs to understand oneself as a member of the family of the victimizers. To that end, I have led many delegations of Americans to conflict situations, feeling that nothing transforms consciousness faster than the actual experience of being on the underside.

Feminism and Reproductive Rights

I have long felt that feminism came naturally to me. My mother and her women friends, born in the mid-1890s, went to college in the era of World War I. In 1920, as young women in their twenties, they cast their first votes after the long struggle for women's suffrage won for women the right to vote. They assumed that they could do anything they wished, that their lives were not defined by marriage and childbearing, although they were happy to do that as well. My mother and her friends worked and traveled in their twenties and thirties and married late. Thirty-three when she married, my mother was forty-one when I was born. Thus, for me, there was no generation gap between the first feminist movement of 1838–1920 and the second beginning in the 1960s. My mother and her friends had embraced an emancipated womanhood that supported me as I awoke to questions and decisions that became the second wave of feminism in the 1960s.

At the same time, I recognized some ambivalence about women in the male traditions of my family on both my mother's and father's sides. While my mother and her woman friends were feminists, the men in the family were traditional. The Radfords of my father's family and the Ords of my mother's family both cherished the memories of their male ancestors' military prowess. My two great-grandfathers, William Radford and E. O. C. Ord, were an admiral and a general, respectively, in the Civil War. My father, Robert Radford, was the only grandson of the admiral to carry on the Radford name. When he married my mother at the age of forty, it was expected that a son or two would issue from the union. My great-aunt Sophie was reputed to have referred to each of my mother's three pregnancies as "the little admiral," only to be disappointed by the birth of yet another girl.

In retrospect, our gender perhaps freed us from having to fulfill these Radford male expectations and allowed us to flourish in the more feminist expectations of my mother's female friends. No one expected us to be "little admirals"! Nor did anyone on the Ord side of the family urge us to attend West Point, even though my great-grandfather graduated from West Point in 1837 (with William Tecumseh Sherman as his roommate), and there had been an Ord at West Point in every generation, including my own. But there was a certain contradiction in these military memories. The swords of our ancestors hung on the wall of our dining room, where we were expected to view them with due reverence. Yet both my mother and her mother experienced the early deaths of their husbands and had to raise their children as single mothers. Thus, the patriarchal prowess of the Radford and Ord men seemed oddly hollow. While honoring their history, the reality was that these men were absent from our lives.

It was women who carried on, who raised the family. When my father died in 1948, my father's sister Mary, a single woman and professional social worker, moved into our house to help my mother raise us three girls. Five women, two adults and three teenagers, kept the family together, with a little help from a Jewish uncle and his wife, my father's second sister. Thus, male power never seemed all that impressive to me. The men had big stories, but when push came to shove, they were disappointingly dead or away at war.

Another disappointment came from the charismatic white and black clergymen who mentored my sisters and me in the civil rights movement, when it came to asking questions about women's rights in the church or society. Before the 1960s, race and class analysis was seen as foundational to critical thought and action for justice, but gender was ignored. Women with social justice concerns were expected to commit themselves to the liberation of others, not to ask questions about their own exploitation as women. This began to change dramatically in the late sixties. Young women in the civil rights and antiwar struggles started to ask questions about the place of women in the movement, only to receive the offhand response of one of its leaders, Stokely Carmichael, who quipped, "The only position of women in the movement is prone." This "joke" infuriated women activists. It became clear to us that the combined exploitation of our work and our sexuality was taken for granted by male leaders we had trusted.

My first talk on sexism and theology, written in 1968, was entitled "Male Chauvinist Theology and the Anger of Women." I was surprised to see how electrified and threatened Christian audiences were by this title. For Christian audiences in churches and theological schools, "anger" had become the expected response of black men to racism, especially after the advent of Black Power, but for women to be angry at sexism was shocking. After this awakening, I increasingly devoted writing and research to the issue of women in Christian history. In 1972, I was invited as a visiting scholar to teach feminist theology at Harvard Divinity School. The next year, 1973–74, I gave a series of public lectures at Yale Divinity School as part of a year-long course on feminist theology and women in Christianity. These courses gave me a wonderful opportunity to research the background of sexism in Christian history from its roots in the ancient Near East to its modern expressions. I also joined with other women in the struggle for women's ordination and women's equality as leaders in the churches.

I had actually been writing on sexism and sexuality since 1963, although this was not at first framed as feminism. In 1957, I married a fellow graduate student, Herman Ruether. Both of us are Catholics, and initially we attempted to space our children through the rhythm method. This proved unworkable in our case. In 1963, with my third pregnancy, I decided to move to using the contraceptive pill, then fairly new as a medical option for birth control. I did not feel particularly angry at the Catholic Church over its views on birth control and sexuality until an incident took place in the hospital where I had just given birth to my second daughter, Mimi.

In the bed next to me was a Mexican woman, Asunción, who had just given birth to her ninth child, born with the umbilical cord wrapped around its neck. Her doctor came in on several occasions to urge her to avoid another pregnancy, which could prove fatal to her. I learned that this woman was very poor and had no heat in her house, except what she could generate from turning on her stove, which leaked gas. She wept every time the doctor mentioned the need to practice birth control, declaring that neither her husband nor the priest would allow it. Listening to this tale of woe, aided and abetted by the irrational laws of the Church, I became enraged. I left the hospital determined to speak out against the Church's teachings. This resulted in an article published in the *Saturday Evening Post* and reprinted in *Reader's Digest*, entitled "A Catholic Mother Speaks Out on Birth Control." The Second Vatican Council was then under way, and I joined other male and female Catholic writers in producing book collections intended for distribution at the council which critiqued the Church's teachings on birth control, among them *Contraception and Holiness* (1964), edited by theologian Gregory Baum.

As a result of these pressures, Pope Paul VI convened the Birth Control Commission to give a thorough review of the teachings, not only by theologians, but by doctors, demographers, and even the Catholic laity, represented by leaders of the Catholic Family Movement. Although the commission voted overwhelmingly to revise the teaching to allow for all medically approved methods of contraception, a few moral theologians persuaded the Pope to reject these conclusions and to reaffirm its traditional position. This has led to a disastrous disconnect between the official teachings of the Catholic Church and the views and practices of most Catholics on sexuality and reproduction. It has also caused enormous hardship for many Catholic women throughout the world.

I have continued to make reproductive rights a major social commitment ever since. In the late 1960s, an organization called Catholics for a Free Choice (CFFC) was developed in New York City, and it was reorganized in Washington DC by Frances Kissling in the 1970s. I have served on the board of this organization from the beginning. CFFC has grown into an international movement, with lively branches and publications throughout Latin America. It takes a broad view of reproductive rights, arguing that effective contraception is essential to avoid what is always an unfortunate choice for abortion, while also working for the legalization of abortion. It has researched such matters as the policies of Catholic hospitals on the "morning after" pill and the way such hospitals make reproductive choice unavailable not just to Catholics, but to anyone, no matter what their views or religious traditions.

These three areas of concern—ecumenism, anti-racism and social justice, and feminism and reproductive rights—continue to be central to my life, although I have also explored many other dimensions of global issues, especially in relation to the ecological crisis. These issues are deeply rooted in my experience as a child and young adult. They remain in my work into my seventies as integral parts of who I am as a theological, and socially concerned, citizen of the world.

Not Too Far from Brooklyn: Growing Up, Growing Old with Art

Linda Nochlin

Y FIRST MEMORIES ARE SOUNDS: the clip-clopping of the milk-man's horse on pavement early in the morning, delivering the Walker Gordon certified milk to our apartment doorstep, that and the reiter-ated clanging of the trolley cars that framed our block of Crown Street between Nostrand Avenue and Rogers Avenue. Then there were the street cries: the "I cash buy old cloes" of the I Cash Clothes Man and the ringing of the perambulating knife-sharpener. Sometimes, to my delight, there would be the hurdy-gurdy music of the traveling merry-go-round beneath my windows—not as exciting as the full-scale version in Coney Island but pleasurable nevertheless. These noise memories are not just there for picturesque effect but to indicate that I was born much closer to the nineteenth century than to the twenty-first. Although I do not live in the house in which I was born, as does the Turkish writer Orhan Pamuk, I have never lived more than seventy-five miles away from where I was born and grew up. Of course I have traveled—Paris is a second home, London not far behind. But the furthest away I have lived in the US, outside of a brief childhood stay in Tucson and some winters in Miami Beach (surely a Brooklyn outpost back then), is Poughkeepsie, New York, where I went to Vassar College and then taught for many years. I got my master's in seventeenth-century English at Columbia, and my doctorate at NYU Institute of Fine Arts where I now teach. None of these is very far from Brooklyn.

My Jewishness, far from being a source of alienation, was a universal identity in our part of Crown Heights. Everyone we knew was Jewish, mostly secular and assimilated, but some "old-fashioned," kosher and religious, black-hatted men whom my elegant, modernist grandfather clearly looked down on. I never entered a Jewish temple until I was thirteen and went to a cousin's, very reformed, bar mitzvah in Forest Hills, which I found boring and slightly embarrassing. I still find the sight of people, of whatever denomination, praying in public, on their knees especially, vaguely disturbing. I didn't know that Jews were different or what it meant to be a Jew until I went to Vassar, and then experienced this difference more deeply on my first trip abroad at seventeen, when I wrote "At Merton College, Oxford," a poem exploring my discovery of Jewish identity (it was published in *Commentary* the following winter). I grew up in a secular, leftist, intellectual Jewish family, like so many in the neighborhood.

Making money as a goal in life was not looked on with favor in my family, although it was certainly convenient. Certainly no one ever talked about it in my presence. That may have been because we had it, even during the Depression. One grandfather, the literary one, was an obstetrician-gynecologist; the other, an opera-lover and inveterate letter-writer to the *Times* and the *Miami Herald*, was the founder and owner of Weinberg News, which delivered all the newspapers in Brooklyn and some in Manhattan. There was a house at the beach and two boats, the *Linda I* and the *Linda II*. There were maids, laundresses, and, for my grandparents, a "couple" to do the housework. One uncle went to Harvard, the other to Dartmouth, and both my father and my uncle went to the Peddie School, where they were definitely a tiny minority, and from which my father was bounced, probably for drinking. Yet the old country, oppression, the shtetl, Yiddish—the language, the theater, the jokes, ultimately, the tragedy of the fate of the Jews in Europe—were always there in the background, and ultimately, during the war, in the foreground, if one looked for them. Intellectual achievement, the creation or appreciation of the arts—literature, music, painting, dance—was considered the highest goal, along with social justice. I understood that before I could understand.

Reading was the drug of choice in my childhood circle, and I really want to emphasize the overwhelming importance of the book, mainly the novel, in my intellectual and emotional formation. A "play date" consisted of two little girls curled up in adjacent armchairs, reading. I often stayed up all night reading a book: Lincoln Steffens's *Autobiography* or *Kristin Lavransdatter* or *Buddenbrooks* or *Dombey and Son*. Did my friend Alice really call me at 2 a.m. so that I could translate the French sentences exchanged by Clavdia Chauchat and Hans Castorp in *The Magic Mountain*, which we were reading simultaneously with flashlights in our own bedrooms? I had already started French, and she was taking Latin. Thus we "did" *The Magic Mountain* at the age of twelve in about a day of continuous reading. The book, like many others I read before there was too much to interfere with its total absorption, is seared into my brain. I still imagine that I remember parts of it perfectly.

My grandfather steered me toward the Russians: Gogol, Tolstoy, Dostoyevsky, of course, but also Ivan Bunin, Chekhov, Turgenev— *Spring Floods* and *Fathers and Sons*. But he was eclectic in his tastes, ranging from Lord Dunsany to James Farrell to Stefan Zweig to dramatists like O'Neill and Ibsen. Knut Hamsun was a particular favorite of both my grandfather and his bohemian Yiddish writer friend Nahum Yeud, who later turned up, much to my surprise, as a character in Henry Miller's *Tropic of Cancer*. At thirteen and fourteen, I was discussing books with them on an equal basis; I had read them, after all, and had my opinions on plots and characters, so why not? I somehow thought of literature as foreign, not part of my Brooklyn daily life. Being English or French seemed an unfair advantage of those literary peers: Jules Romain's Parisian *lycéens* in their closed secret world of intellect, politics, and intrigue filled me with jealousy, as did Elizabeth Bowen's *Death of the Heart*: a kid like me in such interesting grown-up circumstances. How could she be so lucky—and English to boot? (To be English was the height of unattainable desirability.) Gide's *Counter-feiters* was a paradigm of everything of which I felt myself deprived: evil, refinement, self-consciousness.

So Delmore Schwartz came as a revelation: I read *Genesis* of 1942, his long *bildungsroman* in prose and verse, with the youthful hero, Hershey Green, clearly a surrogate of the author, with dawning realization, a sense of my own identity coming into being along with that of the young boy in the text, who was a Jewish kid like myself, a mind nourished by poetry and fiction like my own. His style, deliberately shifting back and forth between formal diction and colloquial speech, became a characteristic of my own verse style. Even the incongruity of the names in Schwartz's work struck a sympathetic chord—above all, the eponymous Shenandoah Fish, hero of his verse play *Shenandoah*. How like it was to Delmore Schwartz's own name—half Anglo, half echt Jewish—and my name, Linda Weinberg. Suddenly, I could talk of the *matière de Brooklyn*, my home, as though it were the stuff of enchanted London or Paris or Moscow—it, too, could be the stuff of high imagination, of literature.

I did do other things besides read: I roller-skated, jumped rope, took ballet lessons and modern dance, went to camp in the summer where I was something of an athlete, learned to ice-skate and of course took piano lessons which were de rigueur for Brooklyn youth at the time. As my piano teacher, who had been my mother's piano teacher, said: "All my pupils are successful, but none of them as pianists." Bach was all I wanted to play. I went down to Florida clutching my beloved Bach-Stokowski records—breakable—in my arms in the upper berth. And what about art, you may wonder? Here I am, an aged art historian, and I haven't yet said anything about the place of art in my youthful formation. Certainly I never, in my early days, even dreamed of being an art historian or even knew such a thing existed, except perhaps vaguely from my uncle who had gone to the Fogg. I became an art historian more or less by accident. After getting my MA in the English department at Columbia, I received a call from the head of the Vassar art department, Agnes Claflin, asking me whether I would replace the youngest member who was leaving to get married. I had nothing better to do, and I had greatly enjoyed my four undergraduate courses in the subject, so I said yes. After a year, I could see that art history suited me, so I decided to get my doctorate at the Institute of Fine Arts, a long commute that ended with a PhD in 1963, a professorship, and eventually an endowed chair at my alma mater, which I finally left for the CUNY Graduate Center in 1980.

But from an early age, I did draw and paint avidly and was said to be "talented," not an unusual label in Brooklyn in those days. I enrolled myself in the Class for Talented Children at the Brooklyn Museum, where I was also taken on field trips from school or by my mother or grandfather, and which certainly played a major role in my artistic formation, although not necessarily in an aesthetic way. I was first of all fascinated by the objects in the museum: their age, their reminders of distant or vanished civilizations. This aspect of the museum experience inspired my first ambitious attempt at epic verse, in 1944, when I was thirteen. The poem in question was called "The Ghosts of the Museum," and began portentously: "We are the ghosts of the past, the dead reincarnate" and spoke from the position of the objects in the museum: "We are the snuff-boxes, the fans, the lace shawls, the mummy cases / costumes once the height of fashion." "We are the jewel hilted daggers / the yellow-leafed hour books . . . / I am an onyx jar that held the eye-black of a princess. . . ." The Egyptian princess especially inspired me to flights of free verse.

I really believed that in sneaking a feel of her mummy case I was somehow directly, mystically, in touch with the distant past—but a distant past that included someone like me, a young girl, after all— and the experience was a decisive one. I ended on a darker hortatory note: "Know this, you yawning, shuffling scornful moppets / That in one short minute of eternity / Your compacts and cigarette cases, / Your bracelets and silk stockings, / Razors and can-openers, / Will be here with us / Passing living death in glass cases . . . / While the men of another era / Yawn and shuffle / Through the damp, musty halls of the museum." An *effet pervers*, this: the museum and the museum experience itself made me realize that I, too, was a part of history. I had unwittingly become a self-conscious subject of the historical experience. Perhaps it is not an accident, then, that my kind of art history is explicitly object-oriented. Certainly, the aesthetics and the formal language of art are important to me, but it is a history and theory of things that I am engaged with: they remain the primary objects of my attention.

My first memory concerning myself and visual imagery, however, was one of iconoclasm, or, one might say, unconscious protofeminist critique. I must have been about six years old when I performed this act of desecration. Slowly and deliberately, I poked out the eyes of Tinker Bell in an expensively illustrated edition of *Peter Pan* with a compass. I still remember my feeling of excitement as the sharp point pierced through those blue, long-lashed orbs. I hoped it hurt, and I was both frightened and triumphant looking at the black holes in the expensive paper. I hated Tinker Bell—her weakness, her sickening sweetness, her helplessness, her wispy, evanescent body so different from my sturdy plump one, her pale hair, her plea to her audience to approve of her. I was glad I had destroyed her baby blues. (I now realize that I had, in effect, repeated the act of Mary "Slasher" Richardson, the militant suffragette who had attacked Velásquez's *Rokeby Venus* in the National Gallery with a meat cleaver to protest the arrest of Emmeline Pankhurst.)

I continued my campaign of iconoclasm with my first-grade reader. *Linda and Larry* it was called, and Larry was always the leader in whatever banal activity the two were called on to perform. "See Larry run. See Linda run. Run Larry run. Run Linda run . . ." etc. Larry was always at least three paces ahead of Linda, as well as being a head taller. I successfully amputated Larry's head with blunt scissors on one page of the reader and cut off his legs in another; now they were equal, and I was satisfied. (Freudians can make of this what they will.) These very deliberate acts of desecration were propelled not so much by rage as by a fierce sense of injustice. Why were girls and women depicted as poofy, pretty, helpless weaklings, men as doughty leaders and doers?

Do not imagine that I was a precocious man-hater—far from it. What I hated was not men—my beloved grandfather was the one who most encouraged me in my intellectual and artistic pursuits—but rather the visual putting-down of girls and women vis à vis a power situation existing in both high and popular culture, and I resorted to extreme measures when confronted by it.

Yet my career as an early feminist art critic was sadly or happily flawed by contradictions. (Let me say, parenthetically, that my life, like most people's, is rife with contradiction and that I approve of this condition, or at least accept it with good grace.) At eight or nine, I pored over my uncle's *Esquire* magazines (not the Harvard uncle!), gazing enraptured at the smooth, airbrushed contours of the scantily dressed, salaciously posed Petty and Varga girls, curvy pinups with large, cup-like, conical breasts and exaggerated bottoms, always wearing the highest of heels and the lowest of décolletés. I knew there was something forbidden about them, though I didn't know exactly what sex as an entity was. But it wasn't their breasts or their backsides that really got to me, but rather their feet—those preternaturally high arches, smooth, round, perfect semicircles uplifted on towering heels. I drew them again and again, as though I could capture some of their manna by the act of drawing them, just as I drew the *Vogue* models in my grandmother's fashion magazines.

At exactly the same time, and for not such different reasons, I was seduced by the reproduction of Jean Fouquet's *Agnes Sorel as the Virgin* in our *Treasury of Art Masterpieces* (one of the first luxe books of reproductions in serious color). The painting is a fetish-image if ever there was one, with the worldly and fashionable Queen of Heaven's bulging white breast protruding over her tightly-laced bodice, her rounded, bare forehead (like the Petty girls' insteps?) domed under an elegant, spiky golden crown, and her entourage of bright, scarlet angels splitting out of their skin-tight breeches like little gods of erection. Here, too, I knew there was something forbidden—I couldn't take my eyes off that white breast, those red thighs. And this, too, was part of the education of an incipient feminist, this sexualized rotundity and expansion that I couldn't quite get a grip on but that fascinated me in its visual expression, which nobody seemed to want to talk about or explain. In these images, women were depicted by male artists as powerful, to be sure, but more because of what they were than because of what they did—or rather, more because of how they looked than what they did.

The Brooklyn Museum was a source of constant instruction— for the usual reasons, of course, but also because its artworks provided access to the naked human body in all its varieties in ways that no other source of the period did. The *National Geographic* provided "native" breasts, but they were usually flaccid and uninteresting, and my grandfather's *Medical Journal* showed naked bodies, to be sure—with the eyes blacked out by a little strip of censorship—with quite wonderful sores and scabs and stitches. But that was not quite what one was after. Of course, the park, the bus, the movie theater, and sometimes the apartment-house roof were places where little Brooklyn girls found out about bodies—or at least the forbidden parts of the male body. Masturbators and exposers abounded in those nostalgically denominated "good old days" or "safer times."

We girls called these mild-mannered deviants "fiends" and divided them up quite systematically by habitat: there were "subway fiends" who lingered, rubbed, and unzipped in the secluded corridors at the ends of subway cars; "bus fiends," who were more devious, often merely eccentric and smelly, like the bulbous-nosed old boy, hung round with onions and mysterious small bundles, feet wrapped in rags, mumbling, who sometimes boarded the Nostrand Avenue trolley on our way home from high school. "Movie fiends" were a dime a dozen, sometimes going so far as to attempt a stealthy touch under cover of darkness, but usually content to massage themselves and breathe heavily in solitude. "Roof fiends" were a more mythic breed, voyeurs who stationed themselves on the building next door at undressing time. One was reputed to have put his hand straight through the open window to pull up the shade, revealing the girl in question stark naked—but I never knew the girl this happened to.

"Park fiends," in Prospect Park or the Botanic Gardens, were more variable: timid and middle-aged on the whole, they could turn aggressive and nasty and follow their victims to lonely places. My best friend and I, contrary to a fault, decided that we should turn the tables, stalk our chosen park fiend, and give him a good scare. We actually did this one lovely spring afternoon. We followed our persecutor through the Gardens and cornered him at the end of an open field just when the Gardens were about to close at sunset. Then, according to plan, we flung roses (illegally picked) at him, turned, and ran for our lives. This gave us immense satisfaction and we built up the incident into a protofeminist triumph, telling our audience and ourselves how scared he had been, how surprised—the look on his face when we hurled the roses! Actually, we never had a chance to see the look on his face—we were running away too fast!

The museum—in my case, Brooklyn and the Metropolitan, as well as the Frick, and later the Museum of Modern Art—gave us bodies in quantity and quality: breasts, penises, backsides, and everything in between. The museum was also a theater of cruelty, and children are both repelled by and fatally attracted to violence and cruelty—everything from Grimm's fairy tales to today's super-violent TV speaks to this fact. In the museum, you could contemplate an African statue with glass in his belly and nails profusely stuck into his skin (it was one of my favorites) or see Saint Erasmus having his bowels torn out by an ingenious machine and Saint Agatha having her breasts cut off and served up on a silver tray—all without a guilty conscience. They were art, after all, not low-class horror films.

Then, of course, there was "The Museum Without Walls," just coming into full-colored splendor in Thomas Craven's *History of Art Masterpieces*. It was there I first saw Grunewald's Isenheim altar *Crucifixion*, an image so horrific I hardly dared look at it, the thrilling effect of the greenish, bruised, tortured body of Christ on the cross doubly verboten to a Jewish child of the Enlightenment like me. That image stayed with me over the years and was the subject of my first published book, an essay called *Mathis at Colmar: A Visual Confrontation*, the result of sitting in front of the Isenheim Altarpiece for five days and writing about what I saw and felt, without scholarly constraint or rational limitation.

Later, in high school, the old Guggenheim was a favorite hangout, where the non-objective paintings were hung at floor level, and one could settle in to do homework to the strains of Bach or late Beethoven quartets. Early on, we learned to discriminate between the Bauers—not good, despite the glowing encomiums provided on request by Hilla Rebay, the director—and the Kandinskys—good, a high point of modernism. The old Whitney was famed in my set for the excellence of its bathrooms as well as its art, and the Frick was where I fell in love with Bellini's *St. Francis Receiving the Stigmata*, its combination of vast, layered spaciousness and obsessive detail—the sandals, the rock formation, the book stand, and the adorable donkey in the middle ground representing, I thought, St. Francis's admirable love of animals. I pretended that the enclosed conservatory was my very own—easy to do on weekdays, when attendance was very low and one might indeed be the only person in residence. At the height of our medieval period, my friend Paula and I would make the long subway pilgrimage from the President Street station in Brooklyn up to the Cloisters on Sunday mornings for the concerts of medieval music in the garden, or "hortus conclusus" as we liked to think of it. This was during and right after the war, and Washington Heights was the only point of reference offered to two girls fixated on the glory of the Middle Ages.

High school was also when we started being regulars at the Museum of Modern Art (reputed in some circles as a place to pick up boys, although I never had any luck in that direction). There was of course the film program. It was one of the few places one could see foreign or vanguard movies: Cocteau's *Blood of a Poet* and Maya Deren's *Meshes of the Afternoon* were standard repertory. I learned to speak scornfully of Hollywood, although I lapped up its products all the same. And I remember being transfixed, like all others of my age, by Pavel Tchelitchew's *Hide and Seek,* strategically set at the top of the stairs, a large and striking canvas with lots of hidden imagery to search out, and, for very different reasons, being enchanted by Morris Graves, an almost forgotten but then very popular northwest coast mystic, whose *Birds of the Inner Eye* were small and modest in scale, but lyrical and mysterious.

And like all my friends, I was awed and moved by Picasso's *Guernica.* It was a kind of shrine, a religious experience for a leftist kid like me, who as a small child had attended rallies for the Loyalists, had seen *Man's Hope* and *Spanish Earth* and could sing all the words of "Viva la Quince Brigada" and "Los Quatros Generales." I remember also being swept away by other Picassos—the *Démoiselles d'Avignon,* in particular. Quite honestly, I don't remember that there was ever a time when I was disturbed, put off by, or even questioned the so-called "distortions" or "ugliness" of modern art, or the lack of a recognizable subject in abstraction. That was simply what art *was* for me; it was something I was trying out in my own art classes. The notion that art was a formal language and that its shapes, color, and structure were as important to its meaning as its content seemed obvious, natural as it were, by the time I was in high school: modernism seemed to me to be the art of our times and I responded to it as such. When I painted a portrait of my mother, it was Matisse who inspired the flattened forms and the decorative background; resemblance seemed secondary and even trivial.

Then, of course, I left Brooklyn for Vassar. Vassar in the late forties, after the war, was an institution with a serious feminist past and a history of brilliant, creative, and often politically activist students like Elizabeth Bishop, Muriel Rukeyser, and Mary McCarthy. But it succumbed in part to the general postwar demand that women return to *Kinder, Kirche, Küche.* A well-publicized survey team of sociologists, psychologists, and educational authorities known as the Mellon Committee blighted the ambition of the women students as well as women's potential for achievement by declaring the college a "homosexual matriarchy" and women who dared to use their minds in competition with men as "overachievers."

Yet here again, contradiction—fortunately—abided. In the classroom, in our courses, by our teachers—the better ones, male and female—we were encouraged to strive, to explore, to excel, even if nothing much awaited most of us after graduation but marriage, parenthood, and membership in the Junior League of St. Louis or Scranton. In my junior year social psych course I decided to do, for a term paper, a so-called "content analysis" of the women's magazines of the period, *Good Housekeeping, Ladies' Home Journal,* and the *Woman's Home Companion,* thereby enabling myself to read in good conscience what I usually felt guilty about as time-wasting. (Parenthetically, I must admit that then, as now, this feminist intellectual enjoyed the occasional wallow in the sluttish pleasures of popular culture.) What was interesting about my content analysis of women's magazines of the late forties was the double message they handed out to their readers: on the one hand, there were the serious articles about major women activists and achievers like Eleanor Roosevelt or Dorothy Thompson or Amelia Earhart, presumably calculated to encourage their readership to do likewise. But the fiction they offered up for female consumption told a different story. In all cases, without exception, women who pursued careers, who didn't pay full-time attention to husbands, children, and domestic affairs were doomed and punished.

Career girls who wanted to keep on working, women artists or writers who dared to compete with male partners, were cast into outer darkness—either they remained "old maids" or lost their mates to more properly domesticated women. The message was clear, and because it was cast in the guise of fiction, it appealed more to the emotions or even the unconscious fears and doubts of the female audience at stake. Such fiction, like similar women's films, reinforced the *doxa* of the day and no doubt helped sell more houses, more washing machines, and more table linen to the would-be model housewives and helpmeets these magazines catered to. It also opened my eyes to my still hypothetical future. Although by no means a card-carrying feminist—and who was in those days, besides some shapeless, tweedy, old leftover suffragettes among the *emeritae?*—I knew from that time onward that I was not going to be one of those model domestic women. I despised them or pitied them, and vowed inwardly that I would be different. Of course there were other models for heterosexual women on view at the college—bohemian wives and mothers, or, in rare cases, married female instructors, but their fate was almost too awful to contemplate; women trying to finish their dissertations, write their poetry, or paint their pictures amid a shambles of urine-soaked diapers, unwashed dishes, and uncontrollable children. No, indeed.

Instead, I pursued as a commuter my doctorate at the Institute of Fine Arts, where I now teach, taught at Vassar, married, had a daughter, and spent a crucial Fulbright year in Paris in 1958–59. I was still not totally convinced about being an art historian when I went to Paris. I worked in the morning on Courbet, my dissertation topic. Courbet, with his unique combination of stylistic innovation and political engagement, is still a major interest, and my collected essays devoted to him appeared in 2007. But in the afternoon, I worked on an experimental novel tentatively called *Art and Life*. I diligently kept a notebook on the order of Gide's in the *Faux-monnayeurs* which I had read before, but which came to life for me in Paris. I used it in my own novel, which lies, still a handwritten manuscript, in a box in my bedroom. The central part of the novel was my trip to Colmar to see the Isenheim Altarpiece.

I also read Jules Romains' *Men of Good Will*. How I envied those students on the rue d'Ulm! I remember thinking that I wanted "my footsteps to ring out on the pavements of Paris." What I envied was the free life of those young male students—free personally and intellectually. I was a young mother with a dissertation to write, but I was trying to forge my own freedom on my own terms. That year in Paris was essential not only to my cultural development—visiting the museums, going to the Comédie, the Cinémathèque, reading the *nouveau roman* which was brand new at the time, adoring Sarraute and Robbe-Grillet—but to my sense of how I wanted to live, who I wanted to be. Still, my friends and I were isolated and confused in attempting to stake out a meaningful future.

It was not until 1969 and the mass impulsion of the women's liberation movement, with its sub-organization the women's art movement, that my feminist impulses assumed a coherent, conscious, coordinated, and eventually, an institutional formulation both activist and theoretical. To those of you who have not read my piece "Starting from Scratch," in the excellent anthology edited by Norma Broude and Mary Garrard called *The Power of Feminist Art*, I recommend that you do so, because it is hard to believe, in 2009, either the situation of ambitious women like myself or the obstacles—institutional, theoretical, or self-imposed—that stood in our way. In that essay, I describe my reading of the early texts of the women's liberation movement—*Off Our Backs, Red Stockings Newsletter*, etc.—as a kind of epiphany that I experienced like Saul/Paul on the road to Damascus, waking me up to a new light of personal and social awareness and the power of communal action. Women artists formed groups to show their work; women academics formed consciousness-raising sessions and changed the subjects of their classes to include feminist material.

I taught the first "Woman and Art" class at Vassar in 1969 and wrote "Why Have There Been No Great Women Artists?" shortly thereafter. No matter how individual and unique we wanted to be as individual women, it seemed clear that power—and change of the status quo—lay in group action. Women—artists included—have always, historically, gathered attention by being spectacular exceptions—women artists like Mme Vigée-Lebrun in the eighteenth century, as a specifically female portrait painter; Rosa Bonheur in the nineteenth century, for being an unusual woman *animalière*; Georgia O'Keeffe, without any doubt one of the best known artists in the United States, with a plethora of calendars and posters to prove it, as a female modernist in the twentieth century. But not until the women's movement of the 1970s was there an attempt—and a mostly successful one—to reframe and recast the whole conception of who artists—or doctors or lawyers—were, and to insist that women artists were an integral element of the art world, with all that it implies. Women artists are no longer "exceptions," brilliant or not, but part of the rule. That is the point of the feminist project, and a point which still needs to be made in many parts of the world where the feminist struggle is going on at many different levels.

We live in contradiction: that is what becomes clearer and clearer to me, as I get older. I am, on the one hand, the most aesthetic of creatures; my appetite for high art is unappeasable. When I saw the recent Velásquez show in London, I can assure you that I and my feminist friends did not, like Mary "Slasher" Richardson, think of taking an axe to the remarkable work on view. Rather, looking at the miraculous squiggles of white-edged painted brocade close up, we thought of the resemblance to the work of Eva Hesse. I try to practice Bach an hour a day; I write sonnets and odes for relaxation. The ballet and modern dance make life complete. When I had myself painted into Manet's *Bar at the Folies Bergère* by feminist artist Kathleen Gilje, it was because I wanted to be there, at the heart of that painting, looking out of it and at the same time being in it, a fantasy come true. But I also drown myself in TV detective shows at night, and love nice clothes, playing with my cats, having silly fun with my family or my friends at dinner parties. I have never—and now that I am old, less than ever—felt the compulsion to impose a spurious unity upon myself. Indeed, more and more, I feel myself to be many selves—a woman, a Jew, a scholar, a feminist, a mother and grandmother, a teacher, an athlete, a friend, a passionate devourer of printed matter—not necessarily connected. I am more and more convinced that "inner life" has no meaning for me: my life is exterior, lived on the surface of experience, devoted to the world and the things in it, for better or for worse. As I get older, I feel closer and closer to my early life, my Brooklyn youth and childhood, and that is why I have spent so much time recalling it, for I am still in many ways that child.

What does it mean to the future self to be so rooted, to be on the whole so protected, so cherished and supported as a child, so—seemingly, at any rate—at home in the world? The flip side of root-edness is complacency, a kind of existential smugness that denies to others—the exiled, the alienated, the uprooted, the disenfranchised, the majority of the human race—their right not merely to angst or estrangement, but to a place at the table alongside the more fortu-nate. As a Jew, especially, I call myself to order: only through luck, sheer chance, am I who I am and not another, am I alive at all. All my grandparents' relatives who stayed in Europe instead of emigrating were, of course, wiped out during World War II. Then, too, it is well to be aware that life and the passage of time eventually tear up your roots even as you cling to them. The protective family dies off, one by one—grandparents, parents, relatives, husbands. On the other hand, travel and mutual interest have greatly expanded my range of friends, acquaintances, and colleagues far beyond the close-knit little world I was born into. Children, grandchildren, students and former students, friends and colleagues, many of them artists, in increasing numbers have changed the focus from roots to shoots—offshoots leading to the future rather than the past. And even though it is true that I have never lived for long more than 75 miles from New York, New York and Brooklyn itself have changed radically over the years. Who would have thought that Brooklyn, rather than the Village, would be the home of aspiring artists or writers today?

Being old gives me the impetus to concentrate on my passions more ferociously than ever. Being a feminist, although an abiding concern, is not a full-time occupation. Still, my passion for justice for women is perhaps my strongest passion of all, and a lasting one: justice for all women, everywhere. I do not feel obliged to love all women, to like them, or to know them. I no more feel that all women are my sisters than I feel that all men are my brothers. Justice is not the same as love or fellow-feeling. But I do feel obligated, within a more restricted domain, to support or speak out for the women artists I like or who arouse my interest, and to teach and disseminate the work of feminist art historians and art critics, who believe, as I do, that art history and criticism are critical practices.

I do not feel that old age confers wisdom; on the contrary, one must be alert to intellectual hardening of the arteries, to closing down and shutting out, to clinging to worn-out verities and outmoded clichés. I have always preferred youthful styles—discovery, invention, experimentation—to old-age ones with their blurry universality and softened generalization of form and content. Grand finales, unifying summaries, are not my thing: give me fragmentation, recalcitrance, contradiction, the beneficent jolt of the unexpected and the antagonistic. That is what I ask of life—and that it continue, of course.

The Making of a
Feminist Musicologist

Susan McClary

NOTHING COULD HAVE BEEN FURTHER from my plans when I started out than an engagement with feminism. The eldest child of a father whose upwardly mobile aspirations very much included me, I grew up trying hard to think of myself as somehow lacking gender. I had no sisters, learned not to identify with my mother (one of those brilliant women who had been yanked from the workforce after World War II and thrust into the role of stay-at-home mom), gravitated toward friendships with boys whom I later would come to recognize as gay, and poured my pent-up emotional energies into my piano-playing.

Only much later was I able to discover how many kinds of denial besides that of gender had gone into my carefully blinkered upbringing. I knew that my parents had emerged from abject poverty in dust-bowl Oklahoma, but until I was in my forties they neglected to tell me that we were Cherokees. By virtue of the G.I. Bill, both of them eventually received advanced degrees—my father in microbiology, my mother in math—and became university professors.

I was born in 1946, the year after the war, just when my father was beginning graduate school. He was determined that I would grow up immersed in a cultural environment he could only imagine and invent: he bought a record player and blasted classical music at me in the crib every waking hour; when I was three or four, he amused his fellow students by teaching me to sing Beethoven's "Ode to Joy" in Schiller's German, which they were then studying for their language-proficiency exams. As a result, I cannot recall a time when I did not know the principal symphonies and operas of the canon, even though my father had been ignorant of them himself until he undertook this intensive educational process. I am his Frankenstein monster.

Although I did not then realize the stakes of this enterprise, I intuited certain taboos. I believed on some level, for instance, that my father's hard-won affluence would evaporate like Cinderella's carriage if I ever listened to popular music. Recall that I was eleven when Elvis appeared on Ed Sullivan's show, that the Beatles appeared when I was finishing high school, that I came of age during the greatest explosion of popular music in history. But I heard virtually none of it, committed as I was to maintaining the family fiction.

In much the same way, I believed that everything I had achieved would crumble if I admitted to myself or anyone else that I was female in any way that truly mattered. Very early memories of my mother's misery in her domestic gulag with the infant me as her principal interlocutor haunted my nightmares. To build an identity around the feminine seemed to invite the kind of sequestering I had witnessed firsthand at that most impressionable age.

My undergraduate and graduate training in the 1960s did little to change such an attitude. Young women were told explicitly that they could not become conductors because they had breasts; these unfortunate appendages would not only prevent the arm motions necessary to the task but would also distract the men in the ensemble. I opted for scholarship. But even here female students encountered severe restrictions: we were warned in no uncertain terms that we had to choose between the life of the mind and having a personal life, and women who formed relationships were asked to leave doctoral programs. (When my department chair learned only after I had advanced to candidacy that I had gotten married, he accused me of having defrauded the faculty: "all that training for naught but diaper-changing," said he.)

Moreover, the possibility that women had ever participated as agents in the production of music was never mentioned. The first individuals who chose to write dissertations on female composers were disdained as not being able to do "real" work; theirs were projects in special pleading, unlikely to add anything of value to the inventory of knowledge that mattered. My dissertation was a hard-core theoretical study of seventeenth-century formal procedures. Armed with that credential I joined the faculty at the University of Minnesota in 1977.

At this point I should probably say something about the work I do. Put simply, I have merely wanted to deal with pieces of music as cultural texts, just as most literary, art, and film critics engage with novels, paintings, and movies in their historical contexts as a matter of course. Yet what has always seemed to me a self-evident endeavor—the critical engagement with music—was virtually prohibited in postwar musicology. Memories of Hitler's and Stalin's policing of music and the other arts had made interpretation of any stripe politically incorrect.

When I entered the discipline in 1968, North American musicologists acknowledged only three modes of professional activity: archival research, the production of scholarly editions, and a quasi-mathematical brand of structural analysis. History and "the music itself" occupied entirely separate and unrelated intellectual compartments. The possibilities that the tensions of certain moments in social history might have affected musical processes or, conversely, that musical processes might have influenced historical events—as they so obviously did in the 1960s—never arose. In essence, those of us who later identified with what our detractors labeled "New Musicology" have sought to bridge that gap between historical contexts and musical practices.

Before I began my graduate work, I had already spent many years as a professional coach. In that capacity, I had assisted other performers (singers, chamber musicians, conductors, opera directors) in bringing notated scores to life by pointing out crucial formal details to them, helping them make sense of such details, and working with them as they converted their readings into dramatic sound. That enterprise continues to be my principal point of departure, and most of my writing addresses would-be performers as well as listeners and other music historians.

My coaching activities had concentrated on the traditional canon—the European art-music repertories from Bach through the early twentieth century. By means of my intensive exposure to this music since childhood, I had internalized the grammar and codes necessary for understanding it long before I studied music theory; I had absorbed classical music as my vernacular, in other words, and had learned how to make sense of it the same way I had learned to speak English. I was entirely confident by the time I started college in 1964 that I could explain any piece of the standard concert repertory I confronted. Looking back forty-five years later, I still believe that to have been the case.

But when I first encountered repertories from before Bach in my undergraduate music history survey, I was both dazzled and challenged. This was the sexiest music I had ever heard, and I had no idea whatsoever what made it tick. I headed off to graduate school with the misguided impression that musicologists knew how to deal with earlier music in ways that paralleled my own approaches to Mozart or Brahms.

Strangely enough, given the prestige of Renaissance and Baroque repertories within the discipline, very little useful work existed along the lines I wished to pursue. A more pragmatic student would have put aside her preconceptions and adapted herself to the agendas condoned by the discipline. But although I went through the paces demanded of me in graduate school, I still headed down from the library to the practice rooms in the basement when no one was looking to puzzle through the pieces that so intrigued me. Because actually playing music was defined as an illicit activity within the program, I usually felt guilty when I emerged in the evening, as if I had been caught masturbating. Each morning I would pledge to stay firmly grounded in front of the reference books all day—only to succumb shamefully once again to my own siren song of musical pleasure.

Finally I acknowledged to myself (and, subsequently, to my disapproving doctoral committee) that I wanted to focus on music per se. Since I was married, however, they assumed I had already given up all professional ambition, and they allowed me—however reluctantly—to go ahead with my foolhardy plans. If they had taken me more seriously as a student, they would have reprimanded me and packed me away to an Italian archive to do proper work. Sexism sometimes has its benefits.

And so I devoted my efforts to reconstructing the grammars and codes necessary for the critical analysis of sixteenth- and seventeenth-century music. With musical scores constantly in the foreground and hunkered over the piano keyboard, I cobbled together my own theories by studying Renaissance treatises, on the one hand, and on the other, borrowing concepts from contemporary linguistics concerning the structures of language change. At last I arrived (to my satisfaction, in any case) at frameworks that allowed me to interpret these remote repertories with the same degree of detail I brought to readings of compositions by Bach or Beethoven. It is not clear to me that anyone read the resulting dissertation, but it was accepted.

I did not anticipate, however, how very alien my projects would seem to my discipline. After I got my teaching position, I faced the difficulty of getting my work accepted. Over and over again, I submitted manuscripts for publication, only to have them returned with a note advising me that early music cannot be analyzed because its composers had not yet grasped how music "is supposed to work." As the tenure clock kept ticking, I tried repackaging my ideas in ways that would make them intelligible—but to no avail.

In the meantime, however, my intellectual orientation had begun to shift, largely as a result of contact with colleagues in other institutions and departments. Through my friend Rose Rosengard Subotnik at the University of Chicago, where I suffered a brief stint as a faculty wife (traumatized the whole time by memories of my mother's thwarted career), I started to read Adorno and Foucault. Adorno in particular seemed to me like a Rosetta Stone, and his ideas helped me to start making connections between musical procedures and social ideologies. I received additional sustenance at the University of Minnesota, which was positioning itself at the forefront of cultural theory with its Theory and History of Literature series and the founding of *Cultural Critique*, and I discovered that many of the tools I needed for my research were being developed in the Center for Humanities Studies. My colleague Richard Leppert was absorbed in similar projects, and together we developed much of what became critical musicology.

As a result of my collaborations with musicians who had developed their own skills in the media of jazz, rock, and even (this was Minnesota, after all!) polka, I finally learned to examine and then to shed my lifelong prejudices concerning popular music. I owe this capitulation especially to Christopher Kachian, who now teaches classical guitar at the University of Saint Thomas, and to Robert Walser, fellow musicologist and my partner of twenty-five years.

Most important, however, was my exposure to feminist theory, which had emerged as the most consequential area of cultural criticism over the course of the 1980s. It was my fortune to have colleagues at Minnesota such as Naomi Scheman in philosophy, Ruth Ellen Joeres in German, Nancy Armstrong in English, and Rey Chow in comparative literature. Everything I read in feminist theory (including the work of many of the women featured in this volume) seemed immediately relevant to my work on music: suddenly it became possible to discuss matters such as bodies, emotions, genders, and sexualities—not as infantile pleasures or subjective impressions, but as crucial contributions to the leading intellectual current.

Both my teaching and my writing changed overnight. If I still had trouble getting musicologists to accept my work, a vast and welcoming interdisciplinary readership opened up to me. My earliest publications appeared in journals far outside my field, and I learned to tailor my writing to be able to accommodate those who wanted to know about the cultural politics of music but who did not necessarily know the professional jargon of music theory. As it turns out, most of that jargon serves as a means of obscuring the intellectual impoverishment of the field: it takes no more insight to label something as a Neapolitan sixth chord than to identify a verbal construction as a gerund, yet many a musician lords it over others simply by virtue of having that arcane skill. The emperor's very old clothes.

My first public statement as a feminist musicologist occurred in an unanticipated format. While living in the Twin Cities, I had become involved in events sponsored by the Walker Arts Center and the Minnesota Composers Forum. My way of talking about the place of music in multimedia postmodernist works attracted the attention of individuals associated with experimental theater, especially Patty Lynch (Brass Tacks Theater) and Matthew Maguire (Creation Theater).

In the summer of 1985, Maguire asked me to serve as dramaturge for his play *The Memory Theatre of Giulio Camillo*. That same summer I was also teaching for the first time a course on women and the arts. One day I had led a class discussion of Norma Broude's classic essay on Artemisia Gentileschi and then engaged in a rehearsal of *Giulio Camillo*, a play that unfolded solely through the manipulation of objects, lighting, and gestures.

In a rare eureka moment, a number of possibilities collided and coalesced in my head. Broude had argued that Gentileschi's portraits of biblical figures broke with the conventions that had presented biblical figures such as Susanna as vain, exhibitionistic, and responsible for their own victimization. Locked away in one of my closets was a facsimile of a seventeenth-century oratorio about Susanna. This was one of the scores on which I had squandered time in the practice rooms when I was a grad student. I had never known quite what to do with the piece, though I hauled it out to perform some of it each year in relevant courses.

Now I realized that I should interrogate the sexual politics of the oratorio. The next morning I played through the oratorio at the piano. Beautiful though its music undoubtedly is, Alessandro Stradella's *La Susanna* posits its eponymous heroine as a seductress; as she awaits execution, she even sings a very long lament in which she blames herself and her beauty for having led the elders to lust after her. Matthew Maguire had been training me to stage theatrical works without spoken dialogue, and those techniques were all I needed for my new task.

I composed my play *Susanna Does the Elders* nearly overnight. I had only to extract and translate parts of the oratorio that best revealed its misogyny and stage them in ways that laid bare their meanings. By re-presenting Stradella's music and lyrics intact but through a feminist staging, I invited the oratorio to deconstruct and indict itself. The play ran successfully at the Southern Theater in Minneapolis in 1987, and it offered me new ways of thinking not only about gender and sexuality but also "the body," "the voice," and "performance"—all terms that have become exalted and, alas, often reified in recent years. I learned in the process of producing *Susanna* that bodies, voices, and performances can lie, sometimes exquisitely so.

In 1991, I published a collection of seven essays titled *Feminine Endings: Music, Gender, and Sexuality*. Some parts of the book had already appeared as articles in journals such as *Genders* and *Discourse*, and typescripts of a few others had circulated samizdat-style, as photocopies of photocopies passed from hand to hand by individuals interested in feminist or queer approaches to the interpretation of music. The book looked quite drab: white lettering on a plain gray background, the only decoration a narrow band of color containing a simple five-line staff. No one glancing at its staid cover could have predicted the disciplinary explosion this slim volume would produce.

Although the ideas presented in these essays were received as radical—even outrageous and preposterous—within musicology, they only brought to music studies the kinds of projects that had long since become standard fare in most other areas of the humanities and social sciences. Central to this cluster of essays were questions concerning gender and sexuality: cultural representations of women and men in opera, constructions of desire and pleasure in music at various historical moments, and the gendered metaphors prevalent in discourse about music. As I wrote the various essays in the collection, I was repeatedly struck by the obviousness of these questions; it is surely no secret that operas feature gendered characters, that many listeners derive great sensual satisfaction from musical patterns, that music theorists and critics often rely on analogies to cultural habits of thought based on the binary opposition between masculine and feminine. In fact, I am rarely certain when I present an idea whether it will receive "huh?" or "duh!" as a response.

Yet few scholars had interrogated even these easily perceived aspects of musical practice. Gradually, I became almost as interested in the relative absence of such discussions in the discipline as in formulating answers to my initial questions. As a result, the book not only surveyed a range of gendered elements in music but also addressed how the traditional priorities of the field had served to shield music against cultural interpretation of any sort.

Perhaps if I had stayed within the realm of music by women no one would have noticed. But the foregrounding of gender also led me to address the music of Bizet, Tchaikovsky, Schoenberg, and even Beethoven (just Google me for traces of the uproar that followed that transgressive act!) as expressions of masculinity. The aftershocks continued for some years, for classical music has long been held sacrosanct as a refuge from the sordid realities of everyday life. The Romans could not have greeted the invading barbarians with less enthusiasm.

Nevertheless, the priorities of the discipline—the questions posed, the methods, the repertories regarded as legitimate for study—have shifted immeasurably since 1991. The barriers prohibiting cultural interpretation have fallen, encouraging the rise of enterprises far beyond my initial questions concerning gender or my approaches grounded in second-wave feminist theory. Much of my own work still focuses on the formal procedures of early-modern music, though I no longer have to explain why I bring historical contexts or radically different models of erotic pleasure to bear in my analyses of, say, seventeenth-century Venetian opera. Indeed, I believe ever more fervently that social values—including assumptions concerning desire, pleasure, and the body—motivate the changes over time in musical imagery and even syntax. Who could have anticipated that feminism would serve as the "open sesame" for the formerly dry-as-dust discipline of music theory?

My graduate-student self of forty years ago would no doubt have been astonished to learn that I would end up recognized as a feminist. Sometimes my career trajectory seems quite unlikely even to me in retrospect. Yet many odd aspects of my intellectual and artistic development—the centrality of classical music in my earliest familial bonding, my channeling of intense adolescent longing into piano-playing, my stubborn refusal to surrender my musical self-pleasuring in the practice rooms for the adult rigor of an academic discipline—all point to the individual I have become. I only needed permission to bring my experiences as an embodied, sentient woman into conjunction with my music scholarship. When I received that permission, the rest simply followed.

"I Will Survive":
Changing Trends in Feminism and Performance

Jill Dolan

MY TITLE REFERS TO THE GLORIA Gaynor song from the height of the disco era that has in some ways become my signature melody, both musically and metaphorically. I first heard the song from my dorm room at Boston University in the mid-seventies, where Gaynor was singing in a Comm. Ave. nightclub that backed onto the three towering blocks of cinder where undergraduate students lived. Something about the driving beat and the insistent determination of that big female voice spoke to me. I heard Gaynor sing before I'd crafted a coherent understanding of my own then-nascent, inchoate feminism. I arrived at BU poised for personal and intellectual changes I couldn't predict. I had been an actor as a kid, using the make-believe of theater to escape the conventional gender socialization I intuitively knew couldn't accommodate my own self-fashionings or my wayward desires. The whole enterprise soured only when I enrolled in college as an acting major and suddenly found myself held hostage to the very gender roles theater had once let me escape. After three semesters suffering unaccustomed failure, I repaired to the English department and then the School of Communications and refashioned myself as a critic.

As I reoriented myself around theater, I took tentative steps toward designing a new identity. At a meeting for prospective arts writers of the BU student newspaper, I found myself telling the editor that I wanted to write about women. Without even knowing it, I'd caught the zeitgeist of the 1970s. Through social osmosis and the greatest, if still unarticulated personal necessity, I clawed my way toward feminism, which I needed to ennoble and validate my sexual desire. I couldn't, at that point, have become a lesbian without becoming a feminist, too. My love for women found a rationale and justification in Robin Morgan, Kate Millett, and Barbara Smith, in notions of sisterhood and power that instilled pride in my gender and, through "women identification," accepted my sexuality. The criticism I went on to write at BU gave me a venue through which to express my new desires, new ideas, new politics, and new sense of the potential of theater.

In 1981, I began graduate school at New York University, joining my program in the second year of its transformation from the graduate drama department into the Department of Performance Studies. The field-in-formation defined itself against the more conventional theater on which I'd been bred. Performance studies, led by the firebrand experimental theater director-cum-theorist Richard Schechner, promoted itself as an inquiry into expressive behavior broadly drawn. Schechner understood performance not just as framed events behind a proscenium arch artfully arranged for spectators' attention, but as ritual, intercultural bartering, popular culture, folklore, global art forms, and performance in everyday life. Schechner theorized performance as "twice behaved" or "restored" behavior, which meant any action purposefully repeated in the presence of others.

The intertexts of performance studies came from, among others, anthropologists Victor Turner and Clifford Geertz, social scientist Erving Goffman, and folklorist Barbara Myerhoff; from avant-garde performance artists like Guillermo Gomez-Peña and Rachel Rosenthal; and from scholars like Schechner, folklorist Barbara Kirschenblatt-Gimblett, and director/historian Michael Kirby. The new department navigated its past in theater and its present across the social sciences, arts, and humanities with unsurprising bumps and grinds. I'd come to NYU to refine and extend the feminist criticism I'd begun to write in Boston, but no one on the Performance Studies faculty identified as feminist, including the two faculty women who'd most recently been hired. In the department's lounge overlooking Washington Square Park, students like me began agitating for the attention to women just beginning to take root in other disciplines. Our frustration with the lack of coursework in feminist performance grew. We petitioned the department to hire Roberta Sklar, of the Women's Experimental Theatre (WET), one of the most important feminist collectives of the moment, to teach a course, and somehow they agreed.

Sklar's teaching inexperience in a graduate program offering a course in a field that barely existed encouraged her to turn to us for guidance about what she should teach. One of the joys and constraints of feminism at the time was that we were all autodidacts—the theorists and the practitioners—and we needed to teach one another. Studying feminism and performance was utterly different from working in, for instance, the history of popular culture, which was a well-established subfield in which students could expect to learn from a distinguished scholar. Sklar's course on women and performance was probably historic as one of the first times, if not *the* first time, a feminist theater artist taught material that she had participated in creating and theorizing.

Sklar included feminist readings on mother-daughter relationships in her syllabus, prompted by WET's work on *The Daughter's Cycle*, their trilogy that revised the Greek story of the house of Atreus from the women's perspective. But she wasn't familiar with the French feminisms then seeping into the consciousness of women academics and intellectuals. I bought Elaine Marks and Isabelle de Courtivron's *New French Feminisms* at a bookstore in Soho and devoured it whole, captivated by the theatrical, sensual, evocative writing. I could see the connections between their thinking and performance, and struggled to teach myself enough to translate their ideas into theories relevant for the stage. Around that time, Herbert Blau came to Performance Studies to offer a three-week mini-course. He was the artist/theorist who lead Kraken, an experimental theater group in the 1960s, and had headed what was expected to become a national theater at Lincoln Center. By the time he offered the NYU class, he was an academic captivated by continental theory. With his inimitable style of reading as closely as a Talmudic scholar, with intense scrutiny and passion for textual exegesis and commentary, Blau tutored us in Derrida and Artaud, peeling away layers of text to illuminate how deconstruction itself could be deconstructed. He encouraged my reading of French feminisms and began to help me connect my politics with a theoretical movement that he viewed as creative and artful, as well as intellectually rigorous.

Through his example, I experienced the metamorphosis I've gone on to wish for my own students. I moved from a pre-critical passion for ideas at which I could only grasp, into enough mastery of complex texts that I could "poach" them for ideas most relevant to my own arguments. Although I'd kept up my theater criticism—and had published a few essays in *Hudson Review,* as well as reviews in community papers like the gay-oriented *New York Nation* and the community-based *The Villager*—I began to write scholarship that used critical theory to bolster my claims for a feminist perspective on performance. I called my master's thesis "Toward a Critical Methodology for Lesbian Feminist Theatre," a title for which I became notorious among other graduate students, especially those who, like me, were gay or lesbian and wondering how their identities would play in the academy. My master's thesis used whatever feminist theory I could find on my own— mostly essays from *New French Feminisms* (1980) and Jane Gallop's *The Daughter's Seduction* (1983), on which I'd somehow stumbled, along with work that Sklar had assigned in our feminist theater class—to discuss three different plays by lesbians, including *The Daughters' Cycle,* through the critical lens it offered. Sklar championed my work, knowing that my efforts would call attention to the theater she, Sondra Segal, and Clare Coss toiled tirelessly to create, often without any critical notice at all.

I learned more than twenty-five years later, when I renewed my connection with Segal and Sklar, that they'd never read my MA thesis. I can't recall why our communication stopped in 1983, but this misstep seems telling of the awkward relationship at the time between feminist performance critics/theorists and feminist artists. After all, much of the theory we read proposed that "the author" was dead. Roland Barthes' essays proposed focusing on the text as a writable artifact, a skein of ideas open to interpretation and "rewriting" that displaced the author's power and centrality. As Barbara Christian wrote at the time in her essay "The Race for Theory," it was ironic that women of color—and really, women at all—were being noticed by the academy just when poststructuralist thought that heralded the author's death became so popular. We'd just rediscovered women novelists and playwrights and begun to write about them when the current of continental theory swept them to the side once again. Perhaps that's why I fell out of touch with Segal and Sklar before they had a chance to read my thesis; already, I was moving away from heralding women playwrights as my critical gesture, and switching to theorizing representation instead.

I didn't get much intellectual direction during my PhD coursework, but performance studies faculty at NYU groomed us enthusiastically for the profession, advising students to publish and to present their work at conferences. In 1982, I presented a paper from my master's thesis-in-progress at what was then the American Theatre Association's (ATA) mammoth convention, held that year in Minneapolis. Somehow, I found my way onto a panel with Sue-Ellen Case, then an assistant professor in the School of Drama at the University of Washington, and Rosemary Keefe Curb, a theater and women's studies scholar at Rollins College, who was soon to become notorious as the coeditor of *Lesbian Nuns: Breaking the Silence* (1985). The three of us, and another graduate student from the University of Minnesota, presented a panel on openly lesbian themes, perhaps the first in the ATA conference's history.

The heady feeling of sitting next to Case and Curb at that panel, looking into an audience of mostly women who were excited by our analyses, proved seductive and indelible. I loved writing criticism, but felt the isolation of writing in private for an imagined public that was difficult to discern and rarely heard. On the conference panel, the response was immediate and visceral. The audience had things to say, questions to ask, affirmations to offer, challenges to put forth. We were all high from it by the time we finished, and although I barely knew Case and Curb, older than me by at least a decade, I rallied my NYU friends to go for an evening field trip with them to the local Minneapolis lesbian bar.

In the early eighties, bar culture provided a center for lesbian (and lesbian feminist) culture. I'd come out in the seventies dancing in Boston women's bars, where the flannel-shirted lesbian feminist college girls would gaze warily at the uniform-wearing softball dykes from Dorchester, who glared back. But once the music started, the divisions melted as everyone approached the floor, our emotions emboldened by the dark interiors, with their covered windows masking the real world, and their disco balls keeping the mood magical. To find a lesbian bar in an unfamiliar city, and to dance with new colleagues who, outside that liminal club space, worked on the ideas I found so compelling, seemed a great gift. The erotics of scholarship mingled with the seductions of the dance floor, charging us all with a palpable sense of the interconnection between knowledge and desire.

After the initial debaucheries of that first evening out, our small group of lesbian feminist scholars continued dancing together at conferences, even as we began to grow into something of a crowd. Because some of the feminists most interested in theory happened to be lesbians, work in feminist performance studies became associated early on with sexuality, a link that made some women uncomfortable. But at conferences, dancing helped ameliorate the discomfort, as heterosexual women mingled with lesbians. After a particularly transcendent moment of scholarship, when Case presented at the 1987 Women and Theatre Program meeting what would become her pioneering "Toward a Butch–Femme Aesthetic" essay, the conference-goers retired to the basement of the Loyola University dorms where we all stayed, sweltering in one of the hottest Chicago summers on record. Straight women danced with lesbians in a miasma of erotic energy inspired by Case's scholarship.

In her lecture, which became a widely cited touchstone in the then-nascent field of queer studies, Case documented how lesbians who adopted butch-femme identities were ostracized by feminists in the seventies. She critiqued the history of feminist disparagement of lesbian style, but also suggested the butch–femme couple could exemplify what she called a new "feminist subject." The piece offered a reparative model that motivated our dancing at the conference. Accompanied by mix tapes broadcast on a cassette player with the volume turned up as high as it would go, the dancing relied on a do-it-yourself ethos that marked our scholarship, too. In 1987, we still had few resources outside ourselves. We made it up as we went along, supporting one another by our engaged, public, collective response to our scholarship, into which we poured our hearts, our souls, and our libidos. The WTP conferences each year became a hotbed for feminist critical thinking about performance. We all anticipated them eagerly, knowing that they provided the crucible in which we would hammer out, try on, and contest new ideas we generated in one another's presence.

But things changed quickly. We began to find our panels at the Association for Theatre in Higher Education meetings, the more formal conference that always followed the WTP, filled with people from across the field eager to hear new ways of theorizing about representation, about embodiment, about gender, race, sexuality, class, and ability, and about the intersection of identity with performance. In only a few years, feminist performance scholarship transformed from a marginalized, activist intellectual endeavor into a trend. We were fashionable; our work about gender and sexuality in performance was sexy in a more public way. We wrote about then-obscure avant-garde troupes like Split Britches and later the Five Lesbian Brothers in downtown Manhattan; about British women playwrights like Caryl Churchill; and about women in the Holocaust, forcing women into visibility across the interdisciplinary concerns of performance studies and performance theory. In remarkably short order, our ideas became central to the project of theater and performance studies. When I began applying for academic jobs in 1986, position descriptions actually advertised for applicants immersed in feminist performance scholarship.

Is that how a social movement with radical ideals acquiesces to institutionalization? My colleagues and I once made our ways through nonexistent programs of study, making it up as we went along in academic environments that were overtly antagonistic or tacitly suspicious and condescending. Suddenly, we found ourselves assistant professors with our own graduate students, in institutions willing to put our courses on the books. We affiliated with women's studies; with folklore; with African American studies; with art and art history; with communications and English and French and Italian. We found our once subaltern feminist performance theory suddenly chic and desirable, the new style in which the cloth of academic fashion was cut.

As feminists, I'm not sure we were prepared for assuming the kind of power our positions suddenly conferred. When I became an assistant professor at the University of Wisconsin–Madison in 1988, potential graduate students looking for feminist performance studies now had several programs from which to choose. Feminist faculty weren't prepared for the sudden competition among us. Our struggle for legitimacy had positioned "us" against "them," the old-school, mostly white male theater faculty and programs that peddled pre-consciousness ideas. Suddenly, we were positioned against one another in the competition for graduate students who wanted to study feminism and theater. I don't think we handled very well our place in the academic marketplace we helped to create. Because of institutional and professional competition from which we suffered, I was estranged for too many years from colleagues who had once been close friends. Our painful gains and losses mirrored the late-1980s, early-1990s capitalization of other aspects of what had been subcultural or countercultural feminist and lesbian feminist movements. We were the academic equivalent of lesbian feminist bookstores that suddenly found their formerly exclusive titles now available at chain stores. We didn't have the skills to navigate gracefully the sudden marketability of our ideas on a much larger scale of exchange.

Despite our inability to maintain our personal and intellectual intimacies as we became more and more empowered professionally, feminist performance theory's exponential growth began to change the landscape of the larger field. At the various institutions where feminist professors of theater and performance studies now plied their trade, grad students developed their own complex and interdisciplinary scholarship, taking women's studies courses now widely available and building their programs with the rich offerings of feminist work across disciplines like history, folklore, anthropology, and the other arts. Whip-smart, they assimilated their mentors' insights and quickly pushed us farther into critical race studies and theories of sexuality as well as gender and class. Where my generation had stammered out the language of deconstruction and poststructuralism, our students wrote and spoke theory with elegant, fluid facility. And while our feet straddled a social movement and the academy, many of our students based their activism in the classroom, assimilating the lessons of movement feminism to their pedagogy and their research. Our students grew up with a ready-made cohort and didn't have to suffer the sometimes dangerous serendipity of searching for congenial colleagues.

This was progress. But it was also painful. Feminist theater and performance theory underwent its own version of the struggle that Nancy Miller, Marianne Hirsch, Evelyn Fox Keller, and other scholars discuss so openly in their conversation in *Conflicts in Feminism*. As those of us who'd struggled to establish the field gained tenure and promotion, our students and junior colleagues made their own reputations often by working against our earlier scholarship. With its academic growth and legitimation, feminism has perhaps become a critical methodology like any other, an assimilation that Terry Eagleton warned against, speaking of Marxist criticism, in the late seventies. What's the continuing utility of feminist performance studies as a radical critique of representational and cultural power and gender, sexuality, race, and other identity inequities? Has it lost its attachment to a movement for social change? As political and intellectual interest in so-called identity politics wanes, is "social justice" a more descriptive term for the work once done under the auspices of feminism in the movement and in the academy? Do we in fact need broader rubrics under which to organize our work, or more thematic concerns such as "trauma" or "affect," terms under which many feminist and lesbian/queer scholars now study culture?

In addition, queer theory—inspired in part by the early 1990s activist group Queer Nation, which resignified what had once been a derog-

atory term in gay and lesbian history into a celebratory label—began
to replace lesbian and gay studies as the moniker for studying sexuality and its meanings in performance and culture. A new intellectual
perspective began to structure performance studies with the advent
of queer theory. Subtly moving aside the feminist energy that once
propelled the field, queer performance theory trumpeted the radical,
subcultural work of performers who brooked the status quo of sexuality as well as gender. While this new scholarship expanded the archive
feminist studies began, work on gender from a feminist perspective
began to be replaced by work in queer studies that often repudiated
women's studies as parsed, coherent, and archaic. The annual ad hoc
gay, lesbian, and queer studies conferences that took place through
the nineties at northeastern universities increasingly presented high
theory in which the objects and subjects of study were less and less
frequently women. And because queer theory positioned itself as
cutting-edge and avant-garde, many of its proponents also privileged
youth over age, exacerbating a generational shift which, as feminism
has often experienced, always requires painful negotiation.

At a queer studies conference in 2007, for instance, Case, who was a
conference organizer, invited me to give a keynote address. I presented
nascent work from a book project tentatively called *From Flannel to Fleece:*
Lesbian Feminist Cultural Production, 1970–1990. The keynote engaged "public feelings" discourse to describe what it felt like to be a young lesbian
in the mid-seventies, listening to music in public settings by singers
like Holly Near and Cris Williamson, lesbian songwriters who carved
out a place for us where there had been none before. I described my
own experiences at the time producing women's music in Boston, and
the challenges of crafting new pathways out of capitalism and into
subcultures that weren't always successful. I'd given other versions
of the lecture before, but this time I felt like I was speaking a foreign
language. I looked into an audience of young scholars, most of whom
looked like men, whether they were biologically male or not. The pre-
dominance of "trans" style—as theory and as sartorial and gender
choice—at the conference made my references to lesbian feminists
in their flannel shirts seem anachronistic and irrelevant. Rather than

curiosity about lesbian feminist history, I saw faces that looked blank and closed if not overtly bored.

In the discussion after my talk, a transman-identified conference participant distinguished his history from my own, insisting that the cut from Cris Williamson's *Changer and the Change* I'd played (and that I'd admitted was the "soundtrack of my life") reminded him only of his own exclusion, and what he called the racism of lesbian feminism. The accusation was familiar; after all, Case's "Toward a Butch-Femme Aesthetic" essay had detailed the historic exclusions of lesbians from feminism, and much cultural theorizing since has described how any community is by definition exclusionary. But does that mean we can't consider the productive aspects of lesbian feminist communities in the seventies? And the charge that lesbian feminist culture was only white and racist also needs debunking. Race—like sexuality and class—was a site of intense struggle at that moment. Barbara Smith and her sister, and Urvashi Vaid, and the Combahee River Collective were all active in Boston in the years I described in my lecture, and the women's music scene included many lesbians of color, from Castleberry and Dupree to Toshi Reagon and many others. I found my questioner's accusations facile.

But the critique rattled me, partly because I'd already felt anxious about presenting a keynote that combined historical and theoretical work with personal reflections and anecdote. I didn't respond to his comments with aplomb but felt put in my place as "old-fashioned" by the spokesman for the current generation of queer theorizing, in which a lesbian feminist past seems to have little place. In fact, a plenary panel on which the speakers were all either gay men or transmen followed my keynote. The moderator—the very person who'd criticized my lecture—referred to all the speakers as "he"; no one identified as a woman or a lesbian. Feminist theory and lesbianism were erased from the stage. The history I'd just laid out for reconsideration was swept back into the dustbin.

Plenty of trans scholars incorporate feminist and lesbian insights as they make their astute arguments about gender and sexuality. I wish we could respect and incorporate our own histories, instead of building reputations by dismissing one another and our various investments. I'm still committed to recovering, retelling, and revisiting an era of lesbian feminist women's culture that modeled ways of thinking, living, and theorizing, whose successes and failures have much left to teach us. In my progressing middle age, in my attachment to being a lesbian, and in my persistent critical and personal practice of feminism, I'm willing to claim my anachronisms. I maintain my commitment to moving the discourse through women's studies, queer studies, and theater and performance studies—that is, through the academy and through public discourse at large.

Inevitably, we participate in the trends that move in and out of academic fashion. That's how new knowledge is formed and contested, advanced and honed. We're complicit in the division of academic spoils through structures of rewards and punishments that sometimes don't feel feminist at all, even as many of us continue trying to resist conservative institutional structures. But as I first heard Gloria Gaynor sing thirty-five years ago, "I will survive" as part of a very necessary, much beloved if mobile and temporary "we," a collective of feminist scholars working across myriad fields, who investigate theater and performance from within the academy and help to proliferate it critically in the world.

Notes on Contributors

Nancy K. Miller, "My Father's Penis"
Nancy K. Miller is a Distinguished Professor of English and comparative literature at the Graduate Center, City University of New York. She is the author and editor of several books, including *The Poetics of Gender* (1986), *Getting Personal: Feminist Occasions and Other Autobiographical Acts* (1991), *Bequest and Betrayal: Memoirs of a Parent's Death* (1996), and *But Enough About Me: Why We Read Other People's Lives* (2002). Her most recent book is a memoir, *What They Saved: Pieces of a Jewish Past* (2011).

Jane Marcus, "A Reasonable Facsimile"
Jane Marcus is a Distinguished Professor of English at the City University of New York and the City College of New York. Her publications include *Virginia Woolf and the Languages of Patriarchy* (1987), *Art and Anger: Reading Like a Woman* (1988), and *Hearts of Darkness: White Women Write Race* (2004). She has recently edited Virginia Woolf's *Three Guineas* and is currently working on projects titled *White Looks, Black Books: Nancy Cunard and Modernist Primitivism*, and *Poets Exploding Like Bombs: Nancy Cunard and Her Comrades on the Spanish Civil War*.

Tania Modleski, "Answering for the Consequences"
Tania Modleski is the Florence R. Scott Professor of English at the University of Southern California. She is the author of *Loving with a*

Vengeance (1982), *The Women Who Knew Too Much* (1988), *Feminism Without Women* (1991), and *Old Wives' Tales, and Other Women's Stories* (1998). She is currently writing about Hitchcock's female collaborators and about male "weepies."

Dyan Elliott, "The Historian, Her Mother, and Her Dead Women: Past, Present, and Places In Between"

Dyan Elliott is the Peter B. Ritzma Professor in the Humanities, Department of History, Northwestern University. She is the author of *Spiritual Marriage: Sexual Abstinence in Medieval Wedlock* (1993), *Fallen Bodies: Pollution, Sexuality, and Demonology in the Middle Ages* (1999), *Proving Woman: Female Spirituality and Inquisitional Culture in the Later Middle Ages* (2004), and *The Bride of Christ Goes to Hell: Metaphor and Embodiment in the Lives of Pious Women, 1200–1500* (2011).

Shirley Geok-lin Lim, "Fleeing and Pioneering Women: Matrophobia and My (Asian American) Feminist Praxis"

Shirley Geok-lin Lim is a professor of English at the University of California, Santa Barbara. She has also taught internationally, most recently serving as Chair Professor at the University of Hong Kong. She is the author of *Nationalism and Literature* (1993) and *Writing South/East Asia in English: Against the Grain* (1994), in addition to several books of poems, a book of memoirs, *Among the White Moon Faces* (1996), and two novels, *Joss and Gold* (2001) and *Sister Swing* (2006). She has served as editor/coeditor of numerous scholarly works, including *The Forbidden Stitch* (1989) and *Transnational Asia Pacific* (1999), and is coeditor of the online *Journal of Transnational American Studies*.

Patricia Yaeger, "Labial Politics"

Patricia Yaeger is the Henry Simmons Frieze Collegiate Chair at the University of Michigan and is the author of *Honey-Mad Women: Emancipatory Strategies in Women's Writing* (1988), and *Dirt and Desire: Reconstructing Southern Women's Writing* (2000). She has published recent essays on Charlotte Delbo, Flannery O'Connor, Eudora Welty, Kara Walker, Alice Randall, "Sea Trash, Dark Pools, and the Tragedy of the Commons," and "Dreaming of Infrastructure." She is working on a book on "Luminous Trash" and currently serves as editor of *PMLA*.

Jane Tompkins, "The Piano Lesson"

Jane Tompkins retired as a professor of English from Duke University and as Director of the Office for the Campus Environment from the University of Illinois at Chicago in 2005. She is the editor of *Reader-Response Criticism* (1980) and author of *Sensational Designs* (1985), *West of Everything* (1992), and *A Life in School* (1996). She lives in Andes, New York; New York City; and Delray Beach, Florida.

Rayna Rapp, "In My Family, We Spoke in Tongues"

Rayna Rapp is a professor of anthropology at New York University. She is the author of *Testing Women, Testing the Fetus* (1999), coeditor of *Conceiving the New World Order, Articulating Hidden Histories,* and *Promissory Notes,* and has published numerous articles, some of which have recently appeared in *Relative Matters: Reconfiguring Kinship Studies* (2002), *Medical Anthropology* (2001), *Public Culture* (2001), and *Living and Working with the New Medical Technologies* (2000). Along with her colleague anthropologist Faye Ginsburg, she is currently writing a book on special education and parent activism.

Sandra M. Gilbert, "Confessions of a Culinary Transvestite"

Sandra M. Gilbert, a Distinguished Professor of English emerita at the University of California, Davis, is the author of seven books of poetry. Gilbert has also published a memoir, *Wrongful Death* (1997), and an anthology of elegies, *Inventions of Farewell* (2001), along with a number of critical works, including *Acts of Attention: The Poems of D. H. Lawrence* (1972) and *Death's Door* (2006). She has also published several works with Susan Gubar, including *The Madwoman in the Attic: The Woman Writer and the 19th-Century Literary Imagination* (1979) and its three-volume sequel *No Man's Land: The Place of the Woman Writer in the 20th Century* (1988, 1989, 1994) as well as *Masterpiece Theatre: An Academic Melodrama* (1995). Together, Gilbert and Gubar have coedited

The Norton Anthology of Literature by Women (2007) and *Feminist Literary Theory and Criticism* (2007).

Leila Ahmed, "Islam in the Family"

Leila Ahmed was the first professor of women's studies in religion at Harvard Divinity School and was appointed the Victor S. Thomas Professor of Divinity in 2003. Prior to her appointment at HDS, she was a professor of women's studies and Near Eastern studies at the University of Massachusetts–Amherst. While at the University of Massachusetts, she was director of the women's studies program from 1992 to 1995 and director of the Near Eastern studies program from 1991 to 1992. In addition to *A Border Passage* (1991), she has written *Women and Gender in Islam: The Historical Roots of a Modern Debate* (1992) and *A Quiet Revolution: The Veil's Resurgence from the Middle East to America* (2011).

Gayatri Chakravorty Spivak, "Foremothers"

Gayatri Chakravorty Spivak, University Professor in the Humanities, Columbia University, holds honorary degrees from the Universities of Toronto and London and Oberlin College. Her recent books include *Thinking Academic Freedom in Gendered Post-Coloniality* (1993), *A Critique of Postcolonial Reason* (1999), *Death of a Discipline* (2003), *Other Asias* (2007), and *An Aesthetic Education in an Age of Globalization* (forthcoming). She holds visiting professorships worldwide.

Hazel Carby, "Lost (and Found?) in Translation"

Hazel Carby is the Charles C. and Dorathea S. Dilley Professor of African American Studies, a professor of American studies, and the director of the Initiative on Race, Gender, and Globalization at Yale University. Her books include *Reconstructing Womanhood* (1987), *Race Men* (1998), and *Cultures in Babylon* (1999). Recent publications include "Becoming a Modern Racialized Subject: 'Detours Through our Pasts to Produce Ourselves Anew'," and a longer version of "Lost (and Found?) in Translation" that appeared in *Small Axe*. Her current book in progress is *Child of Empire*. Hazel Carby is a dual citizen of the UK and the USA.

Neferti Tadiar, "Unreconciled Lives"

Neferti Tadiar is chair and professor of women's studies at Barnard College. She is currently working on two book projects, *Remaindered Lives: Becoming Human in a Time of War* and *Present Senses: Aesthetics, Affect, Asia in the Global* (with Jonathan L. Beller). Her publications include *Things Fall Away: Philippine Literatures, Historical Experience and Tangential Makings of Globality* (2009), *Beyond the Frame: Women of Color and Visual Representation,* coedited with Angela Y. Davis (2005), and *Fantasy-Production: Sexual Economies and Other Philippine Consequences for the New World Order* (2004).

Ann duCille, "Feminism, Black and Blue"

Ann duCille is a professor of English and African American studies at Wesleyan University. She is the author of *The Coupling Convention: Sex, Text, and Tradition in Black Women's Fiction* (1993) and *Skin Trade* (1996), as well as numerous articles on race, gender, class, and popular culture.

Martha C. Nussbaum, " 'Don't Smile So Much': Philosophy and Women in the 1970s"

Martha Nussbaum is the Ernst Freund Distinguished Service Professor of Law and Ethics at the University of Chicago, appointed in law, philosophy, and divinity. Among her books are *Sex and Social Justice* (1999), *Women and Human Development: The Capabilities Approach* (2000), and *Frontiers of Justice: Disability, Nationality, Species Membership* (2006). Her most recent book is *From Disgust to Humanity: Sexual Orientation and Constitutional Law* (2010).

Ann Douglas, "Crashing the Top: Women at Elite Universities"

Ann Douglas, the Parr Professor of Comparative Literature at Columbia University, was the first woman to teach in the Department of English at Princeton (1970–74). She is the author of *The Feminization of American Culture* (1977) and *Terrible Honesty: Mongrel Manhattan in the 1920s* (1995), as well as a number of essays, articles, and book reviews on American culture. She is currently working on a book titled *Noir Nation: American Cold War Culture 1939–1960.*

Lillian Faderman, "Hiding"

Lillian Faderman is a professor emerita of English at California State University, Fresno. She is the author of several books, including *Surpassing the Love of Men* (1981), *Odd Girls and Twilight Lovers: A History of Lesbian Life in Twentieth-Century America* (1991), and *To Believe in Woman: What Lesbians Have Done for America—A History* (1999). She is the recipient of six Lambda Literary Awards as well as the Monette/Horwitz Award, the Publishing Triangle Award, and the AAUW Distinguished Senior Scholar Award.

Jane Gallop, "Feminist Accused of Sexual Harassment"

Jane Gallop is a Distinguished Professor of English and comparative literature at the University of Wisconsin–Milwaukee. She is the author of many essays and several books, including *Around 1981: Academic Feminist Literary Theory* (1991), *Anecdotal Theory* (2002), and *Living with his Camera* (2003). Her latest book—*The Deaths of the Author: Reading and Writing in Time*—will be published by Duke University Press in 2011.

Annette Kolodny, "I Dreamed Again That I Was Drowning, with a Postscript"

Annette Kolodny retired from the University of Arizona in July 2007, and is now a College of Humanities professor emerita of American literature and culture. Although retired from teaching, she still maintains an active agenda of research and publication. Her books include *The Lay of the Land: Metaphor as Experience and History in American Life and Letters* (1975) and *The Land Before Her: Fantasy and Experience of the American Frontiers, 1630–1860* (1984). She wrote candidly about her experiences as a feminist senior administrator in *Failing the Future: A Dean Looks at Higher Education in the Twenty-First Century* (1998). Her most recent book is an edition of a long-lost masterpiece of Native American literature, Joseph Nicolar's *The Life and Traditions of the Red Man* (2007). She is currently completing *In Search of First Contact: The Vikings of Vinland, the Peoples of the Dawnland, and the Anglo-American Anxiety of Discovery*. She also continues to publish articles in the fields of higher education policy studies, feminist ecocriticism, feminist literary criticism, and Native American studies.

Frances Smith Foster, "Anyway, *We* Certainly Don't Want to Be Lumped In with Black Studies!"

Frances Smith Foster is the Charles Howard Candler Professor of English and Women's Studies at Emory University. Recent publications include *Written by Herself: Literary Production by African American Women, 1726–1892* (1993) and *Minnie's Sacrifice, Sowing and Reaping, Trial and Triumph: Three Rediscovered Novels by Frances Ellen Watkins Harper* (1994). Foster is an editor of the *Oxford Companion to African American Literature* (2002), the *Norton Anthology of African American Literature* (2003), *Behind the Scenes* (1998), and *Incidents in the Life of a Slave Girl* (2001). Her most recent book is titled "*'Til Death or Distance Do Us Part": Love and Marriage in African America* (2010).

Hortense J. Spillers, "Quarrels into Ploughshares: Feminism and Race"

Hortense J. Spillers is the Gertrude Conaway Vanderbilt Chair in English at Vanderbilt University and lives in Nashville. Recent essays of hers have appeared in *The New Centennial Review* and *boundary 2*, which special issue on the 1960s she coedited with Chris Connery. Her essays have been collected in *Black, White, and in Color* (2003). She is at work on a project entitled "The Idea of Black Culture."

Tey Diana Rebolledo, "What I Have Learned as a Chicana Professor, or, 'En Bocas Cerradas no Entran Moscas'"

Tey Diana Rebolledo is a Distinguished Professor of Spanish at the University of New Mexico. She is the author of *The Chronicles of Panchita Villa and Other Guerrilleras* (2005) and *Women Singing in the Snow: An Analysis of Chicana Literature* (1995), and coauthor of *Infinite Divisions: An Anthology of Chicana Literature* (1993). She is also the coeditor of *Nuestras Mujeres* (1992) and *Las Mujeres Hablan* (1988), as well as many journals and book chapters.

Nancy J. Chodorow, "The Psychoanalyst, the Sociologist, and the Feminist: A Retrospect"

Nancy J. Chodorow is a professor of sociology emerita, University of California, Berkeley; lecturer on psychiatry, Harvard Medical School; and training and supervising analyst, Boston Psychoanalytic Society and Institute. Her books include *The Reproduction of Mothering* (1978; 2nd ed., 1999), *Feminism and Psychoanalytic Theory* (1989), *Femininities, Masculinities, Sexualities: Freud and Beyond* (2004), and *The Power of Feelings: Personal Meaning in Psychoanalysis, Gender, and Culture* (1999). Her book, *Individualizing Gender and Sexuality: Theory and Practice*, is in press. She has also published extensively on comparative psychoanalytic theory and technique. She is in private practice in Cambridge, Massachusetts.

Rosemary Radford Ruether, "Critical Connections in Religion: An Intellectual Autobiography"

Rosemary Radford Ruether is a visiting professor of feminist theology at Claremont School of Theology and Claremont Graduate University. She formerly was the Carpenter Professor of Feminist Theology at the Pacific School of Religion and Graduate Theological Union. Ruether is the author of many books, including *Sexism and God-Talk: Toward a Feminist Theology* (1993), *Gaia and God: An Ecofeminist Theology of Earth Healing* (1994), and *America, Amerikkka: Elect Nation & Imperial Violence* (2007). She is also editor of *In Our Own Voices: Four Centuries of American Women's Religious Writing* with Rosemary Skinner Keller (1996) and *Introducing Redemption in Christian Feminism* (1998).

Linda Nochlin, "Not Too Far from Brooklyn: Growing Up, Growing Old with Art"

Linda Nochlin is the Lila Acheson Wallace Professor of Modern Art at New York University's Institute of Fine Arts. Prior to assuming this position, Nochlin served as a professor of art history and humanities at Yale University, as a Distinguished Professor of art history at the Graduate School and University Center of the City University of New York, and as the Mary Conover Mellon Professor of Art History at Vassar College. Nochlin has written numerous books and articles, including *Representing Women* (1999), *The Body in Pieces* (1994), *Women, Art, and Power* (1988), and *The Politics of Vision* (1989). She was named Scholar of the Year by the New York State Council on the Humanities, and holds honorary doctorates from Colgate University, the Massachusetts College of Art, the Parsons School of Design, and Harvard University.

Susan McClary, "The Making of a Feminist Musicologist"

Susan McClary is a professor of music at Case Western Reserve University. Best known for her book *Feminine Endings: Music, Gender, and Sexuality* (1991), she is also author of *Georges Bizet: Carmen* (1992), *Conventional Wisdom: The Content of Musical Form* (2000), *Modal Subjectivities: Renaissance Self-Fashioning in the Italian Madrigal* (2004), *Reading Music: Selected Essays* (2007), and *Desire and Pleasure in Seventeenth-Century Music* (2011).

Jill Dolan, " 'I Will Survive': Changing Trends in Feminism and Performance"

Jill Dolan is the Annan Professor in English and Theatre at Princeton University, where she also directs the program in gender and sexuality studies. She has taught at the University of Texas at Austin, where she held the Zachary T. Scott Family Chair in Drama; at the Graduate Center of the City University of New York, where she headed the Theatre Program and the Center for Lesbian and Gay Studies; and at the University of Wisconsin–Madison. She is the author of *The Feminist Spectator as Critic* (1988), *Presence and Desire: Essays on Gender, Sexuality, Performance* (1993), *Geographies of Learning: Theory and Practice, Activism and Performance* (2001), *Utopia in Performance: Finding Hope at the Theater* (2005), and *Theatre and Sexuality* (2010). She blogs at *The Feminist Spectator*, www.feministspectator.blogspot.com.

Acknowledgments

THIS BOOK COULD not have been compiled without the outstanding work of my research assistants at Indiana University, Jamie Horrocks, Shannon Boyer, and Kelly Hanson. I am also indebted to my agent, Ellen Levine, and to my editor, Jill Bialosky. Parts of the introduction derive from four related pieces I composed for four quite different occasions: a response to *A History of Feminist Literary Criticism* edited by Gill Plain and Susan Sellers, a PMLA roundtable on the state of feminist criticism, a City University of New York conference in honor of Carolyn Heilbrun which has been transcribed on the web, and a lecture in Israel to honor the publication of *Venues of Feminist Thinking*, the first gender studies textbook in Hebrew. As always, I profit from conversations with my friends and colleagues, especially Judith Brown, Denise Cruz, Mary Favret, Jen Fleissner, Sandra M. Gilbert, Donald Gray, Alyce Miller, Shane Vogel, Suzanna Walters, Mary Jo Weaver, and Niza Yanay.